LEADERSHIP
IN
ORGANIZATIONS

LEADERSHIP
IN
ORGANIZATIONS

Gary A. Yukl, Ph.D.

State University of New York at Albany

PRENTICE-HALL, INC., *Englewood Cliffs, New Jersey 07632*

Library of Congress Cataloging in Publication Data

Yukl, Gary A. (Date)
    Leadership in organizations.

    Bibliography: p.
    Includes indexes.
    1. Leadership. 2. Decision-making. 3. Organization. I. Title.
HM141.Y84   303.3'4   80-27044
ISBN   0-13-527176-2

©1981 by Prentice-Hall, Inc., Englewood Cliffs, N.J. 07632

Editorial/production supervision and interior design by Margaret Rizzi
Cover design by Miriam Recio
Manufacturing buyer: Gordon Osbourne

Printed in the United States of America

10   9   8   7   6   5   4   3   2

Prentice-Hall International, Inc., *London*
Prentice-Hall of Australia Pty. Limited, *Sydney*
Prentice-Hall of Canada, Ltd., *Toronto*
Prentice-Hall of India Private Limited, *New Delhi*
Prentice-Hall of Japan, Inc., *Tokyo*
Prentice-Hall of Southeast Asia Pte. Ltd., *Singapore*
Whitehall Books Limited, *Wellington, New Zealand*

Contents

Preface

This book is about leadership in organizations. The primary focus is managerial leadership, as opposed to parliamentary leadership, leadership of social movements, or informal leadership in peer groups. The book presents a broad survey of theory and research on leadership in formal organizations. The topic of leadership effectiveness is of special interest. Again and again the discussion returns to the central question of what makes a person an effective leader? Since the definitions of leadership and management are so ambiguous and closely intertwined, much of the book could be said to deal with managerial effectiveness.

The content of the book reflects a dual concern for theory and practice. It is neither a purely theoretical discourse, nor a manual of techniques for practitioners. Theories are explained and evaluated, but the book also has recommendations and guidelines for improving leadership. There is no clear division of chapters into theory versus practice, but some chapters tend to emphasize one more than the other. Most of the guidelines for practitioners appear in Chapters 3, 8, 9, and 10. Chapters 1, 2, and 6 are primarily concerned with introducing and evaluating concepts and theories. Chapters 4, 5, and 7 present a mix of research, theory, and applications.

The field of leadership is in a state of ferment, with many continuing controversies about conceptual and methodological issues. The book addresses these issues rather than merely summarizing findings and recommending practices without concern for the quality of research that lies behind them. The only intentional bias in the review of research is that field studies are accorded greater attention than laboratory studies, and field experiments are given special recognition due to their scarcity and special contributions.

The literature review was intended to be incisive rather than comprehensive. This is not another "handbook" detailing an endless series of individual studies. Integration and extrapolation of findings was a primary objective, although less was accomplished in this regard than was hoped. The book seeks to review what we know about leadership effectiveness. The review shows that we know more than is commonly believed, although much less than we need to know.

Even though the purpose of the book was to review prior theory and research rather than to present new concepts or theories, some original material can be found in several parts of the book. Chapter 5 includes a new taxonomy of nineteen categories of managerial behavior based on my own extensive research on this subject, and Chapter 7 presents propositions about the situational relevance of each type of behavior. Other attempts to develop better taxonomies can be found in Chapters 2 and 9. Chapter 6 presents for the first time my revised and extended Multiple Linkage Model of Leader Effectiveness. Chapter 3 presents some novel ideas about the successful exercise of power by leaders. Finally, Chapter 10 integrates and interprets the leadership literature in a more complete and innovative fashion than has been done previously.

This book is appropriate for use as the primary text in an undergraduate or graduate course on leadership. Courses of this type are found in psychology departments, sociology departments, business schools, departments of educational administration, and schools of public administration. The book could also be used in combination with other texts for courses in management, supervision, group dynamics, administration, and organizational behavior. The extensive coverage of important topics not dealt with except at a superficial level in most other texts makes the book ideal for inclusion on required reading lists for comprehensive graduate student examinations in management, industrial psychology, social psychology, sociology, public administration, and educational administration.

Gary A. Yukl
Albany, New York

Introduction:
the Nature of
Leadership

Leadership is a subject that has long excited interest among scholars and laymen alike. The term connotes images of powerful, dynamic persons who command victorious armies, direct corporate empires from atop gleaming skyscrapers, or shape the course of nations. Much of our conception of history is the story of military, political, religious, and social leaders. The exploits of brave and clever leaders are the essence of many legends and myths. The widespread fascination with leadership may be because it is such a mysterious process, as well as one that touches everyone's life. Why do certain leaders (Gandhi, Mohammed, Mao Tse-tung) inspire such intense fervor and dedication? How did certain leaders (Julius Caesar, Charlemagne, Alexander the Great) build great empires? Why were certain leaders (Winston Churchill, Indira Gandhi, the Shah of Iran) suddenly deposed, despite their apparent power and record of successful accomplishments? How did certain rather undistinguished persons (Adolf Hitler, Claudius Caesar) rise to positions of great power? Why do some leaders have loyal followers who are willing to sacrifice their lives for their leader, and why are some other leaders so despised that their followers conspire to murder them (e.g., as occurred with the "fragging" of some military officers by enlisted men in Vietnam)?

Questions about leadership have long been a subject of speculation, but it was not until the twentieth century that scientific research on leadership was begun. The focus of much of the research has been on the determinants of leadership effectiveness. Behavioral scientists have attempted to discover what traits, abilities, behaviors, sources of power, or aspects of the situation determine how effective a leader will be in maintaining his leadership position, influencing followers, and accomplishing group objectives. The reasons why some people emerge as leaders and the determinants of the way a leader acts are other important questions that have been investigated, but the predominant concern has been leadership effectiveness.

Some progress has been made in probing the mysteries surrounding leadership, but many questions remain unanswered. In this book, major theories and research findings on leadership effectiveness will be reviewed, with particular emphasis on "managerial leadership" in formal organizations such as business corporations, government agencies, hospitals, universities, and so forth. In this first chapter, the subject is introduced by considering: (1) what is leadership? and (2) how do you measure leader effectiveness?

DEFINITIONS OF LEADERSHIP

The term "leadership" means different things to different people. As is often the case when a word from the common vocabulary is incorporated into the technical vocabulary of a scientific discipline, leadership has not been precisely redefined, and it still carries extraneous connotations that create ambiguity of meaning (Janda, 1960). Further confusion is caused by the use of other imprecise terms such as power, authority, management, administration, control, and supervision to describe the same phenomena. Bennis (1959, p. 259) surveyed the leadership literature and concluded: "Always, it seems, the concept of leadership eludes us or turns up in another form to taunt us again with its slipperiness and complexity. So we have invented an endless proliferation of terms to deal with it . . . and still the concept is not sufficiently defined."

Researchers usually define leadership according to their individual perspective and the aspect of the phenomenon of most interest to them. After a comprehensive review of the leadership literature, Stogdill (1974, p. 259) concluded that "there are almost as many definitions of leadership as there are persons who have attempted to define the concept." Leadership has been defined in terms of individual traits, behavior, influence over other people, interaction patterns, role relationships, occupation of an administrative position, and perception of others regarding legitimacy of influence. Some representative definitions are as follows:

1. Leadership is "the behavior of an individual when he is directing the activities of a group toward a shared goal." (Hemphill & Coons, 1957; p. 7)
2. Leadership is "interpersonal influence, exercised in a situation, and directed, through the communication process, toward the attainment of a specified goal or goals." (Tannenbaum, Weshler & Massarik, 1961; p. 24)

3. Leadership is "the initiation and maintenance of structure in expectation and interaction." (Stogdill, 1974; p. 411)
4. Leadership is "an interaction between persons in which one presents information of a sort and in such a manner that the other becomes convinced that his outcomes (benefits/costs ratio) will be improved if he behaves in the manner suggested or desired." (Jacobs, 1970; p. 232)
5. Leadership is "a particular type of power relationship characterized by a group member's perception that another group member has the right to prescribe behavior patterns for the former regarding his activity as a group member." (Janda, 1960; p. 358)
6. Leadership is "an influence process whereby O's actions change P's behavior and P views the influence attempt as being legitimate and the change as being consistent with P's goals." (Kochan, Schmidt & DeCotiis, 1975; p. 285)
7. Leadership is "the influential increment over and above mechanical compliance with the routine directives of the organization." (Katz & Kahn, 1978; p. 528)

The term "leadership" is a relatively recent addition to the English language. It has only been in use for around two hundred years, although the term "leader" from which it was derived appeared as early as 1300 A.D. (Stogdill, 1974). Most conceptions of leadership imply that at various times one or more group members can be identified as a leader according to some observable difference between the person(s) and other members, who are referred to as "followers" or "subordinates." Definitions of leadership usually have as a common denominator the assumption that it is a group phenomenon involving the interaction between two or more persons (Janda, 1960). In addition, most definitions of leadership reflect the assumption that it involves an influence process whereby intentional influence is exerted by the leader over followers. The numerous definitions of leadership that have been proposed appear to have little else in common. The definitions differ in many respects, including important differences in who exerts influence, the purpose of influence attempts, and the manner in which influence is exerted. Key points of divergence in conceptions about who should be regarded as a leader are summarized in Table 1–1. The differences are not just a case of scholarly nitpicking. They reflect deep disagreement about identification of leaders and leadership processes. Differences between researchers in their conception of leadership lead to differences in the choice of phenomena to investigate and to differences in interpretation of the data obtained.

One major controversy involves the issue of leadership as a distinct phenomenon. Some theorists believe that leadership is no differ-

TABLE 1–1

Different Conceptions of a Leader

Broader Conception		More Restrictive Conception
1. A person who influences group members ("distributed leadership").	vs.	1. A person who exerts the most influence on other group members ("focused leadership").
2. A person who influences group members in any manner.	vs.	2. A person who systematically influences member behavior toward attainment of group goals.
3. A person who influences group members to comply with his requests willingly or unwillingly.	vs.	3. A person who obtains the enthusiastic commitment of group members in carrying out his requests.

ent from the social influence processes occurring among all members of a group, and leadership is viewed as a collective process shared among the members. The opposing view is that there is a tendency in all groups toward role specialization with regard to leadership functions. These theorists believe that it is only meaningful to view "leadership" as distinct from "followership." The person who has the most influence in the group and who carries out most of the leadership functions is designated the leader. Other members are followers, even though some may be leaders of subgroups, or may assist the primary leader in carrying out leadership functions.

Related to this controversy is the issue of influence attempts. Some theorists hold that leadership includes only influence processes related to the task and objectives of the group. According to this view, influence attempts that are extraneous or detrimental to the group's mission and are intended only to benefit the leader are not regarded as "acts of leadership." This limitation seems more appropriate to formal task groups in organizations than to groups formed purely for social purposes, since the latter often have no explicit task objectives and exist only to satisfy member needs for companionship and social acceptance.

Some theorists would go even further in limiting the definition of leadership to exercise of influence resulting in enthusiastic commitment by followers, as opposed to indifferent compliance or reluctant obedience. Proponents of this view argue that a person who uses his authority and control over rewards and punishments to manipulate and coerce followers is not really "leading" them. The opposing view is that this definition is too restrictive, because it excludes influence processes that are important for understanding why a manager is effective or ineffective in a given situation. These theorists contend that while it is useful to distinguish between exercising power and providing leadership, the latter process should be viewed with a broader perspective.

It is neither feasible nor desirable at this point in the development of the discipline to resolve the controversy over the appropriate definition of leadership. For the time being, it is better to use the various conceptions of leadership as a source of different perspectives on a complex, multifaceted phenomenon. In research, the operational definition of leadership will depend to a great extent on the purpose of the researcher (Campbell, 1977; Karmel, 1978). The purpose may be to identify leaders, to train them, to discover what they do, to determine how they are selected, or to compare effective and ineffective leaders. As Karmel (1978, p. 476) notes, "It is consequently very difficult to settle on a single definition of leadership that is general enough to accommodate these many meanings and specific enough to serve as an operationalization of the variable." Whenever feasible, leadership research should be designed to provide information relevant to the entire range of definitions, so that over time it will be possible to compare the utility of different conceptualizations and arrive at some consensus on the matter.

LEADERSHIP EFFECTIVENESS

Like conceptions of leadership, conceptions of leadership effectiveness differ from writer to writer. One major distinction between definitions of leadership effectiveness is the type of consequence or outcome selected to be the effectiveness criterion. These outcomes include such diverse things as group performance, attainment of group goals, group survival, group growth, group preparedness, group capacity to deal with crises, subordinate satisfaction with the leader, subordinate commitment to group goals, the psychological well-being and development of group members, and the leader's retention of his status and position in the group.

The most commonly used measure of leader effectiveness is the extent to which the leader's group or organization performs its task successfully and attains its goals. In some cases, objective measures of performance or goal attainment are available, such as profit growth, profit margin, sales increase, market share, sales relative to targeted sales, return on investment, productivity, cost per unit of output, costs in relation to budgeted expenditures, and so on. In other cases, subjective evaluations of performance are used, including ratings of the leader's effectiveness in carrying out his duties and responsibilities, and ratings of the group's success in carrying out its mission. The ratings are usually made by the leader's superiors, peers, or subordinates.

The attitude of followers toward their leader is another common indicator of leader effectiveness. How well does the leader satisfy their needs and expectations? Do followers like him, respect him, admire him? Are followers strongly committed to carry out the leader's requests, or will they resist, ignore, or subvert his requests? Follower attitudes are usually measured with questionnaires or interviews. Various objective measures of behavior such as absenteeism, voluntary turnover, grievances, complaints to higher management, requests for transfer, slowdowns, wildcat strikes, and incidents of deliberate sabotage of equipment and facilities serve as indirect indicators of follower dissatisfaction and hostility toward their leader.

Leader effectiveness is occasionally measured in terms of the leader's contribution to the quality of group processes, as perceived by followers or by outside observers. Does the leader enhance group cohesiveness, member cooperation, member motivation, problem solving, decision making, and resolution of conflict among members? Does the leader contribute to the efficiency of role specialization, the organization of activities, the accumulation of resources, and the readiness of the group to deal with change and crisis? Does the leader improve the quality of work life, build the self-confidence of followers, increase their skills, and contribute to their psychological growth and development?

The selection of appropriate criteria of leader effectiveness depends on the objectives and values of the person making the evaluation. A leader's superiors are likely to prefer different criteria than the leader's subordinates. When there are many alternative measures of effectiveness, it is usually an arbitrary decision as to which is most relevant. The different criteria are often uncorrelated, and may even be negatively correlated. For example, growth in sales or output is sometimes achieved at the cost of reduced efficiency and lower profits. Tradeoffs can occur even within the same criterion at different points of time. For example, profits may be increased in the short run by neglecting activities that have a delayed effect on profits, such as maintenance of equipment, research and development, investment in new technology, and development of employees. In the long run, the net effect of cutting these essential activities is likely to be lower profits. To cope with the problems of partially incompatible criteria, it is usually best to include a variety of different criteria in research on leadership effectiveness and to examine the separate impact of the leader on each of these criteria over an extended period of time. Multiple conceptions of effectiveness, like multiple conceptions of leadership, serve to broaden our perspective and enlarge the scope of inquiry.

OVERVIEW OF MAJOR RESEARCH APPROACHES

Leadership has been studied in different ways, depending on the researcher's conception of leadership and methodological preferences. Most leadership studies have dealt only with one narrow aspect of the phenomenon. Nearly all of the research on leadership can be classified into one of the following four approaches: (1) power-influence approach, (2) trait approach, (3) behavior approach, and (4) situational approach. The implicit assumptions about causal relationships among variables are shown in Figure 1–1 for each approach.

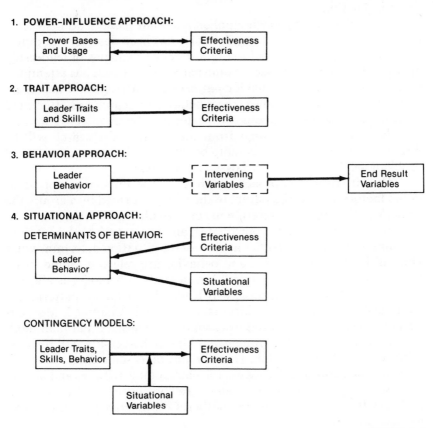

FIGURE 1–1

General Approaches in Research on Leader Effectiveness

The power-influence approach attempts to explain leader effectiveness in terms of the source and amount of power available to leaders and the manner in which leaders exercise power over followers. Recent theory and research has emphasized the reciprocal nature of influence processes and the importance of exchange relationships between leaders and followers. The power-influence approach will be discussed in chapters 2 and 3. The consequences of subordinate participation in leader decisions is an aspect of reciprocal influence that is dealt with in greater detail in Chapter 8.

The trait approach emphasizes the personal qualities of leaders. Early conceptions of leadership attributed the success of outstanding leaders to their possession of extraordinary abilities such as tireless energy, penetrating intuition, uncanny foresight, and irresistible persuasive skill. The results of research on leader traits and skills will be discussed in Chapter 4.

The behavior approach emphasizes what leaders do instead of their traits or source of power. Behavior has been described at different levels of specificity, and many different typologies of leadership behavior have been proposed. Some behavior research has attempted to describe the typical behavior patterns and activities of managers and administrators. However, most behavior research has attempted to identify differences in behavior patterns between effective and ineffective leaders. The findings from the behavioral research will be discussed in Chapter 5. Leadership behavior in the specific context of problem-solving groups is discussed in Chapter 9.

The situational approach emphasizes the importance of situational factors such as the nature of the task performed by a group, the leader's authority and discretion to act, the role expectations imposed by superiors, peers, and subordinates, and the nature of the external environment. These and other aspects of the situation determine what kinds of leader traits, skills, and behavior are relevant. Some situational research is concerned with how a leader's behavior is affected by the immediate situation and why leadership behavior patterns differ across situations. This subject is dealt with in Chapter 7. Most situational theory and research has sought to identify situational moderator variables that determine what kind of leadership will be most effective in a given situation. This orientation is sometimes called the "contingency approach" because the particular attributes and behavior essential for leader effectiveness are contingent on the situation and vary from one situation to another. Contingency theories will be discussed in Chapter 6.

Leadership research has been characterized by highly segmented and narrowly focused studies with little integration of findings from the trait, behavior, and power-influence approaches. The research on leader power and influence has not dealt with leadership behavior except for direct influence attempts, and there has been little concern for traits except those that are a source of leader influence (e.g., expertise, persuasive ability). The trait research has shown little concern for direct measurement of either leader behavior or influence, even though it is evident that they both somehow mediate the effects of leader traits on end-result variables such as subordinate performance. Research on leadership behavior has seldom included measurement of leader traits or influence processes, even though a leader's behavior is clearly affected by the leader's traits, and much of the behavior involves attempts to influence the attitudes and behavior of subordinates. Finally, situational research and theory has focused narrowly on the way the situation enhances or nullifies the effects of some leader traits or some aspects of leader behavior, rather than examining how traits, behavior, and influence interact with each other and the situation to determine leader effectiveness. In Chapter 10 we examine points of correspondence between findings from the different research approaches, summarizing what has been learned about leader effectiveness, reviewing ways of applying this knowledge, and making recommendations for future research.

REVIEW AND DISCUSSION QUESTIONS

1. What features are shared in common by most definitions of leadership?

2. What are some major differences in the way leadership has been defined?

3. Does it really matter how you define leadership? Why or why not?

4. How is leadership effectiveness determined?

5. Why is it important to include multiple criteria of leadership effectiveness in research on leadership?

6. Briefly describe the four perspectives or approaches that account for most of the research on leadership.

2
Reciprocal Influence
Processes in Leadership

The essence of leadership is influence over followers. Without followers, there cannot be leaders. However, the influence process between leader and followers is not unidirectional. Leaders influence followers, but followers also have some influence over leaders. In this chapter we will examine the reciprocal nature of influence processes in leadership and the various sources of influence for leaders and followers. In the next chapter we will examine how influence processes are related to leadership effectiveness.

THE NATURE OF INFLUENCE PROCESSES

There is more conceptual confusion about influence processes than about any other facet of leadership. Influence is a word that everybody seems to intuitively understand; it is merely the effect of one party (the "agent") on another party (the "target"). However, closer examination reveals ambiguities and complexities in even this relatively simple concept. The process by which the agent affects the target person can take many different forms, and the nature of the effect differs depending on the process. The agent's actions may result in a change in the target person's attitudes, values, perception, behavior, or some combination of these outcome variables. The consequence of the agent's influence attempt may be one that was intended by the agent, or it may be an unintended outcome. The magnitude of the change in the target person may be equivalent with the agent's intended effect, or it may fall short of the agent's objectives. The agent's influence may be strong enough to assure "control" over the target person's behavior, or so weak that the target person feels "pressure" but is not induced to do anything he otherwise would not do.

It is desirable to distinguish between different forms of influence, because the required conditions vary somewhat, as do the consequences of each form of influence. Several behavioral scientists have proposed influence typologies, but none of these typologies spans the full range of useful distinctions that are apparent. The typology proposed in this book is a composite of several earlier ones (Cartwright, 1965; Dahl, 1957; Etzioni, 1961; French & Raven, 1959; Lee, 1977; Patchen, 1974; Peabody, 1964; Webber, 1975). The typology has 11 distinct forms of influence. The different forms of influence are not necessarily incompatible, and some of them may be used together at the same time. A list of the 11 forms of influence and a summary of agent and target person requirements for use of each form are presented in Table 2–1.

TABLE 2–1
Typology of Different Forms of Influence

Form of Influence	Agent Requirements	Target Person Requirements
1. Legitimate Request	Legitimate Justification	Relevant Values
2. Instrumental Compliance	Control over Rewards; Credibility of Promise	Relevant Needs, Openness to Manipulation
3. Coercion	Control over Punishments; Credibility of Threat	Fear, Openness to Intimidation
4. Rational Persuasion	Insight; Technical Expertise; Persuasive Ability	Relevant Values and Needs
5. Rational Faith	Technical Expertise; Credibility	Low Expertise, Relevant Need; Trust of Agent
6. Inspirational Appeal	Insight into Values and Beliefs; Persuasive Ability	Relevant Values and Beliefs
7. Indoctrination	Control of Social Situation; Relevant Skills	Alienation, Relevant Needs
8. Information Distortion	Credibility as Information Source	Use of Information for Impression Formation and Decision Making
9. Situational Engineering	Control of Relevant Aspects of Situation	Willingness to Accept Situation
10. Personal Identification	Attractiveness, Charisma	Admiration of Agent
11. Decision Identification	Willingness to Allow Participation; Relevant Skills	Desire to Participate, Goals Consistent with Agent Goals

Legitimate Request

A very common form of influence in organizations is the "legitimate request." This form of influence occurs when a target person complies with the request of an agent because the target person recognizes the "right" of the agent to make such a request. The legitimacy of the request may be based on the agent's formal authority, on his designation as the official or legal representative of someone with formal authority, on tradition, on group norms, or on the need for the person to make the request in order to fulfill his role responsibilities. The motivation for compliance may be an internalized belief in the desirability of obedience to authority figures, or other internalized values such as cooperation, courtesy, respect for tradition, and loyalty to the organization. Formal authority as a source of legitimacy is discussed in more detail in a later section of this chapter.

Instrumental Compliance

Instrumental compliance occurs when a person is induced to alter his behavior by an agent's implicit or explicit promise to insure some tangible outcome desired by the person. The potential for using this form of influence is referred to as "reward power" (French & Raven, 1959). Instrumental compliance includes delayed effects of an agent's manipulation of rewards, as well as immediate effects of an overt promise or incentive. For example, as a result of knowledge about the way an agent has rewarded behavior in the past, a person may infer that similar reward contingencies continue to exist, even though this perception may in fact be erroneous.

The likelihood of instrumental compliance is greatest when the target person is dependent on the agent for attainment of an important reward, he is convinced that the reward can only be attained by compliance, and he perceives that he is capable of performing the requisite behavior. It is easier to induce a target person to do something that is consistent with his attitudes and values than to do something contrary to them. Furthermore, instrumental compliance is more likely when the target person considers it appropriate and ethical in the specific situation to accept the agent's offer, regardless of whether the behavior requested is desirable (Cartwright, 1965).

Coercion

Compliance may also be induced by the agent's explicit or implicit threat to ensure adverse outcomes such as physical pain, economic loss, expulsion from the organization, or public embarrassment if the target person fails to comply. The likelihood of compliance is greatest when the agent's threat is credible; that is, the agent is perceived to be capable and willing to cause the undesirable outcomes to occur. Compliance is less likely if the behavior is contrary to the target person's values, or if he is unwilling to be intimidated by threats. Coercion is compliance motivated primarily by fear, and a person's potential for using this form of influence is sometimes referred to as use of "coercive power" (French & Raven, 1959).

Rational Persuasion

In order to induce instrumental compliance, an agent must appear to have control over the benefits that are promised. Rational persuasion is a form of influence that does not require any control over desirable or undesirable outcomes by the influence agent. With rational persuasion, the agent convinces the target person that the suggested behavior is the best way for the target person to satisfy his needs or attain his objectives. In order for the agent to do this successfully, it is essential for him to understand the target person's needs, objectives, and perception of the situation. The agent must be skilled in making logical arguments and presenting evidence that appears credible. Sometimes it is necessary to arouse the need first before persuading the target person to satisfy it in the prescribed manner. An example of logical persuasion is the manager who convinces an ambitious subordinate that the best way to get promoted is to attend optional management development workshops and volunteer for special assignments to gain visibility. The agent's influence is usually less than if he actually had control over the outcomes themselves (e.g., authority to promote the subordinate).

Rational Faith

With rational persuasion, the agent must communicate a logical argument that includes evidence supporting the instrumentality of the recommended behavior. In contrast, rational faith is a form of influence in which the suggestion of a particular agent is sufficient to evoke compliance by the target person, without any explanation necessary. The target person acts out of faith in the expertise and credibility of the agent (Webber, 1975). A good example of rational faith is provided by a patient who takes medicine recommended by his doctor without knowing what the medicine is or how it will cure him. Some other examples of rational faith include an athlete who follows the advice of his coach regarding how to improve his performance, a manager who follows the advice of his legal counsel to avoid a lawsuit, and a production supervisor who follows the directions provided by a maintenance technician in order to repair one of his machines. Rational faith is a form of influence that is most likely to occur when the target person has a problem, he has little or no knowledge of how to solve it, and he perceives that the agent can be trusted to indicate the best course of action. As with rational persuasion, the agent has no actual control over the outcome desired by the target person, only apparent knowledge about ways to attain the outcome.

Inspirational Appeal

An inspirational appeal occurs when a target person is induced to do something that appears to be a necessary expression of his values and ideals. For example, a manager may induce a subordinate to accept a special assignment out of loyalty to the organization, and a soldier may be induced to volunteer for a dangerous mission as an expression of his patriotism. The agent must persuade the target person that there is a necessary link between the requested behavior and some value that is important enough to justify the behavior. The agent does not offer any tangible rewards to the target persons, only the prospect that they will feel good as a result of "doing something that is noble and just," "making an important contribution to humanity," "performing an exceptional feat," or "serving God and country." It is often helpful to invoke the salience of the value in an emotional manner (e.g., with symbols, rituals, music, etc.). As with rational persuasion, the agent needs to understand the target person's beliefs, feelings, and values.

A particularly effective set of values for building and expanding organizations throughout recorded human history is the "classical patriarchal ideology" (McClelland, 1975). The themes in this ideology include: gaining power through submission to a father figure or superordinate entity, self-discipline and self-sacrifice so that the system may prevail, and justice in distribution of rewards and punishments, with rewards for the obedient and faithful in the afterlife if not in their present lifetime. Reviewing evidence from historical records, McClelland (1975, p. 285) concluded: "The core values in the ideology of patriarchal authority have led to some of the strongest organizations and most expansive empires in history." This occurred when there were leaders who were able to mobilize the resources of the system for expansion and who inspired member dedication to the system by building on the influence potential of the core values.

Indoctrination

Inspirational appeals are feasible only when the target person has strong values that are relevant to the behavior one wants to induce. One way to insure that the appropriate values are present is to establish selection procedures for the organization to reject potential members who have not acquired these values in their earlier experience and training (Etzioni, 1961). Another approach is to directly induce internalization of values and beliefs that will facilitate influence over the behavior of organizational members (Strauss & Sayles, 1972). These values include things like obedience to authority figures, reverence for tradition, patriotism, self-sacrifice, loyalty to the organization, and so forth. The indoctrination of new members may entail a detailed code of ethical behavior and beliefs as well as abstract values.

Internalization of values and beliefs usually requires a prolonged period of indoctrination, but some faster "brainwashing" and "conversion" techniques have been developed to speed up the process. These techniques seem to work best on people who feel alienated, lack a strong value structure, and have a strong need for affiliation. The indoctrination is typically carried out while the recruit is isolated from regular social contacts and is in a weakened state due to lack of sleep and inadequate nourishment. The process appears most effective when carried out in a group setting by persons who enthusiastically explain and endorse the doctrines, values, and objectives of the organization or movement. The recruit is induced by the group to proclaim agreement with the prescribed ideology, denounce any earlier values, beliefs, and loyalties contrary to it, and confess to thinking and acting improperly in the past. All of this occurs in an atmosphere of heightened emotionality and expression of group acceptance of the new convert.

An effective tactic to strengthen commitment to the organization and faith in the ideology is to induce the new convert to take some concrete action to demonstrate his sincerity. For example, religious cults typically ask new converts to donate money and assets to the cult and participate actively in recruiting new members. New members may also be asked to participate in an unpleasant initiation ritual, or to commit an act that is contrary to earlier beliefs and values. The need to rationalize this behavior tends to strengthen the new values and loyalties. It is hard to justify donating one's savings, committing an act of violence, or enduring a harrowing initiation unless the person feels deeply committed to the ideology and the organization, so this kind of commitment is likely to occur.

Information Distortion

A person's impressions and attitudes can be influenced by an agent who is able to limit the information received by the person. Selective presentation of facts, false information, presentation of statistics that favor a particular interpretation of data, and selective editing of records, transcripts, and videotapes are all examples of tactics used by "information gatekeepers" to influence persons who depend on them for certain kinds of information (Pettigrew, 1972). This form of influence differs from rational persuasion in that the agent does not make any overt attempt to persuade the target person to agree with him or comply with a request. The target person is influenced without being aware of it. Information distortion is also useful for enhancing the effectiveness of some other forms of influence such as rational persuasion, rational faith, and indoctrination.

Situational Engineering

A person's attitudes and behavior may be influenced indirectly by manipulating relevant aspects of the physical and social situation. Since a person's behavior is determined in part by his perception of situational opportunities and constraints, behavior can be altered in subtle ways by rearranging the situation (Cartwright, 1965). One form of situational engineering is to limit the number of alternative actions available to the target person. For example, a person is likely to use a certain product if it is the only one conveniently available that will satisfy his needs. Another form of situational engineering is to prevent undesirable behavior by removing the opportunities for such behavior to occur. For example, storing dangerous machinery in a locked room greatly reduces the likelihood that people will injure themselves on it. Technology is an important means of accomplishing situational engineering. Machine–paced assembly lines set the speed at which employees work, and the workflow determines which employees interact with each other and who initiates action for whom. The major requirements for effective use of situational engineering are control over relevant aspects of the situation and willingness of the target persons to accept the situation imposed on them.

Personal Identification

Personal identification occurs when people imitate the behavior of a greatly admired agent and develop attitudes similar to those he expresses. This form of influence is most evident with popular heroes, movie stars, rock music stars, and charismatic religious and political leaders. It is a form of influence often exploited in product advertising. Identification may occur even without the agent's knowledge or intention, and when this happens, some aspects of the imitative behavior may be considered undesirable by the agent. It is not completely understood whether the motivation for identification is a desire to feel important and powerful as a result of becoming more like the agent, or a desire to please the agent and gain his approval. Both motives are probably involved to some degree.

Identification can be a useful source of intentional influence for an agent who is highly attractive to the people he wants to influence. The agent can "model" certain behaviors for the people to imitate, and he can endorse certain values and beliefs in order to induce similar attitudes among the people who identify with him. Attraction is one source of personal loyalty. If the agent asks admirers to do something extra or unusual, they may be motivated to comply merely to please him and receive his approval. The potential influence of an attractive agent is sometimes called "referent power" (French & Raven, 1959; French & Snyder, 1959).

Decision Identification

In the process of participating in making a decision where a person perceives he has substantial influence over the final choice, the person is likely to identify with the decision and perceive it as "his decision." As a result of this identification and ego involvement, the person will be strongly committed to implement the decision effectively. When an agent makes a decision that must be implemented by other people, allowing them to participate in the decision making is a potential way to influence them to implement the decision enthusiastically. Of course, decision participation will only be a form of positive influence to the extent that the target persons agree on a choice that is consistent with the agent's objectives and is comparable to what he would have decided by himself. This outcome is likely if the objectives of the target persons are compatible with the objectives of the agent. Participation illustrates the apparent paradox of increasing an agent's influence by giving the target person more influence over the agent's decisions. Decision participation is discussed in more detail in Chapter 8.

INFLUENCE, POWER, AND AUTHORITY

The conceptual confusion surrounding influence processes in leadership is aggravated by controversy over the proper way to define concepts such as power and authority. These terms have been defined in different ways by different writers, and some writers have used the terms without providing any explicit definition. It is worthwhile to examine some of the variations in interpretation of these terms before stating the meaning of the terms as they will be used in this book.

Power

Power generally refers to an agent's potential capacity to influence a target person, but the term has been used in different ways (Dahl, 1957; Grimes, 1978; Pollard & Mitchell, 1971; Jacobs, 1970). Sometimes power means the agent's potential to influence the target person's behavior in the direction desired by the agent. Other writers use power to mean influence over a target person's attitudes and values as well as over behavior. Sometimes power means potential unilateral influence, whereas at other times it refers to an agent's potential to influence a target person without being penalized for doing so. The latter usage involves the bilateral or reciprocal influence processes in a relationship, and emphasizes the agent's "net power" or "usable power." Sometimes power refers to an agent's potential influence over a particular target person, and at other times it means potential influence over a collection of people, or over processes and decisions.

In this book, power will be defined broadly as an agent's potential at a given point in time to influence the attitudes and/or behavior of one or more specified target persons in the direction desired by the agent. Power is considered to be a dynamic variable that depends on the relationship between agent and target person(s). Since the agent's power depends ultimately on the target's needs, changes in these needs or the agent's control over means of satisfying them result in changes in the agent's power.

Authority

Power is the agent's capacity to exert influence, but authority is the agent's *right* to exert influence (Jacobs, 1970). Authority can be defined in terms of the relationship between formal positions in an organization. It is the right of one position occupant to influence specified aspects of the behavior of the other position occupant.

The exercise of authority by some persons over others is necessary for most organizations to be effective, especially large, bureaucratic organizations. The complex pattern of role specialization and the great amount of role interdependence in large organizations make it essential for each member to conform to role expectations. The organized, coordinated effort responsible for system effectiveness is disrupted by failure of key individuals to perform reliably their expected functions (Katz & Kahn, 1978). The necessary compliance of members with role expectations cannot be accomplished by relying only on the shared values of members or the demonstrated expertise of leaders. It is sometimes necessary to ask members to carry out activities they dislike, and since managers come and go in large organizations, it is not always possible to elicit compliance with sources of influence that require time to become established, such as expertise and personal loyalty (Hamner & Organ, 1978). Thus, organizations rely instead on authority as a basic mechanism for obtaining minimal compliance with role expectations.

Individual members of an organization can justify submitting to rules and leader commands as a necessary condition for membership. The sacrifice of some personal freedom of action is worthwhile as long as the benefits derived from membership outweigh the costs of less autonomy. The conditions for membership in the organization may be set forth in a formal, legal contract, or there may simply be a mutual understanding, an "implicit social contract." In either case, the ultimate basis for the legitimacy of authority is the collective consent of the governed. In privately owned organizations, authority also requires the approval of the owners or their representatives. From the perspective of the owners, the flow of authority downward through the management hierarchy is necessary for maintenance of owner control as well as for organizational effectiveness. However, traditional management theorists have overemphasized the importance of property rights and management prerogatives as explanations of authority and have failed to recognize the importance of member consent (Jacobs, 1970). Today it is recognized that, although control over material things is a source of some forms of power, ownership is never a sufficient basis for the right to influence people.

One prerequisite for acceptance of a leader's authority is the perceived legitimacy of the person as an occupant of the leadership position. This aspect of legitimacy depends on how the leader was selected. Formal leaders may be selected in a variety of ways, depending on the nature of the organization. In most organizations, leadership positions are filled either by appointment or election. Unless the particular selection procedure is consistent with the expectations of organization members regarding what is proper and legitimate, the authority of the leader will be in question. These expectations are based on tradition, and in many cases, on the provisions of a legal charter or constitution. Expectations about legitimate selection of a leader from among group members tend to reflect the informal status hierarchy in the group. If a low-status member is promoted to a position of authority over other members, the legitimacy of the new leader will be less than if a high-status member were promoted. The importance of legitimate selection is evident in the concerted efforts of most leaders to establish a recognized basis for their authority. Elected leaders are concerned about being able to claim a "mandate" by voters, leaders who gain their position as a result of a power struggle often hold "elections" to obtain a vote of confidence and claim popular endorsement, and thrones are usually claimed on the basis of blood relationship and succession to earlier rulers. Elaborate inauguration ceremonies are held by many kinds of leaders to formalize the transfer of power and enhance the legitimacy of their selection.

Legitimacy of authority involves not only who has the right to make legitimate requests, but also the scope of activities and behaviors about which the requests may be made. A person's scope of authority depends to a great extent on the influence needed to accomplish recognized role requirements and organizational objectives (Barnard, 1952). The legitimacy of managerial authority is likely to be high for things such as work procedures and work schedules, but low for such things as where subordinates live, what political party they join, and what kind of car they drive (Davis, 1968). A leader's scope of authority may be more or less delineated in writing by documents such as job descriptions, employment contracts, the organization charter, regulations manuals, labor laws, and other legal codes. However, there still may be considerable ambiguity and disagreement about a particular leader's scope of legitimate authority. Reitz (1977; p. 468) provides some good examples of the kinds of questions that may be raised about scope of authority:

An executive can rightfully expect a supervisor to work hard and diligently; may he also influence the supervisor to spy on rivals, spend weekends away from home, join an encounter group? A coach can rightfully expect his players to execute specific plays; may he also direct their life styles outside the sport? A combat officer can rightfully expect his men to attack on order; may he also direct them to execute civilians whom he claims are spies? A doctor can rightfully order a nurse to attend a patient or observe an autopsy; may he order her to assist in an abortion against her will?

When subordinates disagree with a leader about the legitimacy of a particular request, they may refuse to comply with this request. Unless the leader is able to persuade subordinates that the request is essential to carry out his role responsibilities, the leader will have to rely on some form of influence other than a legitimate request to obtain compliance. Although authority is an important source of influence in organizations, its potential is often much more limited than is apparent, especially in large bureaucracies. Theodore White (1960, pp. 366–367) relates the comments of a former aide to President Truman on the problems of exercising authority:

> The most startling thing a new President discovers is that his world is not monolithic. In the world of the Presidency, giving an order does *not* end the matter. You can pound your fist on the table or you can get mad or you can blow it all and go out to the golf course. But nothing gets done except by endless follow-up, endless kissing and coaxing, endless threatening and compelling. There are all those thousands of people in Washington working for you in the government—and every one is watching you, waiting, trying to guess what you mean, trying to get your number. Can they fool you? Can they outwait you? Will you be mad when you hear it isn't done yet?

LEADER POWER OVER SUBORDINATES

Under the right conditions, a leader may use any of the 11 forms of influence described in the early part of this chapter. Some leaders find themselves in a situation permitting use of all 11 varieties of influence, whereas other leaders find that they have only a limited choice of influence forms in their particular situation. In most organizations, the specification of a leader's legitimate authority includes provisions about forms of influence as well as scope of influence. Some forms of influence are explicitly prescribed in the role expectations for a leader, and other forms of influence may be expressly prohibited. The potential influence inherent in the nature of an administrative position and the authority vested in its occupant by superiors and subordinates is called "position power." The potential influence derived from the characteristics of the individual who occupies the administrative position is called "personal power." The two sources of influence are not entirely independent, but it is useful to distinguish between them.

Position Power

Organizations usually have some formal prescriptions regarding the use of compensation as a form of influence. Some managers are allowed to offer economic incentives (e.g., commissions, bonus, merit pay increase, stock options) to deserving employees. The conditions for offering such incentives may be specified exactly or left up to a manager's judgment within prescribed limits. Other tangible benefits may also be administered at the discretion of managers, including promotion, assignment to a better job, assignment of a more desirable work schedule, assignment of a better vacation schedule, delegation of more authority and autonomy, formal recognition of accomplishments (e.g., awards, commendations), and allocation of status symbols (e.g., bigger office, reserved parking place). The extent of a manager's authority and discretion in dispensing noneconomic rewards varies greatly from one organization to another, and across levels of management. Some managers have the opportunity to use all of these rewards, whereas other managers are severely restricted in how they may administer rewards.

The formal authority system of an organization and its traditions deal with the use of punishment as well as with the use of rewards. The authority of a manager to reprimand, suspend, demote, fine, transfer, or dismiss a subordinate is the source of his coercive power. Over the last two centuries, there has been a sharp decline in the legitimate use of coercion in organizations (Katz & Kahn, 1978). For example, supervisors once had the right to dismiss employees for any reason they thought was justified. The captain of a ship could flog sailors who were disobedient or who failed to perform their duties diligently. Army officers could threaten to shoot a soldier for desertion or failure to obey an order during combat. Nowadays, these forms of coercion are prohibited or sharply restricted in Western nations.

A leader's position power includes other things besides the right to make legitimate requests and administer rewards and punishments. The extent to which a leader is able to modify working procedures, organize the work, redesign jobs, and make changes in the technology determines the opportunities for situational engineering. Leaders with the discretion to modify the design of subordinate jobs have a potentially strong influence over subordinates' work motivation and satisfaction (Oldham, 1976). Research indicates a person's intrinsic motivation tends to be greater when the job requires a variety of skills, provides a sense of completing a meaningful task, provides direct feedback about performance to the person, and allows the person considerable autonomy in how the work is done (Hackman & Oldham, 1975). Thus, by redesigning subordinate jobs to increase these motivating characteristics, a leader may be able to increase subordinate motivation indirectly.

The degree of leader authority to make task-related decisions also has a bearing on the use of decision participation. If all major decisions about how the work is done and who does which job are made by higher management, then a lower-level manager has little opportunity to use participation by subordinates as a source of influence over them.

An especially important aspect of position power is control over vital information (Pettigrew, 1972). As will be discussed in more detail in Chapter 5, managers and administrators are the "nerve center" of an information network. They often have exclusive access to certain kinds of information from higher levels in the organization, from other parts of the organization, and from outside of the organization. Some of this information is received automatically through the formal communication system as a result of merely occupying a managerial position, but much of it can be obtained only if the leader establishes and maintains effective relationships with superiors, peers, and outsiders.

The degree to which a leader controls the flow of vital information determines his opportunity to interpret outside events for subordinates and to exert influence over their perceptions and attitudes (Kuhn, 1963). A tactic used by many political leaders is to generate hostility against some outside group or institution by feeding followers a steady flow of unfavorable propaganda that creates a negative impression, supports unfavorable stereotypes, arouses fears, and creates distrust. Exaggeration of an external threat can be used to influence followers to believe in the necessity of more restrictions on their behavior and the suppression of dissent.

Another tactic used by some leaders who control vital task information is to increase subordinate dependence on them by hoarding this information and making all key decisions alone. The leader's expertise relative to that of subordinates will be greater if he is the only person who "knows what is going on." He can claim that certain decisions are justified by circumstances, and subordinates will lack any evidence to dispute this claim. It is not surprising that many leaders try to prevent followers from getting information that will cause them to question controversial decisions made by the leader (Pfeffer, 1977).

Although tight restriction of information facilitates the use of influence methods such as information distortion, rational faith, rational persuasion, and indoctrination, it inhibits use of methods like decision participation and job redesign. If a leader wants to use group decisions and delegation of authority to increase subordinate motivation and have subordinates share the administrative burden, then it is essential to share relevant information openly and provide subordinates with direct access to outside sources of information. Of course, security considerations sometimes limit the extent to which a leader can disseminate strategic information to subordinates, but the need to maintain security is more often a convenient excuse for hoarding information than a valid constraint on sharing it.

Personal Power

The opportunity to use forms of influence such as rational persuasion, rational faith, and personal identification depends more on the characteristics of the leader than on the attributes of his position. In order to use rational persuasion effectively, a leader must have technical expertise, persuasive ability, and insight into the motives and perceptions of subordinates. The leader's apparent expertise relative to that of subordinates determines the extent to which they can be influenced by rational faith or rational persuasion (French & Snyder, 1959). A leader is more likely to be perceived as an expert if he acts confident, has a history of demonstrated knowledge and skill, has extensive practical experience, and has received a diploma, license, or other certification of education and training. A leader's "expert power" also depends on his credibility as a trustworthy source of advice and information. Use of rational faith requires a high degree of subordinate trust as well as belief in the leader's expertise.

Charisma and personal magnetism are another source of personal power. A leader with these attributes is better able to use personal identification, inspirational appeals, and rational faith to influence subordinates. They will tend to identify with him, imitate his behavior, and emulate his beliefs. The exact qualities required for charismatic leadership are not well understood. One important characteristic seems to be insight into the needs, hopes, and values of followers (McClelland, 1975). Another attribute of charismatic leaders is a dramatic, persuasive manner of speaking, which enables the leader to enunciate the hopes, ideals, and fears of followers and inspire faith in his ability to lead them to "victory," "success," or a "better world" (Berlew, 1974). As Gardner (1965, p. 3) pointed out, such leaders "can conceive and articulate goals that lift people out of their petty preoccupations, carry them above the conflicts that tear a society [or organization] apart, and unite them in the pursuit of objectives worthy of their best efforts." Charismatic leaders usually radiate the impression of complete confidence and intense inner conviction, which implies either that they really have extreme self-confidence, or that they possess the acting ability necessary to project this impression to followers (House, 1977). The charismatic leader appears somewhat mysterious and larger than life, a person who can be trusted to succeed where most people would fail. To create this impression, it is helpful to have a good understanding of the use of symbols, myths, rituals, staged events, and techniques of impression management through the mass media.

The opportunities for charismatic leadership depend on the nature of the situation, and there are fewer opportunities in business organizations than in political or religious organizations (Katz & Kahn, 1978). In addition, Berlew (1974) contends that most managers and administrators fail to recognize and take advantage of opportunities to inspire enthusiastic commitment among subordinates. In part, the low incidence of charismatic leadership in business organizations may be due to the scarcity of leaders possessing the necessary traits and skills. Charismatic leadership is discussed in more detail in the next chapter.

Upward and Downward Power

In the next section we will review sources of subordinate influence over their leader. It is important to remember that a leader has opportunities to use many of these same forms of influence in his relationship with his own superiors and peers. A leader's downward power is dependent to a considerable extent on the leader's upward and lateral power, especially his capacity to influence superiors to provide necessary resources and make needed changes (Cashman, et al., 1976; Evans, 1974; House, et al., 1971; Patchen, 1962; Pelz, 1952; Wager, 1965; Zaleznik, 1970).

SUBORDINATE POWER OVER SUPERIORS

In order to understand influence processes in leadership, it is necessary to consider the influence of subordinates on the leader as well as the leader's influence over subordinates. The potential influence of subordinates is sometimes called their "counterpower," and it serves as a restraint on the leader's exercise of power. The primary source of subordinate counterpower is the leader's dependence on subordinates. This dependency can take several forms. It is most obvious when the leader is selected by subordinates and can be replaced at their discretion. In groups with emergent or elected leaders who lack appreciable position power, the subordinates clearly hold the balance of power. Leaders are provided with the opportunity to exercise influence based on their expertise, attractiveness, and legitimate status, but their power will quickly vanish if they fail to satisfy the expectations and needs of followers. Thus, the most basic form of dependence is the need to satisfy followers in order to retain the leadership position.

For leaders who have substantial position power and are accountable to superiors or some power elite (e.g., a board of directors, the military), retention of the leadership position can be influenced but not completely controlled by subordinates. The removal of such leaders is difficult to accomplish by subordinates, and it would likely require an intense rebellion or a mass protest by a sizable percentage of them. The principal source of counterpower in organizations with appointed leaders is the leader's dependence on subordinates for attainment of other desirable outcomes besides retention of his office. One form of dependency occurs where leaders are formally evaluated by subordinates, and this evaluation influences the leader's compensation, reputation, and prospects for promotion to a better position. However, organizations seldom provide a formal mechanism for subordinates to evaluate their leaders. In most cases, subordinates influence the evaluation of leaders only indirectly. If subordinates perform well, they can help their boss gain a reputation as an effective manager. On the other hand, if they restrict production, sabotage operations, go out on strike, initiate grievances, hold demonstrations, and complain directly to higher management, subordinates can damage the reputation of their boss (Mechanic, 1962).

The counterpower of subordinates is more visibly displayed and more effectively exerted when subordinates organize to take collective action (Lee, 1977). Even the threat to establish a subordinate union or association may serve as a restraint on superiors. Counterpower is also enhanced when one or more subordinates forms an alliance with powerful persons in the organization (e.g., peers or superiors of the leader) or with outside groups (e.g., special interest lobbying groups, professional associations) that are able to exert pressure on the leader and on his superiors (Pfeffer, 1977).

Subordinates seldom need to exert their counterpower in overt threats and coercion. The mere fact that subordinates have substantial power to affect a leader's outcomes usually serves as a restraint on his abuse of position power and causes him to be more open to subordinate influence by noncoercive methods such as legitimate requests, rational persuasion, and normative appeals. However, if a leader badly underestimates subordinate counterpower and is unresponsive to subtle influence attempts by subordinates, then they are likely to resort to threats or overt acts of hostility.

As was true of leaders, individual subordinates derive power from control over vital information (Pettigrew, 1972). When subordinates have exclusive access to information that is used by superiors to make decisions, this advantage can be used as a source of subtle influence over the superior's decisions through information distortion. Information control also facilitates use of rational persuasion by subordinates, and in extreme cases may enable them to use rational faith as a form of influence over their boss. One tactic used to increase the leader's dependence on a particular subordinate is for the subordinate to assume responsibility for collecting, storing, and reporting operating information. Preparing reports with complex analyses that cannot be readily understood by the boss makes him dependent on the subordinate for interpretation of the reports, which may cause him to invite the subordinate to participate directly in decision making, such as by attending meetings and making recommendations (Korda, 1975).

Another source of subordinate influence is demonstration of special skill and expertise in dealing with critical problems in the organization. The ability to perform some function that the leader cannot do himself increases leader dependence on a subordinate (Mechanic, 1962). The same is true for a subordinate with special outside contacts and the ability to obtain resources needed by the leader. The power derived from this form of dependence is greatest when no substitute person is available to replace the subordinate, and the subordinate has opportunities to move to an attractive position in another organization if not satisfied in his present position (Pfeffer, 1977).

One problem with expert power is that it is quickly dissipated if special knowledge and expertise are shared to the point where people are no longer dependent on the agent. Subordinates may try to protect their expert power by keeping procedures and techniques shrouded in secrecy, by using technical jargon to make the task seem more complex and mysterious, and by destroying alternate sources of information such as operating manuals and written descriptions of computing procedures (Hickson, et al., 1971). For example, Goldner (1970) found that an industrial relations department intentionally negotiated a vague contract with the union in order to increase organizational dependence on the department and enhance its ability to get more resources from the organization. A related power tactic is to cause periodic crises covertly in order to increase the apparent uncertainty in the task and demonstrate competence in dealing with these crises (Pfeffer, 1977).

In highly bureaucratic organizations, knowledge of organizational rules and regulations is another type of expertise that may become a source of counterpower. Rules and tradition provide a basis for legitimate requests by subordinates. If the manager is newly appointed from the outside, subordinates will have an advantage for a time knowing rules and regulations better than the manager (Jacobs, 1970). Even in a situation where the boss is familiar with rules and regulations, if some of these rules are obsolete and contradictory, subordinates may be able to find an excuse for not doing something requested by the boss. A complex system of formal rules and operating procedures also provides subordinates with a coercive tactic that can be used with little risk of being dismissed or disciplined. Since written rules and procedures usually fail to cover all contingencies or to specify all behaviors necessary to do the work effectively, subordinates can seriously disrupt performance merely by following these rules and procedures exactly (Mechanic, 1962).

A final source of upward influence for a subordinate is demonstration of approval and loyalty. People who have lower power and status often try to use flattery and praise to ingratiate themselves with high-status persons. If flattery and praise appear insincere, they are unlikely to be effective, but if used in a subtle, skillful manner over a period of time, they may help a subordinate to establish a closer relationship with his boss. Other tactics for improving relations with the boss include being dependable and displaying loyalty when the boss is criticized by others (Dubrin, 1978).

SOCIAL EXCHANGE THEORY

Social Exchange Theory is an attempt to explain how the reciprocal process of influence between leaders and followers occurs over time. The theory uses interaction processes between individuals as the basis for explaining complex social behavior in groups. The most fundamental form of social interaction is an exchange of benefits or favors, which leads to mutual attraction when repeated over time. Many kinds of social exchange can occur, including material benefits and psychological benefits such as expressions of approval, respect, esteem, and affection. Individuals learn to engage in social exchanges early in their childhood, and they develop expectations about reciprocity and equity in these exchanges. Several versions of Social Exchange Theory have been proposed (Blau, 1964; Homans, 1958; Thibaut & Kelley, 1959), but the versions by Hollander (1979) and Jacobs (1970) are most relevant, because they are explicitly concerned with leadership.

Emergent Leaders

It is easier to begin by considering emergent leaders in small groups. During the course of interaction, some members of a group will appear to have more competence at the task than other members. By demonstrating competence and loyalty to the group, a member accumulates credits that contribute to his relative status in the group and affect expectations about the role he should play in the group. Hollander (1958, 1960, 1961) called these credits "idiosyncrasy credits," because a person who has a large accumulation of them is allowed by other members to deviate more from group norms without apparent penalty. Thus, in addition to gaining a higher position of status and influence, a member who is emerging as a leader is allowed some latitude for innovation. Since the person has demonstrated good judgment in the past, the group is willing to allow him considerable influence over task decisions. Group members are usually willing to suspend immediate judgment and go along with the emergent leader when he proposes innovative approaches for attaining group goals. In return for his higher status, increased influence, and freedom to devviate from nonessential norms and traditions, the emergent leader is expected to contribute his unique expertise and assume the responsibilities of the leadership role. The amount of status and influence accorded the person is proportionate to the group's evaluation of his potential contribution relative to that of other members. The contribution may involve the person's unique control over scarce resources and his access to vital information, in addition to skill and expertise in dealing with critical task problems.

When an emergent leader makes an innovative proposal that proves to be successful, the group's trust in his expertise is confirmed, and he may be accorded even greater status and influence. On the other hand, if the leader's proposals are implemented and they prove to be a failure, a different outcome is likely. If it is apparent that failure was due to circumstances beyond the leader's control, he may not be blamed for it, unless the group needs a scapegoat. However, if it appears to members that failure was due to the leader's poor judgment or incompetent behavior, then the terms of the exchange relationship will be reassessed. The reaction is more negative if the leader is perceived to have pursued his own selfish interests at the expense of the group than if he appears to have loyally served the group and tried his best. Selfish motives and irresponsibility are more likely to be attributed to a leader who willingly deviates from group norms and traditions. Thus, innovation by the leader can be a double-edged sword that cuts both ways. Success resulting from innovation leads to greater credit, but failure leads to greater blame.

The extent of a leader's reduction in status following failure depends in part on how serious the loss of potential and actual benefits is to the group. A major disaster results in greater loss of esteem than a minor setback. Loss of status by the leader also depends on how much status he had prior to the failure. The higher a leader's prior status, the more is expected of him and the greater the loss of status if he is believed responsible for the failure. These propositions of exchange theory are all supported by results from laboratory studies (Hollander, 1979).

Social Exchange Theory portrays the leader role as one in which some innovation is not only accepted, but is expected when necessary to deal with serious problems and obstacles. The risk of failure cannot be avoided by a leader who refuses to show initiative in the face of serious problems. The credits accumulated by a leader will begin to disappear if no action is taken to deal with such problems. The process of evaluating the exchange relationship by followers is an ongoing one, and an emergent leader cannot maintain a dominant position in the group unless it is showing progress toward attainment of its goals, or he can at least create the appearance of progress.

The foregoing discussion should not imply that the only basis for evaluating emergent leaders is their contribution to attainment of group goals. As a person consolidates his position as the acknowledged leader of a group, he tends to gain influence over a broader range of decisions, including role assignments, distribution of rewards, and modification of the group's goals. The leader is expected to carry out a variety of leadership functions and will be judged according to how well they are handled. The extent to which rewards are distributed fairly by the leader has an especially significant effect on his evaluation. Another important basis for evaluation by members is the extent to which the leader is dependable rather than unstable and impulsive. Still another basis for evaluation is the degree to which a leader helps to define reality for the group in a way that is consistent with their underlying needs and values.

In the process of interpreting the group's immediate experience, the leader is expected either to reaffirm established group objectives or to propose modifications in them as circumstances change drastically. For example, the original objective may be attained, or changing conditions may cause it to become impractical, in which case the group may experience an identity crisis. Expertise and initiative in problem solving, equitable distribution of rewards, dependable performance of duties, and definition of reality and purpose are the leader's major contributions to the group in return for his position of status and influence. The extent to which followers use these and other criteria for evaluating the leader's success will depend on their expectations for the leader, and these expectations tend to be somewhat different in different kinds of groups and task situations.

Formal Leaders and Legitimacy

Social Exchange Theory is also useful for analyzing leadership processes in organizations with formally designated leaders. The analysis is more complex, however, because the leader–follower exchanges are superimposed on an underlying exchange relationship between each follower and the organization. This more basic exchange relationship involves the formal or implicit social contract governing the terms of a person's membership in the organization and occupancy of his formal position. As noted earlier in this chapter, one condition for continued membership is acceptance of legitimate authority. Members are expected to follow the directions of their designated leaders as long as these directions do not exceed a leader's legitimate scope of authority. This authority and the considerable degree of position power that comes with the office makes formal leaders less dependent than informal leaders on subordinate evaluation of their contribution to the group. Even a formal leader who is obviously incompetent may be able to retain his position for a time because of his term of office (if there is no recall provision) or his employment contract. However, ability to retain his position does not prevent an incompetent leader from losing status and esteem among subordinates, and demonstrated incompetence may eventually undermine the leader's legitimate authority (Evan & Zelditch, 1961). The exchange process by which leaders gain influence from repeated demonstration of their expertise probably occurs for formal leaders in much the same way as it does for emergent leaders. As will be seen in the next chapter, the incremental influence derived by a formal leader in the exchange process with subordinates tends to be a more important determinant of leader effectiveness than the influence derived from formal authority.

The basis of legitimacy probably differs somewhat for elected and appointed leaders in formal organizations. The process of election may create higher expectations among followers and a greater feeling of responsibility for the leader's actions. Laboratory research on small groups finds that elected leaders enjoy more initial support from followers than appointed leaders and tend to be more assertive and innovative in their behavior (Hollander & Julian, 1970; 1978). However, elected leaders are more vulnerable to follower rejection by a group that is unsuccessful in attaining its goals.

VERTICAL DYAD LINKAGE THEORY

Up to this point, leader–follower transactions have been discussed in a general way without concern for possible differences in the kinds of exchange relationships established by a leader with different subordinates. The process of developing different exchange relationships is the theme of one version of Social Exchange Theory called Vertical Dyad Linkage Theory (Dansereau, Graen & Haga, 1975; Graen & Cashman, 1975).

The term "vertical dyad" refers to the relationship between a leader and one individual subordinate. The basic premise of the theory is that leaders usually establish a special relationship with a small number of trusted subordinates (the "in-group") who function as assistants, lieutenants, or advisors. The nature of this relationship is considerably different from the relationship established with the remaining subordinates (the "out-group"). Early in the history of the dyadic interaction between leader and subordinate, the leader initiates either an in-group or out-group relationship. It is not clear just how a leader selects members of the in-group, but Graen and Cashman (1975) suggest that selection is made on the basis of personal compatibility and subordinate competence and dependability. Over time, the dyadic exchanges with in-group subordinates follow a different developmental sequence than that occurring with out-group subordinates.

In the exchange relationship with out-group subordinates, there is a relatively low level of mutual influence. The primary source of leader influence is legitimate authority in combination with coercive power and a limited degree of reward power. The only requirement for out-group subordinates to satisfy the terms of the exchange relationship is their compliance with formally prescribed role expectations (e.g., rules, job duties, standard procedures) and with legitimate directions from the leader. As long as such compliance is forthcoming, the subordinate receives the standard benefits (e.g., compensation) for his position in the organization.

The basis for establishing a deeper exchange relationship with in-group subordinates is the leader's control over outcomes that are desirable to most subordinates. These outcomes include such things as assignment to interesting and desirable tasks, delegation of greater responsibility and authority, access to "inside information," participation in making some of the leader's decisions, allocation of tangible rewards (e.g., pay increase), provision of special benefits (e.g., better work schedule, bigger office), facilitation of a subordinate's career (e.g., recommendation for promotion, making assignments that assure greater visibility), and provision of personal support and approval. These things are provided to in-group subordinates in return for greater loyalty to the leader, commitment to work unit objectives, and sharing of administrative duties. The development of in-group relationships occurs gradually over a period of time, through reciprocal reinforcement of leader and member behavior as the exchange cycle is repeated over and over again. Unless the cycle is broken, the relationship is likely to develop to a point where there is a high degree of mutual dependence, loyalty, and support.

The benefits to the leader from an in-group relationship are evident. The assistance of committed subordinates can be invaluable to a manager who lacks the time and energy to carry out all of the duties for which he is responsible. In a large group, the assistance and commitment of some subordinates may be necessary to insure successful attainment of work unit objectives. However, the special relationship with in-group subordinates creates certain obligations and constraints for the leader. In order to maintain the in-group relationship, the leader must continue to provide support and attention, and he must remain responsive to the needs and feelings of the subordinates. The leader cannot resort to coercive, authoritative methods of influence without endangering the relationship. Instead, he must rely on persuasion and negotiation in the context of decision participation, and these consultative approaches require more time and effort on his part, especially when there is a controversial decision.

The benefits of a special exchange relationship to in-group subordinates are also evident, as long as the leader controls outcomes that they value highly. The in-group subordinates will have greater status and influence, more interesting and satisfying jobs, fewer problems with their boss, more opportunity for advancement, and a larger share of tangible rewards. With these benefits, however, come certain obligations and costs beyond those required of out-group subordinates. In-group subordinates are expected to be more devoted to their jobs, and in the process of assuming more responsibility, they also assume the risk of failure to handle this responsibility in a competent manner. There are other risks as well, such as possible alienation from friends who are not included in the in-group, and the danger of being too closely associated with a boss who may turn out to be a "loser" in some future power struggle in the organization.

Vertical Dyad Linkage Theory is not a situational contingency theory like those in Chapter 6, but the importance of situational factors is recognized. In a study by Cashman, Dansereau, Graen and Haga (1976), vertical dyads were studied at two levels in the authority hierarchy, in contrast to the initial research on dyads at only one level. The results indicated that the relationship between a manager and his subordinate was influenced in part by the relationship of the manager to his own boss. Managers who had a favorable in-group relationship with their boss were better able to establish in-group relationships with some of their own subordinates. The effects of the manager's upward relationship were felt by subordinates regardless of their own relationship with the manager. The managers who had in-group relationships with their own boss were described by subordinates as having more technical skill, providing more outside information, allowing more participation in decision making, allowing more subordinate autonomy, and providing more support and consideration. It is obvious that a manager who has more upward influence is in a better position to obtain benefits for subordinates and facilitate their performance by obtaining support and cooperation, cutting red tape, and gaining approval of changes desired by subordinates. The results from the study point out a major situational constraint on a leader's ability to establish a special exchange relationship with subordinates. If the leader has little to offer in the way of extra benefits, then there is little reason for subordinates to incur the extra obligations of a special exchange relationship.

Summary

It is desirable to distinguish between various forms of influence, because the prerequisite conditions and likely consequences are different. Eleven distinct forms of influence were proposed: legitimate request, instrumental compliance, coercion, rational persuasion, rational faith, inspirational appeal, indoctrination, information distortion, situational engineering, personal identification, and decision identification. Power was defined in terms of a person's potential to influence unilaterally the attitudes and behavior of certain persons in the desired direction.

Authority is the right of a person to influence others in specified ways. Acceptance of authority depends on the perceived legitimacy of the agent as an authority figure, which depends in turn on how the person was selected for his position in the organization. Scope of authority for a manager or administrator is dependent on the influence needed to accomplish role requirements, and there is usually some ambiguity about the appropriate scope. Since authority is useful as a source of influence only when regulations, directions, and requests are perceived to be legitimate, leaders cannot rely on authority as the sole basis for influencing subordinates.

Position power is the potential influence of a leader derived from the nature of the administrative position and the authority vested in its occupant, including control over organizational rewards and punishments, control over vital information, and control over the work environment and working procedures. The amount of position power varies greatly from one kind of leadership position to another.

Potential influence derived from characteristics of the person who occupies a leadership position is called personal power. Principal sources of personal power are the expertise, attractiveness, and charismatic qualities of a leader. These qualities facilitate the use of influence forms such as rational faith, rational persuasion, personal identification, and inspirational appeals.

Subordinate counterpower serves as a restraint on the leader's exercise of his position power. Subordinates derive power from the leader's dependence on them to keep him in office and to maintain his reputation as a competent manager. Subordinate power is increased by organizing to present a united front, by forming alliances with powerful persons or groups, by maintaining exclusive access to vital information, by developing special skills and coping with major problems facing the organization, by demonstrating dependability and loyalty, and by developing alternative job opportunities.

Social Exchange Theory is useful for explaining how the reciprocal influence processes between leaders and followers occur over time. Groups accord greater status and influence to a member who demonstrates loyalty to the group and competence in contributing to group activities and goal attainment. Innovative proposals can be a source of increased status when successful, but they will result in lower status if failure occurs and it is attributed to the leader's poor judgment and/or irresponsibility. Members continually evaluate the exchange relationship with their leader and will not continue to accord him the benefits associated with his high-status position unless the group appears to be making satisfactory progress toward attainment of its goals.

Vertical Dyad Linkage Theory deals with the development of different kinds of exchange relationships with different subordinates. Leaders usually establish special exchange relationships with some subordinates who are given extra influence, autonomy, and other benefits in return for greater loyalty, commitment, and help in performing administative duties. A leader's exchange relationship with his own boss and the resulting upward influence is an important determinant of the potential for establishing special exchange relationships with subordinates.

REVIEW AND DISCUSSION QUESTIONS

1. What are some different ways of defining power?

2. Why is authority necessary in formal organizations?

3. What is the basis for a leader's authority in an organization?

4. What forms of influence can leaders use over subordinates?

5. What are the sources of subordinate counterpower, and which forms of influence can be used by subordinates over their leaders?

6. Why is upward influence important for a leader?

7. Briefly explain Social Exchange Theory.

8. What are the practical implications of Social Exchange Theory for leaders?

9. Briefly explain Vertical Dyad Linkage Theory.

10. Define and explain each of the following terms: reciprocal influence process, power, authority, scope of authority, legitimate request, instrumental compliance, coercion, rational persuasion, rational faith, inspirational appeal, indoctrination, brainwashing, situational engineering, per-

sonal identification, decision identification, position power, personal power, charismatic leader, emergent leader, idiosyncrasy credit.

3

Power and Leader Effectiveness

Social Exchange Theory provides insight into reciprocal influence processes in leadership, but the comparative effects of different amounts and patterns of leader influence is an issue that is not directly addressed. Vertical Dyad Linkage Theory holds that in-group relationships facilitate group performance, but the theory does not indicate whether a leader who establishes separate in-group and out-group relationships will be more effective than a leader who is able to establish a special exchange relationship with all of his subordinates.

In the present chapter, we will examine how leader power and influence are related to leader effectiveness. Three questions will be considered: (1) what pattern of power usage is best? (2) how do effective leaders exercise power? and (3) how much power is optimal for a leader? In addition, House's (1977) theory of charismatic leadership will be reviewed to gain further insight into the reasons why charismatic leaders are able to exert so much influence over followers.

RESEARCH ON CONSEQUENCES OF POWER USAGE

A number of studies have been conducted to compare the effects of using different forms of power. Most of these studies have used influence measures based on the power typology proposed by French and Raven (1959). The five different bases of power in their typology are as follows:

1. REWARD POWER: The subordinate does something in order to obtain rewards controlled by the leader (same as instrumental compliance).

2. COERCIVE POWER: The subordinate does something in order to avoid punishments controlled by the leader (same as coercion).

3. LEGITIMATE POWER: The subordinate does something because the leader has the right to request it and the subordinate has the obligation to comply (same as legitimate requests).

4. EXPERT POWER: The subordinate does something because he believes that the leader has special knowledge and expertise and knows what is necessary (includes rational persuasion and rational faith).

5. REFERENT POWER: The subordinate does something because he admires the leader, wants to receive his approval, and wants to be like the leader (same as personal identification).

Relevant results from field studies on comparative effects of influence sources are summarized in Table 3–1. The use of different measures of leader effectiveness complicates comparison of the results across studies, but some trends in the results are evident. Influence based on the attractiveness and expertise of a leader was usually associated with greater subordinate satisfaction, less absenteeism and turnover, and higher performance. Use of legitimate power and coercive power tended to result in lower satisfaction and performance, or to be uncorrelated with them. The results for use of reward power were quite inconsistent, with no clear trend across studies.

The finding that effective leaders rely more on use of personal power derived from their expertise and attractiveness can be explained in terms of the complex nature of work roles in most task groups. Reliance on position power emphasizes the performance of formal role requirements prescribed by rules, regulations, and specific directions from the leader. It is unlikely that a group will achieve exceptional levels of performance if members merely meet these role requirements without showing enthusiasm or taking the initiative to do things that are necessary but not formally specified. In terms of Social Exchange Theory, the leader must establish "incremental influence transactions" beyond those based on authority and formal incentive systems in order to obtain subordinate commitment (Jacobs, 1970).

Limitations of Power Studies

The discovery that use of personal power is important for leader effectiveness does not necessarily imply that position power is unimportant. Although the power usage studies appear to favor that conclusion, interpretation of the findings is limited by some serious methodological problems in the research. One issue is the validity of the influence measures. It is difficult to measure accurately the manner in which one person exerts influence over another person. The power studies have depended on subordinates to report the relative usage of different forms of influence by their leader. Subordinates who are satisfied with their leader may attribute different forms of influence to him than subordinates who are dissatisfied and critical. For example, one would expect satisfied subordinates to attribute greater

TABLE 3-1

Summary of Selected Studies on Effects of Different Forms of Power

Study Date and Investigators	Sample Description	Criterion Variable	Leg.	Rwd.	Power Base Coer.	Expert	Ref.	Misc.
Bachman (1966)	685 Professors rate Deans	SAT/Dean	-.18**	-.31**	-.20**	.18**	.22**	
Bachman, Smith & Slesinger (1966)	36 Office Managers rated by 656 Salesmen	Group Perf.	-.17	-.55**	-.31	.36*	.40*	
		Group SAT/Mgr.	-.57**	-.51**	-.71**	.69**	.75**	
		Ind. Perf.	-.08	-.12**	-.09*	.13*	.09*	
		Ind. SAT/Mgr.	-.24**	-.16**	-.19**	.17**	.22**	
Dunne et al. (1978)	49 Military & Civilian Project Personnel (Interviews)	Commitment to:						
		Project Mgr.	.18	-.04	-.15	.63**	.26	.68**
		Functional Mgr.	.03	-.15	-.11	.43**	.20	.35**
		Willingness to Disagree with:						
(MISC.: Legitimacy Due to Work Responsibility)		Project Mgr.	.00	.10	-.06	.28*	.15	.20
		Functional Mgr.	-.14	.20	-.01	.20	.16	-.13
Hammer (1973)	227 Glaziers (g) & 39 Iron Workers (i) rate Supervisors	Motivation Index g		.16*	-.10	.26**		
		i		.40*	.32*	.05		
		Overall Perf. Rating g		-.10	-.35**	.07		
		i		.02	.00	.30		
		SAT/Supervisor g		.09	-.24	.50**		
		i		.20	-.06	.71**		
Ivancewich (1970)	34 Agency Managers rated by Agents	SAT/Status	-.12	.39*	-.21	.69**	.72**	
		SAT/Autonomy	.38*	.28*	-.10	.63**	.71**	
Ivancewich & Donnelly (1970)	31 Branch Managers rated by 394 Salesmen	Sales/Potential Sales	.11	-.09	.14	.21*	.25*	
		Sales/Number Orders	.07	.11	.08	-.02	.19	
		Orders/Number Calls	-.16	.23*	-.12	.16	.21*	
		Selling Cost Index	.13	-.04	.19	.22*	.10	
		Calls/Miles	.01	.12	.18	.09	.31*	
		Excused Absenteeism	-.16	-.19	-.04	-.29*	-.29*	

Ivancewich & Donnelly (cont'd) (1970) 31 Branch Managers rated by 394 Salesmen						
Unexcused Absenteeism	.04	.10	.11	-.14	-.22*	
Turnover	.06	-.07	.02	.04	.01	
Sheridan & Vredenburgh (1978) 216 Nurses rate Head Nurses						
Job Tension	.11	-.09	.34	-.21	-.09	
Perf. Rating	.02	.17	-.24	.12	.17	
Terminations	.01	-.08	.12	-.04	-.08	
Slocum (1970) 96 Scientists & Engineers rate Supervisors						
a. Professionally Oriented Subordinates						
Perf. Ratings	.07	-.52*	-.31*	.57**	.30*	
SAT/Supervisor	-.37*	.02	-.08	.45**	.30*	
b. Company-Oriented Subordinates						
Perf. Ratings	-.12	-.41**	-.22*	.22*	.23*	
SAT/Supervisor	-.32**	-.04	.01	.36**	.24*	
Student (1968) 39 Production Supervisors rated by 486 Workers						
Accidents	-.20	-.03	-.16	-.28*	-.12	
Excused Absenteeism	-.12	-.18	.16	-.28*	-.35*	
Unexcused Absenteeism	-.08	.18	.02	.02	-.02	
Turnover	.01	.14	.08	-.01	.23	
Indirect Cost Perf.	.00	.15	.22	.10	.40**	
Maintenance Cost Perf.	.10	-.20	-.30*	.18	.00	
Supply Cost Perf.	.08	.31*	.08	.32*	.21	
Scrap Cost Perf.	.06	.26	.12	.13	.33*	
Quality of Production	.11	.13	-.08	.31*	.32*	
Thambain & Gemmill (1974) 22 Project Managers rated by 66 Project Personnel						
Degree of Commitment	-.10	-.20	-.45**	.15	.00	.10
Willingness to Disagree	-.20	-.10	.00	.30*	.00	.25*
Involvement in Work	-.35*	-.15	.00	.00	.00	.45**
Performance Rating	-.30*	-.15	-.02	.40**	.17	.25*
(MISC.: Work Challenge)						
Warren (1968) 18 Principals rated by 528 Teachers						
Total Conformity	-.37*	.36*	.34*	.25	.75*	
Beh. Compliance	.02	.34*	.66*	-.15	.14	
Infl. on Atts.	.40*	.22	.09	.60*	.37*	

* p < .05
** p < .01

use of referent power to their leader. Subordinate perception of how well the group is performing may also bias attribution of leader influence; members of successful groups probably attribute greater expertise to their leader than members of poorly performing groups. Furthermore, it is difficult to separate the effects of different power sources. The possession of substantial reward and coercive power probably enhances the effectiveness of leader requests based on other forms of influence. Even though not invoked, the possibility that rewards and punishments may be used is likely to encourage compliance (Kahn, et al., 1964; p. 204). The leader's influence may be attributed by the subordinate to expert or referent power, but this influence would likely be less if the leader lacked reward and coercive power. Failure to utilize alternative methods to measure leader influence makes it impossible to know whether subordinates describe accurately how their leader exerts influence.

Another limitation of most studies on comparative effects of power usage is omission of intervening variables such as behavioral compliance and attitudinal change. An effort was made to measure these variables in only two of the studies. Warren (1968) found that use of reward and coercive power was correlated with behavioral compliance by subordinates but not with attitudinal commitment. Use of legitimate power, expert power, and referent power was associated with attitude change. In a study by Thambain and Gemmill (1974), the primary reason subordinates gave for compliance was the supervisor's legitimate power, and reward power was also important as a determinant of compliance. However, use of legitimate power and reward power was not associated with subordinate commitment.

The lack of clear association between use of reward power and leader effectiveness in the power studies is inconsistent with the findings of some other research on leadership and motivation. Several recent studies (Brass & Oldham, 1976; Keller & Szilagyi, 1976; Sims, 1977; Sims & Szilagyi, 1975, 1978; Oldham, 1976; Yukl & Kanuk, 1979) have found that use of rewards such as monetary incentives and recognition can be a very effective technique for improving subordinate satisfaction and performance. In light of this research, the possibility of biased results in the power usage studies seems even more likely.

Thus, it appears that the power research may tell us more about the manner in which a leader influences subordinates than about the power source behind this influence. Position power can be an important source of leader influence, but it will be related to group performance only when used in a manner that elicits subordinate commitment to task objectives. If position power is used in a manner that results in apathetic compliance by subordinates, or worse in covert resistance, then it will not facilitate group performance and may actually impede it. As shown in Figure 3–1, the manner in which a leader uses position and personal power determines whether the outcome will be subordinate commitment, compliance, or resistance. Both sources of power facilitate influence attempts, but power itself is not a direct cause of the intervening or end-result variables.

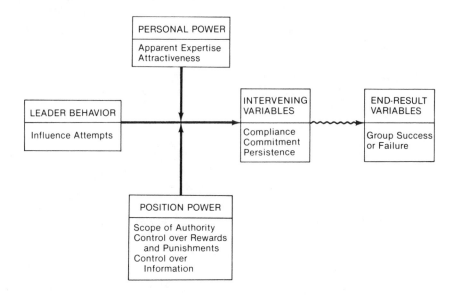

FIGURE 3–1
Leader Power and Leadership Effectiveness

GUIDELINES FOR EFFECTIVE USE OF POWER BY LEADERS

There is ample evidence that existence of a power differential is generally disturbing to the party with less power and status (Jacobs, 1970). Subordinates are aware that a powerful boss has the potential to cause them great inconvenience or harm. For this reason, even the subordinates of a benevolent leader tend to be very sensitive to his behavior, including subtle indications of approval or disapproval. Involuntary dependence on the whims of a powerful authority figure may create resentment as well as anxiety. Furthermore, unfavorable status comparisons with superiors may threaten a subordinate's self-esteem. Whyte (1969, p. 312) describes the hostile reaction of one employee to a new foreman:

He wants us to call him Mister Thomas. Every time he walks past I feel like walking up to him and punching him in the jaw. One of these days I'm going to do it.

Leaders who are sensitive to the disturbing aspects of a power differential seek to deemphasize this differential. They do not try to eliminate status differences altogether, but the status gap is reduced by actions that have symbolic importance to subordinates as an expression of the leader's acceptance and personal regard. Whyte (1969, p. 312) provides an example in a subordinate's description of an effective production foreman:

He spent his time out on the floor, not in the office. He used to wear work clothes, and when anything went wrong, he wasn't afraid to step in and get dirty.

Whyte points out that subordinates do not expect a supervisor to do their work or to be constantly available when they need help, but that a supervisor who is willing to help out in a difficult situation is building subordinate loyalty for a small expenditure in time and effort.

It is unfortunate that there has not been more research on the consequences of using different forms of influence. Most of the leader power research has been too superficial and simplistic to provide managers with much practical guidance. Nevertheless, by drawing on diverse kinds of research and theory in the behavioral sciences, it is possible to offer some guidelines that appear reasonable in light of what we do know. The following sections suggest ways to use each of French and Raven's five forms of power to elicit subordinate commitment, or at least to obtain willing compliance rather than resistance to the leader's requests and commands. Table 3–2 provides a brief summary of the likely outcome when each form of power is used in different ways.

Building and Using Referent Power

Referent power depends on a feeling of personal affection, loyalty, and admiration by a subordinate. Personal loyalty to a leader is something that develops slowly over a long period of time. Only rarely does a leader have sufficient charismatic attraction to engender immediate identification by subordinates. Charismatic leaders are discussed in more detail later in this chapter.

The way a manager or administrator treats subordinates is usually the most important determinant of referent power. A leader is

TABLE 3–2
Major Sources of Leader Influence over Subordinates and Likely Outcomes

Source of Leader Influence	Type of Outcome		
	Commitment	Compliance	Resistance
REFERENT POWER	LIKELY** If request is believed to be important to leader	POSSIBLE If request is perceived to be unimportant to leader	POSSIBLE If request is for something that will bring harm to leader
EXPERT POWER	LIKELY** If request is persuasive and subordinates share leader's task goals	POSSIBLE If request is persuasive but subordinates are apathetic about task goals	POSSIBLE If leader is arrogant and insulting, or subordinates oppose task goals
LEGITIMATE POWER	POSSIBLE If request is polite and very appropriate	LIKELY** If request or order is seen as legitimate	POSSIBLE If arrogant demands are made or request does not appear proper
REWARD POWER	POSSIBLE If used in a subtle, very personal way	LIKELY** If used in a mechanical, impersonal way	POSSIBLE If used in a manipulative, arrogant way
COERCIVE POWER	VERY UNLIKELY	POSSIBLE If used in a helpful, nonpunitive way	LIKELY** If used in a hostile or manipulative way

more likely to have loyal, devoted subordinates if he shows consideration for their needs and feelings, treats each person fairly, and defends their interests when acting as the group representative. Since referent power depends on the quality of the leader–subordinate relationship, a leader should spend some time in face-to-face interaction with each subordinate to cultivate the optimal kind of relationship (Sayles, 1979). A leader who spends most of his time with a few "favorite" subordinates risks alienating the remaining ones.

The development of personal loyalty, like the development of expert power, can be viewed as a social exchange process. The leader's relationship with subordinates will be improved by his expression of affection, trust, acceptance, and concern for their welfare. The relationship will be impaired if the leader expresses hostility, distrust, rejection, or indifference toward subordinates.

One way for a leader to gain referent power is to select subordinates who are likely to identify with him. A good example of this is the successful sales VP in a manufacturing company who, as an immigrant, began at the "bottom of the ladder" in the company. When he became a sales manager, he began recruiting other immigrants from his homeland. These immigrants constituted 85 percent of his workforce by the time he became a vice president. Their identification and loyalty were so strong that he could get them to implement new marketing programs in much less time than any of the company's competitors.

The most common way to exercise referent power is to make a "personal appeal." One variation of personal appeal is for the leader to say that he would be really pleased if the subordinate would carry out a particular request for him. Another variation is for the leader to say to subordinates that he is depending on them and needs their cooperation and support to deal with a problem. When making a personal appeal, the leader should indicate that the request is important to him. If subordinates think that the leader is not really concerned about a particular policy or action plan, then they are unlikely to make a concerted effort to implement it effectively. In this case, a personal appeal is likely to result in subordinate compliance but not enthusiastic commitment.

Even though a personal appeal based on strong referent power is usually successful, this form of influence clearly has its limitations. What subordinates are requested to do should be commensurate with the extent of their affection and loyalty. Some things are simply too much to ask, and if a leader asks for too great a sacrifice by subordinates, the request itself may irritate subordinates and cause them to think less highly of the leader. Personal appeals also reduce the leader's referent power if used too often. Here again, the leader is likely to be perceived as "taking advantage" of subordinates. An exchange theorist would contend that a leader who is continually making personal appeals is using up his "credits" faster than they can be replenished. Finally, the requested action should not be something that subordinates perceive to be harmful to the leader. A loyal subordinate is not likely to do anything to harm the leader he admires so much.

Another way to exercise referent power is through "role modeling." Since subordinates who identify with a leader tend to imitate his behavior, the leader should intentionally try to set an example of appropriate role behavior for subordinates. The leader should perform duties in a dedicated manner, fulfill job responsibilities diligently, maintain a positive attitude about the work, and avoid improper behavior.

Building and Using Expert Power

Possession of superior expertise is not a sufficient condition for a leader to influence subordinates. It is also necessary for the subordinates to recognize the leader's expertise and perceive him to be a credible source of information and advice. In the short run, the subordinates' perception of leader expertise is likely to be more important than his actual expertise. A new leader may be able to "fake it" for a time by acting confident and pretending to be an expert. However, over time as the leader's knowledge is put to the test, subordinate perceptions will become more accurate. The dynamic process wherein a leader gains or loses expert power is explained by Social Exchange Theory and was discussed in the preceding chapter.

There are a number of guidelines for acquiring and using expert power:

1. Promote an image of expertise. Since perceived expertise in many occupations is associated with a person's education and experience, a leader should make sure subordinates, peers, and superiors are aware of his formal education, relevant work experience, and significant accomplishments. One common tactic to make this information known is to display diplomas, licenses, awards, and other evidence of expertise in a prominent location in one's office. Another tactic is to make subtle references to prior education or experience (e.g., "When I was chief engineer at GE, we had a problem similar to this one"). However, this tactic can easily be overdone, and it is usually more effective to enlist the aid of others to promote your expertise than to do it yourself. For new leaders, it is advisable to avoid projects with a low likelihood of success. Instead, the leader should initially undertake projects that he is likely to complete successfully and for which success is highly visible. Such projects will rapidly enhance the new leader's reputation and expert power.

2. Maintain credibility. Once established, one's image of expertise should be carefully protected. The leader should avoid making careless comments about subjects on which he is poorly informed. If subordinates discover that the leader has made incorrect statements or has provided bad advice, his expert power will be diminished somewhat. Expert power also depends on subordinate trust of the leader. A leader will quickly lose credibility if subordinates discover that he has lied to them or is trying to manipulate them for his own personal benefit. If a serious "credibility gap" occurs, subordinates will begin to doubt the accuracy of anything the leader says, and it may never be possible for the leader to regain his initial credibility.

3. *Act confident and decisive in a crisis.* In a crisis or emergency, subordinates prefer a "take charge" leader who appears to know how to direct the group in coping with the problem. In this kind of situation, subordinates tend to associate confident, firm leadership with expert knowledge (Mulder et al., 1970). Even if the leader is not sure of the best way to deal with a crisis, to express doubts or appear confused risks the loss of influence over subordinates. The leader's capacity to exert expert power is increased in a crisis, often to the level of rational faith, but it may also be completely undermined if the leader displays panic and vacillates in his behavior.

4. *Keep informed.* Expert power is exercised through the processes of rational persuasion and rational faith. For managers and administrators, rational persuasion is by far the most common process. The leader's technical knowledge is the source of the facts and logical arguments used to persuade subordinates. Thus, it is essential for a leader to keep informed about the technical aspects of the work and about related developments in other parts of the organization. If subordinates are professionals, the leader will find it difficult to maintain an image of expertise unless he keeps up with developments in the field and remains professionally active.

5. *Recognize subordinate concerns.* As noted earlier in Chapter 2, a leader needs to have considerable persuasive ability to overcome the reservations and doubts of subordinates about changes or new policies. However, a highly persuasive leader may be tempted to overwhelm subordinates with a barrage of facts and logical arguments, without stopping to consider how subordinates perceive the situation. Consequently, the arguments presented by the leader may fail to address the major concerns of subordinates. Use of rational persuasion should not be regarded as a form of one-way communication from the leader to subordinates. Leaders who use this tactic successfully treat it as a form of two-way communication. These leaders actively seek to discover the feelings and attitudes of each subordinate and try to deal with them in making a persuasive appeal. Rather than telling subordinates "You have nothing to worry about," the skillful leader probes to discover what subordinates are in fact worried about, then tries to dispel these doubts and fears. If subordinates are concerned about the possible unfavorable consequences of a policy or action plan, the man-

ager should propose ways to avoid such consequences or to deal with them if they cannot be avoided.

6. Avoid threatening the self-esteem of subordinates. Expert power is based on a knowledge differential between leader and subordinates, but the very existence of such a differential can cause problems if the leader is not careful about the way he exercises expert power. As noted earlier, subordinates dislike unfavorable status comparisons where the gap is very large and obvious. They are likely to be upset by a leader who acts superior and arrogantly flaunts his greater expertise. In the process of presenting rational arguments, some leaders lecture at subordinates in a condescending manner and convey the impression that subordinates are "ignorant." The impression that a leader looks down on subordinates may also be created if the leader is completely unreceptive to subordinate objections, criticisms, and suggestions regarding his action plans. Competent, well informed subordinates are likely to have something to contribute to a leader's plans, even though the leader is acknowledged to have more skill and experience than any of the subordinates. These subordinates are likely to feel hostility toward a leader who rudely interrupts anyone trying to raise an objection, or who says that any objections by subordinates are ridiculous. A leader is more likely to be successful in using rational persuasion if he shows respect for the ideas and concerns of subordinates and attempts to modify his action plans to incorporate their ideas and deal with their concerns.

Even when rational persuasion is used in the most skillful manner, it is not always useful as an influence tactic. It is most appropriate when subordinates share the leader's task goals and are really interested in doing the work effectively. In this situation, the leader can use rational persuasion to convince subordinates that his plan of action is the best way to attain their mutual task goals. In a situation where subordinates are opposed to the leader's goals, or where it is obvious that the leader's action plan would entail unacceptable costs to subordinates, rational persuasion is unlikely to be successful.

Using Legitimate Power

Authority is exercised by making a legitimate request. Such a request may be communicated either orally or in written form, and may be expressed as a demand, command, order, directive, instruction, or request. The outcome may be subordinate commitment, compliance, or resistance, depending on the nature of the request and the manner in which it is made. There is less likelihood of subordinate resistance if the leader observes the following guidelines:

1. Make polite requests.   An arrogant demand (e.g., "I don't care if you like it, just do it!") is unlikely to result in subordinate commitment, and such a demand will probably engender resistance. A polite request is usually more effective, because it does not emphasize a status gap or imply subordinate dependence on the leader. It is advisable to include the word "please" in a legitimate request. For example, "Joe, would you please work on the ACME account after you finish the job you are doing now?" Use of a polite request is especially important for subordinates who are likely to be sensitive about status differentials and authority relationships, such as a subordinate who is older than the leader, or a subordinate with multiple supervisors (e.g., members of a project team or committee).

2. Make requests in a confident tone.   Making polite requests does not imply that the leader should plead with subordinates or appear apologetic about the request. To do so risks giving the impression that the request is not worthy and legitimate. A halfhearted, unenthusiastic request communicates doubt that subordinates will comply, and may thereby reduce the likelihood of compliance (Sayles, 1979). In an emergency, it is especially important for the leader to appear confident in directing the group's response, and here it is more important for requests to be assertive than polite. A direct order in the "command tone of voice" is sometimes necessary to shock subordinates into immediate action in an emergency.

3. Make clear requests and check for comprehension.   A leader should make legitimate requests in a clear, concise manner, using language that subordinates can understand. If the instructions are complex, it is advisable to provide written directions or have subordinates take notes. When a leader makes an ambiguous request, subordinates may hesitate to act for fear of doing the wrong thing. A leader should be sensitive to cues that subordinates fail to understand what they are supposed to do (e.g., puzzled expressions, confused or hesitant reactions). The leader can check for comprehension by asking a subordinate questions or by asking a subordinate to repeat the directions back to him.

4. Make sure that requests appear legitimate.   An illegitimate request is likely to be ignored or otherwise resisted, especially if it is something subordinates are opposed to doing. If there is any doubt as to a leader's authority to make a particular request, the leader should try to verify its legitimacy to subordinates. One way to do this is to refer subordinates to documentation such as written rules, policies, bylaws, charter provisions, union contract provisions, employment contract provisions, or established precedents and traditions. If the authority has been delegated by higher-level management, or is the result of reorganization imposed from above, the leader can call upon superiors to verify his authority. A manager or administrator should be very cautious about making requests that are not clearly within the scope of his authority. If an unusual request is necessary the leader should plan on using supplementary influence tactics (e.g., personal appeal, inspirational appeal, group decision) to gain acceptance for it.

5. *Explain reasons for the request.* A legitimate request is more likely to result in subordinate compliance or even in commitment if subordinates understand that the requested action is necessary to attain task objectives they share with the leader. It is advisable for a leader to explain the reasons for a legitimate request to subordinates, unless there is no time to do so or the reasons are already obvious. In effect, such an explanation involves using rational persuasion to enhance the acceptance of a legitimate request. One approach that is sometimes helpful is to review for subordinates the decision process used to arrive at the action plan they are being asked to implement. By taking subordinates through the process step by step, they will be able to see why the decision was made and why other alternatives were rejected. Thus, what might appear at first to be a foolish decision will be recognized by subordinates as the only realistic and sensible course of action available to the group. Of course, if the decision is in fact a foolish one, explaining why it was made will not convince subordinates otherwise.

6. *Follow proper channels.* Managers and administrators should give formal orders and directions through proper channels. When intermediaries are used to convey legitimate requests, it may create unnecessary problems. If one subordinate is asked to tell another of higher or equal status to do something, the latter subordinate may feel resentment, or may doubt that the request really came from the leader. Use of intermediaries to convey oral requests also risks the chance of distortion in the message, and the leader gives up the opportunity to observe the subordinate and directly evaluate the degree of comprehension and acceptance.

7. *Exercise authority regularly.* One way to increase subordinate responsiveness to leader authority is to exercise authority regularly. Subordinates will get used to being directed by the leader and are more likely to accept such direction as legitimate and normal (Sayles, 1979). For a new leader, or for one with unclear authority, it is best to begin with the most acceptable and obviously legitimate kinds of or-

ders and requests; these are not likely to be resisted by subordinates. Then the leader should gradually expand the scope of his orders and requests until the limits of his authority are mutually determined. In some cases, these limits will be well beyond what would have been acceptable to subordinates initially. Use of this tactic does not imply that the leader should resort to close supervision or meddling in subordinate activities. It is a matter of degree, and the appropriate amount of direction varies depending on the nature of the task, the subordinates, and the type of organization. Too much direction by the leader is oppressive and will engender resentment by subordinates. As Sayles (1979, p. 43) points out, "Subordinates don't want mindless or needless orders from managers who relish demonstrating their authority by commanding deference."

8. *Insist on compliance and check to verify it.* It is important for leaders to avoid instances of outright refusal by subordinates to carry out an order or request. Any nonresponse by subordinates begins to undermine the authority of the leader in the eyes of subordinates and increases the likelihood of future disobedience. A leader should be persistent in insisting that legitimate demands are met by subordinates. Often, subordinates will delay in complying with an order or request to see how serious the leader really is about it. If the leader does not follow up his initial request quickly with additional, more insistent ones, subordinates are likely to conclude that the request can safely be ignored. Leaders should be aware of this possibility and find ways to determine if immediate compliance has occurred.

9. *Be responsive to subordinate concerns.* Despite leader persistence, subordinates may still fail to carry out an authoritative request. Coping with initial nonresponse is an important requirement for effective leadership (Sayles, 1979). One approach is to apply more pressure on a subordinate to comply. This can be done by using other influence tactics such as rational persuasion, the promise of rewards for compliance, or the threat of punishment for noncompliance. These tactics are least effective when the subordinate has strong, personal reasons for resisting the leader's request, and the leader offers inducements or makes arguments that are irrelevant to the subordinate's primary concerns. Sayles (1979) recommends trying to discover the underlying reasons for the subordinate's resistance rather than immediately applying more pressure. According to Sayles, the leader should try to understand the subordinate's values, interests, anxieties, and desires by using nondirective interviewing. The subordinate is encouraged to talk about his objections, and the leader listens without interrupting,

arguing, or making judgments. Then the leader seeks through discussion to mutually redefine the problem in such a way that the subordinate has some opportunity to contribute to its solution. Together, they look for a way to satisfy the subordinate's concerns as well as the requirements of the task.

Using Reward Power

The most common way of using reward power is to offer tangible rewards to subordinates in an attempt to elicit instrumental compliance. Contingent rewards ("incentives") are often effective for influencing subordinate compliance with organizational rules or specific leader requests. The promise of a reward may be either explicit or implicit. Compliance is most likely under the following conditions:

1. Compliance can be verified. It is not feasible to use incentives unless the behavior of subordinates can be measured accurately enough to determine that compliance has occurred or that performance standards have been attained. Either the behavior itself must be observable, or there must be available measures of the consequences of subordinate behavior, such as performance measures.

2. The request is feasible. Unless subordinates perceive that they are capable of doing what is necessary to obtain the incentive, it is unlikely to induce them to make a serious effort. The perceived difficulty of the required behavior or performance standard depends on the nature of the task, the skills of the subordinate, the subordinate's self-confidence, and the presence of extraneous factors that could nullify subordinate efforts (e.g., insufficient supplies, machine breakdowns).

3. The incentive is attractive. In order to motivate compliance for something that a subordinate would not otherwise do, it is necessary to find a reward that is attractive to the subordinate. Since different kinds of rewards satisfy different needs, and subordinate needs vary in strength over time, it is vital to determine what needs are dominant for each subordinate at the time of the influence attempt. Rather than assuming that money is important to a subordinate, the leader should try to discover whether there are other, more desirable rewards, such as more time off, more responsibility, or more recognition. An incentive must not only be attractive, it must also provide benefits that exceed the likely costs to be incurred by a subordinate in the process of carrying out the leader's request. Moreover, the incentive must be something that cannot be attained by another, less costly course of action by the subordinate.

4. The leader is a credible source of the reward. In order to be motivated by the promise of a reward, subordinates must perceive that the leader can deliver on his promises. The leader needs to have enough authority and upward influence with higher management to obtain rewards valued by subordinates. In addition, subordinates must trust the leader enough to believe he will do what he has promised.

5. The request is proper and ethical. An incentive is more likely to influence subordinates if they perceive the leader's request to be ethical and proper under the circumstances. If a promised reward appears to be a "bribe" to do something improper, subordinates may be unwilling to be manipulated in this way. For example, a subordinate may not be willing to help cover up improper practices by the leader in return for a pay raise.

It should be obvious that the ideal conditions for using incentives are not always present. Many leaders lack control over attractive rewards. Subordinates often have interdependent tasks, which reduce a person's control over his own performance and make it difficult to use individual incentives, although group incentives may be feasible. Finally, for many kinds of tasks, no objective indicators of performance are available, and behavior is not readily observable.

Even when conditions are ideal for using incentives, there are a number of potential problems with this form of influence. Incentives are useful for obtaining subordinate compliance with rules or policies, but subordinate commitment is much more difficult to obtain. Even though a subordinate is eager to obtain the promised reward, the required behavior or task performance is likely to be seen as merely a means to an end. The subordinate may be tempted to take shortcuts and neglect less visible aspects of the task in order to complete it quickly and obtain the reward. The reward is unlikely to motivate the subordinate to put forth extra effort beyond what is required, or to show initiative in carrying out the task.

Use of reward power can lead to subordinate resistance if the leader uses it in a manipulative manner. The leader's power to give or withhold rewards may cause resentment among subordinates who dislike being dependent on a powerful authority figure, or who believe that the leader is manipulating them to his own advantage. When rewards are used as contingent incentives, it is difficult to avoid the appearance of manipulation.

Subordinates of a leader who uses incentives frequently are likely to define their relationship with him in purely economic terms. They will come to expect special rewards very time the leader wants them to do something new or unusual. The tendency for subordinates to view their relationship with the leader as an impersonal exchange of tangible benefits is greatest when the leader establishes an excessively mechanistic incentive system that specifies the exact payoff for every possible level of subordinate performance (e.g., piece rate incentive, sales commissions).

Rather than using rewards as explicit incentives, a leader should use them in a more subtle manner to recognize and reinforce desired behavior. A leader can make it clear to subordinates that they will be rewarded for their contributions, accomplishments, and diligent efforts without having to establish an elaborate incentive system. It is still essential to find reasonably accurate indicators of performance, and it is still desirable to establish performance standards and goals, but the reward contingencies do not have to be established in detail. This proposition is consistent with the commonly accepted belief that meetings to provide performance appraisal feedback should be separated from discussion of salary increases. Whenever possible, a leader should try to use reward power to supplement and strengthen his referent power. Rewards should be given in a way that expresses a leader's personal appreciation for a subordinate's efforts and accomplishments. Used in this way, reward power can be a source of increased referent power, because people who repeatedly provide rewards in an acceptable manner gradually come to be liked more by the recipients of the rewards (French & Raven, 1959). It is more satisfying for both leader and subordinate to view their relationship in terms of mutual friendship and loyalty than as an impersonal economic exchange.

Coercive Power and Discipline

Effective leaders try to avoid using coercive power except when absolutely necessary, because it is likely to create resentment and erode their referent power. With coercion there is no chance of gaining subordinate commitment, and even willing compliance is difficult to achieve. Subordinates typically react to coercion with physical withdrawal (e.g., quit, stay away from work), psychological withdrawal (e.g., daydreaming, alcoholism), or hostility and aggression (e.g., sabotage, theft, strikes, slowdowns). Although coercion has been one of the most commonly used forms of influence throughout history, its frequent use is probably due more to convenience and ignorance than to demonstrated effectiveness. There are some situations where coercion is appropriate, and historical accounts provide evidence of its effective use in maintaining discipline and dealing with rivals, rebels, and criminals. The threat of punishment for violation of laws and sacred tradition is recognized as an essential aspect of legitimate authority in most social systems. Nevertheless, coercion and punishment are effective only when applied to a small percentage of the membership under conditions considered legitimate by most members. When leaders are tempted to use coercion on a large scale against followers, it undermines their authority and creates a hostile opposition seeking to restrict their power or remove them from office (Blau, 1956).

In work organizations, the potential for effective use of coercion is quite limited. Even under extreme conditions, where administrators have the power to torture and murder workers, coercion is usually ineffective. Webber (1975) relates an example of disastrous consequences resulting from reliance on coercion in a Nazi bomb factory manned by slave labor during World War II. The workers hindered production by persistently requesting detailed instructions and doing nothing constructive on their own initiative. They sabotaged production by improperly fitting the bomb fuses, and the sabotage was discovered only after the bombs were dropped and they failed to explode. It was impossible for the guards to detect the sabotage and ensure minimal performance of role requirements unless they watched each worker closely. Close surveillance required nearly as many guards as workers. As Webber noted, it would have been more sensible to have the guards do the work instead of the slaves.

Use of coercion is usually discussed in the context of maintaining discipline. Coercion is most appropriate when it is used to deter behavior that is very detrimental to the organization (e.g., theft, sabotage, violation of safety rules, fighting, direct disobedience of legitimate orders). Coercion is more likely to result in compliance rather than resistance if the leader uses an approach sometimes referred to as "positive discipline." Rather than trying to scare a subordinate with threats or sample doses of punishment, the leader tries to induce the subordinate to assume responsibility for helping to resolve the discipline problem. The following guidelines combine suggestions for effective discipline from several different writers (Arvey & Ivancevich, 1980; Haimann & Hilgert, 1977; Preston & Zimmerer, 1978; Schoen & Durand, 1979; White, 1975).

1. Inform subordinates about rules and penalties for violations. When coercion is used as a deterrent of undesirable behavior, it is essential to specify clearly what kinds of behavior are unacceptable. Otherwise, subordinates may not be aware of various rules and regulations. Subordinates should also be made aware that violations are a serious matter. It is not desirable to specify in detail exact punishments for every violation, but subordinates should understand how serious the consequences would be if violations occur.

2. Administer discipline consistently and promptly. A leader should not overlook or ignore infractions, nor should he delay too long in responding to them. Failure to act invites repetition of the infraction, because subordinates may conclude that they can "get away with it." Consistent enforcement of rules and regulations over time is essential to insure that subordinates understand what is expected and to avoid perception of the leader as arbitrary and impulsive. Discipline should also be consistent from one subordinate to another so that the leader doesn't appear to be showing favoritism.

3. Provide sufficient warning before resorting to punishment. A few types of infractions are so serious that the violator should be immediately dismissed, expelled, or arrested. However, for most kinds of violations, it is best to use a pattern of progressive disciplinary steps, beginning with one or more oral warnings, then written warnings, before using actual punishment such as an official reprimand, suspension, demotion, or dismissal. Gradual escalation of coercion increases the likelihood that subordinate compliance can be obtained without having to resort to punishment. When giving a warning, the leader should indicate clearly what is expected of the subordinate and what must be done to avoid punishment. The required conditions should be something the subordinate is capable of doing if he makes a serious effort.

4. Get the facts before using reprimands or punishment. When a leader has an indication that discipline is needed, a prompt investigation should be made to gain a better understanding of the problem. It is essential to avoid jumping to conclusions. Even when a violation appears obvious, there may be extenuating circumstances. For example, the leader's directions may have been countermanded by the leader's boss, or a rule violation may have been necessary to deal with an emergency. A hasty reprimand or punishment can be very embarrassing to a leader if it turns out to be unjustified. This kind of incident seriously impairs relations with subordinates.

5. Stay calm and avoid appearing hostile. Situations involving discipline tend to be highly charged with emotion, and there is always a danger of losing one's temper. If the leader is hostile and insulting, the subordinate is likely to react with anger and resentment. Warnings should be communicated calmly and in a way that avoids the appearance of hostility or personal rejection of the subordinate. The subordinate should be given ample opportunity to respond to any charge of improper behavior or inadequate performance, and the leader should convey a sincere desire to help the subordinate comply with role expectations and avoid the need for punishment.

6. *Maintain credibility.* It is very important for a leader to maintain credibility with respect to his coercive power. Loss of credibility is likely for a leader who makes threats and warnings but fails to follow up with the appropriate punishment when the infractions continue. Credibility is also lost by threatening extreme sanctions that exceed the leader's authority and cannot possibly be enforced. Finally, credibility is lost when the leader announces a punishment, then changes his mind and rescinds it.

7. *Use appropriate punishments.* The type of disciplinary action taken by a leader should be consistent with organizational rules, policies, and traditions. The magnitude of punishment should be commensurate with the seriousness of the infraction. Subordinates are more likely to accept the legitimacy of punishment if it is consistent with established practice and is not excessive. Subordinates should not be punished for something beyond their control if they have acted in a responsible, appropriate fashion.

8. *Administer warnings and punishments in private.* It is advisable to avoid giving reprimands to a subordinate in front of other persons. A subordinate who is publicly embarrassed may become extremely defensive and resentful. He may decide to act openly defiant in order to show coworkers that he is not intimidated by the supervisor. In either case, the likelihood of compliance is reduced.

TWO FACES OF POWER

The discussion of how to use power effectively reflects an assumption that there are two fundamentally different approaches to the use of power (McClelland, 1970). One approach seeks to dominate and subjugate subordinates by keeping them weak and dependent on the leader. All five forms of power can be used to this end. Rewards and punishments are used to manipulate and control subordinates. Authority is used as an excuse to command obedience by subordinates, and it is highly centralized in the leader, with little delegation or participation. Expert power is maximized by skillful impression management designed to maintain an image of infallibility, as well as by preventing subordinates from gaining access to vital information. Referent power is accumulated by using public relations tactics and media management to glorify the leader and make him appear benevolent. Leaders who use power in this way are sometimes very successful in maintaining their preeminent position and developing a "cult of personality." However, over time the organization will suffer from this kind of leadership. There will be less initiative and creativity in dealing with new problems, and any commitment that is generated will be to the leader personally rather than to the goals and ideals of the organization. If the leader dies or leaves the organization, there is likely to be a serious crisis caused by the abrupt power vacuum. If followers begin to tire of their dependence and come to resent their lack of influence and autonomy, they may eventually rebel against the leader, just as children of authoritarian parents often do when they grow older.

In contrast, the other approach to power seeks to build the skills and self-confidence of subordinates rather than to make them weak. Power is exercised in a cautious, responsible manner, consistent with the objective of maximizing internalized motivation and self-control among subordinates. This kind of leader seeks to build commitment to the organization and its ideals rather than to himself. Authority is delegated to a considerable extent, information is shared openly, and participation in decision making is encouraged. The enlightened leader also seeks to raise the consciousness of followers by appealing to higher ideals and moral values, rather than to baser motives such as fear, prejudice, jealousy, and greed (Burns, 1978).

Charismatic leaders appear to represent a blend of both uplifting and domineering styles of exercising power, but it is obvious from historical accounts that a charismatic leader may emphasize either one style or the other. A Hitler or Reverend Jones (of the Jonestown massacre) represents one extreme; a Gandhi or Martin Luther King, Jr., represents the other extreme. Which path is chosen depends on the personality of the leader, and this will be discussed further in Chapter 4.

HOUSE'S CHARISMATIC LEADERSHIP THEORY

Since charismatic leaders are so successful in influencing follower commitment, it is worthwhile to take a closer look at the way in which these leaders exercise personal power. The most comprehensive theory of charismatic leadership is the one proposed by House (1977). His theory is based on theoretical propositions and research findings from a variety of social science disciplines. The theory helps to reduce some of the mystery surrounding charismatic leadership by identifying how such leaders differ from other people, how they behave, and the conditions under which charismatic leadership is most likely to occur.

The extent to which a leader is charismatic is assessed with several indicators:

1. Followers' trust in the correctness of the leader's beliefs.
2. Similarity of followers' beliefs to the leader's beliefs.
3. Unquestioning acceptance of the leader by followers.
4. Followers' affection for the leader.
5. Willing obedience to the leader by followers.
6. Emotional involvement of followers in the mission of the organization.
7. Heightened performance goals of followers.
8. Belief by followers that they are able to contribute to the success of the group's mission.

The theory consists of several propositions identifying essential leader traits, behaviors, and situational conditions. Each proposition will be explained briefly.

Propositions

Charismatic leaders are likely to have high self-confidence, a strong conviction in their own beliefs and ideals, and a strong need to influence people (need for power). A strong need for power motivates the leader to attempt to persuade followers and influence their behavior. Self-confidence and strong convictions increase the likelihood that subordinates will trust the leader's judgment. A leader without confidence in himself or his beliefs is less likely to try to influence people, and when an attempt is made, it is less likely to be successful.

Charismatic leaders are likely to engage in behaviors designed to create the impression among followers that the leader is competent and successful. This kind of impression management bolsters subordinate trust in the leader's decisions and increases willing obedience by followers. In the absence of such behavior, problems and setbacks may erode subordinate confidence and undermine the leader's influence.

Charismatic leaders are likely to articulate ideological goals for subordinates. These leaders relate the work and mission of the group to deeply rooted values, ideals, and aspirations shared among followers. By providing an appealing vision of what the future could be like, charismatic leaders give the work of the group more meaning and inspire enthusiasm and excitement among followers. The net effect is a greater emotional involvement by followers in the mission of the group and greater commitment to group objectives.

Since charismatic leaders rely heavily on appeals to the hopes and ideals of followers, a necessary condition for occurrence of charismatic influence is the possibility of defining follower roles in ideological terms that will appeal to them. It is evident that some work roles have low potential for ideological appeals, particularly simple, repetitive work in business organizations. Some possibility exists that stressful conditions are also a prerequisite for charismatic leadership, but there is still too little evidence to justify stating an additional proposition to this effect.

Charismatic leaders are likely to use role modeling wherein they set an example in their own behavior for followers to imitate. This process involves changes in the perception, attitudes, values, and emotional responses of followers as well as the imitation of the leader's behavior. In other words, if followers admire a leader and identify with him, they are likely to imitate his behavior and emulate his beliefs and values. Through this process, charismatic leaders are able to exert considerable influence on subordinates' job satisfaction and motivation.

Charismatic leaders are likely to communicate high expectations about follower performance, while simultaneously expressing confidence in followers. Leaders with strong referent power can induce subordinates to set higher performance goals and gain their commitment to these goals. However, such commitment will not occur unless subordinates perceive that the goals are realistic and attainable. If subordinates lack confidence in their ability to meet the leader's high expectations, they may resist the leader's influence attempts and decline to make a serious effort. The expression of confidence by a highly admired leader is likely to boost subordinates' self-esteem and give them hope that success is indeed possible.

Charismatic leaders are more likely to behave in ways that arouse motives relevant to the accomplishment of the group's mission. Arousal of achievement motivation is relevant for complex, challenging tasks requiring initiative, calculated risk taking, personal responsibility, and persistence. Arousal of power motivation is relevant for tasks requiring subordinates to be competitive, persuasive, and aggressive. Arousal of affiliation motivation is relevant for tasks requiring cooperation, teamwork, and mutual support among subordinates. Motives can be aroused by giving inspirational talks with emotional appeals to follower values, with emphasis on such things as "team loyalty," "being the best," "defeating the enemy," and so on.

Evaluation of the Theory

In support of his theory, House (1977) reviews relevant evidence from earlier research in a number of disciplines. The theory was based on these findings and appears to be consistent with them. However, the theory is so recent that there has been little new research to test the propositions as presently stated.

The major contribution of the theory is to explain charismatic leadership in terms of a set of testable propositions. These propositions involve straightforward behavioral processes rather than the typical forklore and mystique surrounding charismatic leadership. The theory includes leader traits, influence, behavior, and situational factors, giving it a comprehensive scope rarely found in the leadership literature.

HOW MUCH POWER IS DESIRABLE FOR LEADERS?

The extent to which a given amount of power is adequate depends in part on the leader's strategy in applying this power to specific ends. There are always finite limits to a leader's influence, and a given amount of power can be used in more or less effective ways. Less power is needed by a leader who has the skills to use power effectively and who recognizes the importance of concentrating on essential objectives. Bauer (1968, p. 17) explains the need for careful application of power so as to maintain a favorable relationship with subordinates, peers, and superiors.

> In any ongoing institution, the ability to get important things done is dependent upon maintaining a reservoir of goodwill. The person who fights every issue as though it were vital exhausts his resources including, most especially, the patience and goodwill of those on whom he has to depend to get things done. Therefore, it should be considered neither surprising nor immoral that, when an issue is of low salience, the sensible individual may use it to build goodwill for the future, or pay off past obligations, by going along with some individual for whom the issue is of high salience.

In the final analysis, the amount of necessary power and the effectiveness of different patterns of influence depend on the perspective of the person making the evaluation and on the priorities assigned to different criteria of leadership effectiveness. Most research on power usage has focused on subordinate performance as the primary criterion, and it has usually been assumed that some combination of subordinate compliance and commitment is necessary to achieve exceptional performance. This research indicates the importance of personal power, but it does not resolve whether a leader can maintain high levels of group performance if he has no substantial position power.

The amount of position power necessary for leader effectiveness is likely to vary from situation to situation. Position power is more important when a leader needs to influence subordinate compliance with unpopular rules or procedures, and there is inadequate potential for influencing subordinates by use of personal power or appeal to subordinate values. Some control over rewards is necessary if rewards are to be used in establishing a deeper exchange relationship. Some authority to make decisions is necessary for the leader to use decision participation. Thus, in general, it is desirable for a leader to have a moderate amount of position power. However, too much position power can be as detrimental as too little. Leaders with a great deal of position power may be tempted to make excessive use of instrumental compliance, coercion, information distortion, and situational engineering, instead of making an effort to develop and use personal power. The notion that power corrupts is especially relevant for position power. In an experiment by Kipnis (1972), leaders with greater reward power used it more often to influence subordinates, perceived subordinates as objects of manipulation, devalued the worth of subordinates, attributed subordinate efforts to their own power use, and preferred to maintain social distance from their subordinates. Although only a laboratory study with students, the research clearly points out the potential dangers of excessive position power.

The question remains whether it is desirable for leaders to have a great amount of personal power. Personal power is less susceptible to misuse, since it is eroded rapidly when a leader acts contrary to the interests of followers. Nevertheless, the potential for corruption remains. It is quite possible that the experience of great influence over followers due to a leader's charismatic appeal or superior expertise will tempt him to act in ways that will eventually lead to his downfall (Zaleznik, 1970). McClelland (1975, p. 266) describes this phenomenon:

> How much initiative he should take, how persuasive he should attempt to be, and at what point his clear enthusiasm for certain goals becomes personal authoritarian insistence that those goals are the right ones whatever the members of the group may think, are all questions calculated to frustrate the well-intentioned leader. If he takes no initiative, he

is no leader. If he takes too much, he becomes a dictator—particularly if he tries to curtail the process by which members of the group participate in shaping group goals. There is a particular danger for the man who has demonstrated his competence in shaping group goals and in inspiring group members to pursue them. In time both he and they may assume that he knows best, and he may almost imperceptively change from a democratic to an authoritarian leader.

Studies of the amount of influence exercised by organizational members at each level in the authority hierarchy in several different kinds of organizations reveal that the most effective organizations have a high degree of reciprocal influence (Bachman, Smith & Slesinger, 1966; Smith & Tannenbaum, 1963). The results suggested that leaders in the more effective organizations created relationships in which they had strong influence over followers but were also receptive to influence from followers.

One of the best ways to insure that a leader remains responsive to follower needs is to provide formal mechanisms to promote reciprocal influence and discourage arbitrary actions by the leader. Rules and policies can be enacted to regulate the exercise of position power and limit the use of coercion. Grievance and appeals procedures can be enacted, and independent review boards can be established to protect subordinates against misuse of power by their leader. Bylaws, charter provisions, and official policies can be drafted to require a leader to consult with subordinates and obtain their approval on specified types of decisions. Regular surveys can be conducted to measure subordinate opinions about the leader and determine if they are satisfied with him. In organizations where it is appropriate, periodic elections or votes of confidence can be held to determine if the leader should continue to occupy his position of authority. Leaders can facilitate reciprocal influence by inviting subordinates to participate in making decisions that affect them. Decision participation is discussed in detail in Chapter 8.

Summary

Research on the use of different forms of power by leaders suggests that effective leaders rely more heavily on personal power than on position power Nevertheless, position power is also important. Whether a leader is able to obtain subordinate commitment depends to a great extent on the manner in which power is exercised. Effective leaders are likely to exercise power in a subtle, careful fashion that minimizes status differentials and avoids threats to the self-esteem of subordinates. In contrast, leaders who exercise power in an arrogant, manipulative, domineering manner are likely to engender resistance by subordinates.

Power can be used either to dominate subordinates and make them weak, or to uplift subordinates and build their competence and self-esteem. The latter approach is more beneficial to the organization and its members. Charismatic leaders appear to represent a blend of both the domineering and uplifting styles of exercising power.

House has proposed a theory to explain charismatic leadership in terms of the leader's traits, behavior, and influence, and the situational conditions enhancing subordinate receptivity to ideological appeals. The theory appears promising, but it has not been directly tested as yet.

The amount of position power necessary for leader effectiveness depends on the nature of the organization, task, and subordinates. If the leader has too much reward and coercive power, he is tempted to rely on them excessively instead of using referent and expert power. This path leads to resentment and rebellion. On the other hand, if the leader lacks sufficient power to provide equitable rewards, make necessary changes, and punish chronic troublemakers, then he will find it difficult or impossible to develop a high-performing group.

REVIEW AND DISCUSSION QUESTIONS

1. How are position power and personal power related to leader effectiveness?

2. How much power is optimal for a leader?

3. What problems have impeded research on leader power and influence?

4. What should a leader do to acquire and effectively use expert power?

5. What should a leader do to acquire and effectively use referent power?

6. What should a leader do to exercise authority effectively?

7. Under what conditions are incentives most likely to result in subordinate compliance?

8. Some writers have asserted that leaders should never use coercion and punishment. Do you agree? Explain your answer.

9. What should a leader do if a subordinate fails to carry out an order or request?

10. How are charismatic leaders able to exert so much influence over followers?

11. Define and explain each of the following terms: reward power, coercive power, legitimate power, expert power, referent power, commitment, compliance, resistance, positive discipline.

4

Leadership Traits and Skills

One of the earliest approaches for studying leadership was the trait approach. Underlying this approach was the assumption that some persons are "natural leaders". Such persons were assumed to be endowed with certain traits not possessed by other people. The early leadership researchers were not sure what traits would be essential for leadership effectiveness, but they were confident that these traits could be identified by empirical research. Trait research was facilitated by the rapid development of psychological testing during the period from 1920 to 1950. The kinds of traits studied most frequently in the early leadership research included physical characteristics (e.g., height, appearance, energy level), personality (e.g., self-esteem, dominance, emotional stability), and ability (general intelligence, verbal fluency, originality, social insight).

In this chapter, the various approaches for studying the personal attributes of successful leaders will be reviewed. The emphasis will be on traits relevant for leadership effectiveness, rather than on traits related to leader emergence. The objective will be to identify traits that appear to contribute to a person's capacity to assume an administrative position and perform its role requirements successfully.

RESEARCH ON LEADER TRAITS

Over a hundred studies on leader traits were conducted in the period from 1904 to 1948. In the majority of studies, the general approach was to compare leaders with nonleaders to see what differences existed with respect to physical characteristics, personality, and ability. A smaller number of studies compared successful leaders with less successful leaders, or correlated measures of various traits with measures of leadership effectiveness. Success and leadership effectiveness were sometimes measured in terms of group performanance, and sometimes in terms of personal advancement up the authority hierarchy of the organization (i.e., successful leaders get promoted to higher levels of management and earn a larger salary relative to persons of the same age). Studies in which leaders are rotated among similar work groups are occasionally regarded as part of the trait approach, but these studies (Feldman, 1937; Jackson, 1953; Rosen, 1969; Wyndham & Cooke, 1964) tell us more about the effect of changing leaders than about the specific traits of effective leaders.

The trait research has been reviewed at various times by different scholars (Gibb, 1954; Jenkins, 1947; Mann, 1959; Stogdill, 1948, 1974). The two reviews by Stogdill can be compared to discover how conceptions about the importance of leader traits have evolved over a quarter of a century.

Stogdill's 1948 Review

In his early review, Stogdill examined the results of 124 trait studies from 1904 to 1948. A number of traits were found to differentiate repeatedly between leaders and nonleaders in several studies. The pattern of results was consistent with the conception of a leader as someone who acquires status through active participation and demonstration of his capacity to facilitate the efforts of the group in attaining its goals. Traits relevant to the assumption and performance of this role include intelligence, alertness to the needs of others, understanding of the task, initiative and persistence in dealing with problems, self-confidence, and desire to accept responsibility and occupy a position of dominance and control. For a few traits, such as dominance and intelligence, there were some negative correlations, which may indicate a curvilinear relationship.

Despite the evidence that leaders tend to differ from nonleaders with respect to certain traits, Stogdill found that the results varied considerably from situation to situation. In several studies that measured situational factors, there was evidence that the relative importance of each trait depends upon the situation. Thus, Stogdill (1948, p. 64) concluded: "A person does not become a leader by virtue of the possession of some combination of traits, . . . the pattern of personal characteristics of the leader must bear some relevant relationship to the characteristics, activities, and goals of the followers."

In effect, the early studies failed to support the basic premise of the trait approach that a person must possess some particular set of traits in order to become a successful leader. Although some traits appeared widely relevant for different kinds of leaders, these traits were neither necessary nor sufficient to insure leadership success. A leader with certain traits could be effective in one situation but ineffective in a different situation. Furthermore, two leaders with different patterns of traits could be successful in the same situation. None of the traits in these studies correlated very highly with leadership effectiveness when considered alone. Various combinations of traits correlated more highly with leader effectiveness, but only within certain limited situations.

Stogdill's 1974 Review

In his 1974 book, Stogdill reviewed 163 trait studies conducted during the period from 1949 to 1970. In this more recent set of trait studies, a greater variety of measurement procedures was used, including projective tests (e.g., Thematic Apperception Test, the Miner Sentence Completion Scale), situational tests (e.g., In-Basket, Leaderless Group Discussion), and forced choice tests (e.g., Ghiselli's Self-Description Inventory, Gordon's Survey of Interpersonal Values). More of the recent trait studies have dealt with managers and administrators, as opposed to other kinds of leaders. One reason for this trend is that the 1948 literature review by Stogdill greatly discouraged many leadership researchers from studying leader traits, whereas industrial psychologists interested in improving managerial selection continued to conduct trait research. The emphasis on selection focused trait research on the relation of leader traits to leader effectiveness, rather than on the comparison of leaders and nonleaders. This distinction is an important one. Predicting who will be selected as a leader is not the same as predicting who will be the most effective leader. The interest in managerial effectiveness led researchers to extend the list of traits under investigation to include specific administrative and technical skills, and specific aspects of managerial motivation compatible with the requirements of an administrative role.

The differences in methodology and perspective led to stronger, more consistent results in the second set of trait studies. Most of the same traits were again found to be related to leader effectiveness and some additional traits and skills were also found to be relevant (see Table 4–1). Stogdill (1974, p. 81) suggested that the following trait profile is characteristic of successful leaders:

> The leader is characterized by a strong drive for responsibility and task completion, vigor and persistence in pursuit of goals, venturesomeness and originality in problem solving, drive to exercise initiative in social situations, self-confidence and sense of personal identity, willingness to accept consequences of decision and action, readiness to absorb interpersonal stress, willingness to tolerate frustration and delay, ability to influence other persons' behavior, and capacity to structure social interaction systems to the purpose at hand.

TABLE 4-1
Traits and Skills Found Most Frequently to Be
Characteristic of Successful Leaders

Traits	Skills
Adaptable to situations	Clever (intelligent)
Alert to social environment	Conceptually skilled
Ambitious and achievement-oriented	Creative
Assertive	Diplomatic and tactful
Cooperative	Fluent in speaking
Decisive	Knowledgeable about group task
Dependable	Organized (administrative ability)
Dominant (desire to influence others)	Persuasive
Energetic (high activity level)	Socially skilled
Persistent	
Self-confident	
Tolerant of stress	
Willing to assume responsibility	

In retrospect, it is apparent that many leadership researchers overreacted to the earlier pessimistic literature reviews by rejecting the relevance of traits altogether. As Stogdill (1974, p. 72) noted:

> The reviews by Bird, Jenkins, and Stogdill have been cited as evidence in support of the view that leadership is entirely situational in origin and that no personal characteristics are predictive of leadership. This view seems to over-emphasize the situational, and underemphasize the personal, nature of leadership.

However, Stogdill makes it clear that recognition of the relevance of leader traits is not a return to the original trait approach. The old assumption that "leaders are born" has been discredited completely, and the premise that certain leader traits are absolutely necessary for effective leadership has never been substantiated in several decades of trait research. Today there is a more balanced viewpoint about traits. It is now recognized that certain traits increase the likelihood that a leader will be effective, but they do not guarantee effectiveness, and the relative importance of different traits is dependent on the nature of the leadership situation.

MANAGERIAL SELECTION RESEARCH

Since the most promising results on leader traits have come from studies of managerial assessment and selection, it is worthwhile to examine this line of research more closely. Up until the mid-1960s, attempts to predict managerial effectiveness with measures of personality and ability did not meet with much success. As was characteristic of trait research in general, certain aptitude, personality, and interest measures correlated with effectiveness criteria, but the correlations were sporadic and usually of low magnitude (Ghiselli, 1966; Guion & Gottier, 1966; Korman, 1968). Selection research in this earlier period relied heavily on standardized paper-and-pencil tests. It was common in the earlier research to measure general intelligence, scholastic aptitude, and specific aptitudes such as verbal comprehension, arithmetic computation, numerical reasoning, and perceptual accuracy, but there was seldom any attempt to measure specific, job-relevant technical knowledge or administrative skills. One exception was the use of some mechanical principles tests to predict the effectiveness of production foremen, but even these tests were general in content rather than assessing knowledge specific to the particular technical processes supervised by the foremen. A few selection studies have attempted to assess human relations skills with paper and pencil tests such as the Leadership Evaluation and Development Scale (Mowry, 1964; Tenopyr, 1969) and the How Supervise test (Rosen, 1961). However, it is very difficult to measure human relations skills with a written test, and this approach did not prove very useful for predicting managerial effectiveness.

Assessment Center Approach

Around the same time that pessimistic reviews of managerial selection appeared in print, the field was undergoing a major revolution in the methodology of managerial selection. The assessment center approach to managerial selection was being perfected. The term "assessment center" refers to a standardized set of procedures used to identify managerial potential. Although no two programs are exactly alike, they all utilize multiple methods of assessing traits and skills, including projective tests and situational tests in addition to traditional methods like interviews and written tests. Moreover, candidates for selection or promotion to a managerial position are usually given some kind of writing exercise (e.g., a short autobiographical essay) and a speaking exercise to evaluate their oral and written communication skills. The assessment process in the centers typically takes two to three days.

The projective tests used in assessment centers contain ambiguous stimuli such as incomplete sentences to be completed by the candidate, or pictures to be interpreted. Examples of these projective tests are described later in the chapter. Two commonly used situational tests are the In-Basket and Leaderless Group Discussion. The In-Basket test consists of letters, memos, and reports that supposedly have accumulated in the in-basket of a hypothetical manager. The candidate has a limited amount of time to indicate how to deal with each of the managerial problems contained in these materials. The Leaderless Group Discussion places candidates in a group situation where there is no designated leader. Sometimes the candidates are asked to represent competing viewpoints, with each candidate trying to persuade the others to adopt his viewpoint. Another variation is to have the candidates assume the roles of different managers trying to make a group decision, such as whether to merge with another company. Observers rate each candidate on qualities such as initiative, assertiveness, persuasiveness, dominance, and cooperation.

An overall evaluation of each candidate's management potential is made by several staff members who interview the candidate, examine his test scores and biographical information, observe his behavior in the situational exercises, then meet to discuss their assessment and resolve any disagreement. The assessors attempt to integrate the information from these diverse sources into a coherent picture of the motives, skills, and behavioral tendencies of each candidate. Studies on the validity of assessment center predictions of managerial potential usually examine the correlation between this composite evaluation and later managerial success. Some validity studies go a step further and examine the unique predictive power of each trait and skill measured in the assessment center. These more elaborate studies provide considerable insight into the leader traits relevant to managerial success in a large, formal organization.

The research evidence suggests that assessment centers can effectively predict managerial success (Huck, 1973). Hundreds of organizations are currently using assessment centers to improve their managerial selection and promotion decisions. One of the best examples of assessment center research is the longitudinal study conducted at American Telephone and Telegraph Company (AT&T) by Bray, Campbell and Grant (1974). Eight years after an early group of candidates was assessed, each candidate's progress in terms of advancement into middle management was related back to the candidate's assessment scores, which had been kept confidential so as not to affect promotion decisions. Sixty-four percent of the candidates predicted to reach middle management did so, whereas only 32 percent of the remaining candidates reached middle management. The significant correlations found between individual traits and managerial success are shown in Table 4–2.

TABLE 4-2
Most Effective Trait Predictors of Managerial Advancement in the AT&T Study

Trait Description	Correlation
1. **ORAL COMMUNICATION SKILL:** How good this person would be in presenting an oral report to a small conference group on a well-known subject.	.33**
2. **HUMAN RELATIONS SKILL:** How effectively this person can lead a group to accomplish a task without arousing hostility.	.32**
3. **NEED FOR ADVANCEMENT:** How much this person wants to be promoted significantly earlier than his or her peers.	.31**
4. **RESISTANCE TO STRESS:** How well this person's work performance will stand up in the face of personal stress.	.31**
5. **TOLERANCE OF UNCERTAINTY:** How well this person's work performance will stand up under uncertain or unstructured conditions.	.30**
6. **ORGANIZING AND PLANNING:** How effectively this person can organize his or her work and plan ahead.	.28**
7. **ENERGY:** How continuously this person can sustain a high level of work activity.	.28**
8. **CREATIVITY:** How likely this person is to solve a management problem in a novel way.	.25**
9. **RANGE OF INTERESTS:** The extent to which the person is interested in a variety of fields of activity, such as science, sports, music, and art.	.23**
10. **INNER WORK STANDARDS:** The extent to which the person wants to do a good job, even if a lesser performance is acceptable to his or her boss and others.	.21*
11. **BEHAVIORAL FLEXIBILITY:** How readily this person, when motivated, can modify his behavior to reach a goal.	.21*
12. **NEED FOR SECURITY:** The extent to which this person desires a secure job.	−.20*
13. **ABILITY TO DELAY GRATIFICATION:** The extent to which this person is able to work over long periods without great rewards to attain later rewards.	−.19*
14. **DECISION MAKING:** The person's readiness to make decisions, and the quality of his or her decisions.	.18*

Trait Description	Correlation
15. **PRIMACY OF WORK:** The extent to which this person finds satisfactions from work more important than satisfactions from other areas of life.	.18*
16. **GOAL FLEXIBILITY:** The ability of the person to change his life goals in accordance with reality opportunities.	−.18*

SOURCE: Adapted from: D. W. Bray, R. J. Campbell and D. L. Grant, *Formative Years in Business: A Long Term AT&T Study of Managerial Lives*. New York: John Wiley & Sons, Inc. 1974.
 * $p < .05$
 ** $p < .01$

Another important discovery in the longitudinal research at AT&T is the effect of the job situation on the relevance of individual traits for managerial success. The prediction of success based on a candidate's assessed traits was more accurate if the person had a job situation favorable to individual development. A favorable situation existed when a person's boss provided encouragement for him to develop management skills, gave him challenging assignments with increased supervisory responsibility, and served as a role model by setting an example of how a successful, achievement-oriented manager should act. Without this kind of stimulation and encouragement, a person was less likely to become a successful middle manager, regardless of his traits. Thus, success was due to a combination of the relevant personal qualities and the opportunity for these qualities to be translated into competent managerial behavior. Demonstration of managerial competence and growth led in turn to advancement and additional opportunities for a person to prove himself.

The trait measures in the AT&T study and other assessment center studies are not entirely independent aspects of personality or ability, so these studies usually include a factor analysis of the predictor measures to obtain a smaller number of more distinct traits and skills. Dunnette (1971) reviewed four such studies and found that there was considerable agreement about the following six traits related to managerial success: (1) overall activity (energy) level, (2) organizing and planning skills, (3) interpersonal competence, (4) cognitive competence, (5) work-oriented motivation, and (6) personal control of feelings and resistance to stress. The manner in which these traits jointly influence managerial success can be seen in Bentz's (1967, pp. 117–18) description of the successful Sears executive as indicated by that company's assessment center research:

> It would seem that powerful competitive drive for a position of eminence and authority provides a strong impetus for these men; the need to be recognized as men of influence and status, and ambition to govern, and the desire to excel appears to be of primary importance in enabling these men to utilize their talents fully and appropriately. . . . They are fully confident of their abilities to cope with and control unfamiliar situations, have the facility to deal with problems impersonally, and possess the physical vitality to maintain a steadily productive work pace. . . . While they prefer a dominant position within a group, they are also cooperative teamworkers who willingly listen to the ideas and suggestions of others. . . . Their strong power motive is tempered somewhat by consideration for other people, so that they are not likely to run roughshod over others in their efforts to gain success and renown.

MINER'S RESEARCH ON MANAGERIAL MOTIVATION

The importance of managerial motivation as a predictor of leadership effectiveness has been established in the general review of trait studies, and particularly in the assessment center research. Additional evidence about the importance of managerial motivation is provided by the research of Miner (1965, 1978).

The first step in the research was formulation of a theory of managerial role motivation to describe the type of motivational traits required for success in most management positions in large, hierarchical organizations. The initial traits selected for investigation were based on an analysis of role requirements common to these managerial positions, as well as on aspects of role theory and psychoanalytic theory, and results from early research on effective leadership. The managerial role prescriptions and associated motivational patterns are described by Miner (1978, pp. 741–42):

1. A manager must be in a position to obtain support for his actions at higher levels. This requires a good relationship with superiors. It follows that a manager should have a generally positive attitude toward those holding positions of authority over him. Any tendency to generalize hatred, distaste, or anxiety in dealing with people in positions of authority will make it extremely difficult to meet job demands.
2. There is a strong competitive element built into managerial work. Managers must strive to win for themselves and their subordinates and accept such challenges as other managers may offer. In order to meet this role requirement a person should be favorably disposed

toward engaging in competition. If he is unwilling to compete for position, status, advancement and his ideas, he is unlikely to succeed.

3. Although the behaviors expected of a father and those expected of a manager are not identical, both are supposed to take charge, to make decisions, to take such disciplinary actions as may be necessary, and to protect other members of a group. Thus, one of the common role requirements of the managerial job is that the incumbent behave in an active and assertive manner. Those who prefer more passive behavior patterns, no matter what their sex and those who become upset or disturbed at the prospect of behaving in an assertive manner would not be expected to possess the type of motivation needed.

4. The manager must exercise power over subordinates and direct their behavior. He must tell others what to do and enforce his words through appropriate use of positive and negative sanctions. The individual who finds such behavior difficult and emotionally disturbing, who does not wish to impose his wishes on others or believes it is wrong to do so, would not be expected to meet this particular role requirement.

5. The managerial job requires a person to stand out from his group and assume a position of high visibility. He must deviate from the immediate subordinate group and do things which inevitably invite attention, discussion, and perhaps criticism from those reporting to him. When this idea of standing out from the group elicits feelings of unpleasantness, then behavior appropriate to the role will occur much less often than would otherwise be the case.

6. There are administrative requirements such as constructing budget estimates, serving on committees, talking on the telephone, filling out forms, and so on in all managerial work, although the specific activities will vary. To meet these prescriptions a manager must at least be willing to face this type of routine and ideally gain some satisfaction from it. If such behavior is consistently viewed with apprehension or loathing, a person's chances of success are low.

SOURCE: John Miner, "Twenty Years of Research on Role Motivation Theory." *Personnel Psychology*, 1978, 31, 739–60.

Miner measures managerial motivation with a projective test called the Miner Sentence Completion Scale. The test provides separate scores on different aspects of managerial motivation, including positive attitudes toward authority figures, desire to compete with peers, desire to exercise power, desire to be actively assertive, desire to stand out from the group, and willingness to carry out routine administrative functions.

The relationship between managerial motivation and managerial success was assessed for 21 samples of managers in large, bureaucratic organizations. In each sample, the overall score on managerial motivation was found to correlate significantly with promotion into management and advancement to higher levels of management. The particular motivation subscales that correlated most consistently with managerial success included desire to exercise power, desire to compete with peers, and positive attitude toward authority figures. Desire to be assertive, desire to stand out from the group, and desire to perform routine administrative functions were less frequently associated with managerial success and appear to be less important aspects of managerial motivation.

In an experimental training study by Miner (1965), additional evidence about the importance of managerial motivation was found. A group of research and development managers in an oil company participated in a management development program designed to increase their managerial motivation. The managers were compared to untrained managers to determine if the training affected subsequent job success. Managers in the experimental group turned out to be more successful, and this success was attributed to significant increases in certain aspects of their managerial motivation as a result of the training.

Miner (1967, 1977) also investigated managerial motivation in samples of leaders who were not in large, hierarchical organizations. These samples included managers of branch offices in a consulting firm, administrators in a business school, and educational administrators in small school districts. The managerial motivation of these leaders was not correlated significantly with managerial success. Criterion problems may account for the lack of significant correlations, but it is also possible that the aspects of managerial motivation measured by Miner's test are unimportant for leadership success in smaller, less bureaucratic organizations. More research is needed to explore this question.

McCLELLAND'S RESEARCH ON MANAGERIAL MOTIVATION

Extensive research on managerial motivation has also been conducted by McClelland and his associates. This research examines the importance of achievement, power, and affiliation needs for managerial effectiveness. In most of the studies, need strength has been measured with a projective technique called the Thematic Apperception Test (TAT). The test consists of a series of pictures of people in ambiguous situations. A person taking the test is asked to make up a story about each picture, and the feelings, needs, and attitudes of the person are "projected" into his stories. The test provides a good indication of what the person thinks about in idle moments—his daydreams, fantasies, and aspirations. The TAT appears to be a better measure of needs than direct questions about them. The person taking the test, as with Miner's projective test, typically reveals much more about himself than he realizes.

When a person's stories indicate he thinks a lot about attaining a challenging goal, attaining a standard of excellence, or successfully completing a difficult task, the person probably has a high need for achievement. People with a strong need for achievement prefer a job with the following characteristics:

1. Performance outcomes depend on a person's own effort and ability rather than on chance factors beyond the person's control.
2. The tasks are moderately difficult and risky, rather than easy or impossible.
3. There is frequent, concrete feedback about how well the person is performing.
4. There is considerable opportunity to initiate action rather than merely deciding how to react to immediate problems.

Such characteristics are likely to be found in occupations such as sales representative, real estate agent, producer of entertainment events, and owner-manager of a small business (McClelland, 1965).

When a person's stories indicate he thinks a lot about influencing other people, defeating an opponent or competitor, winning an argument, or attaining a position of greater authority, the person probably has a high need for power. Such persons may act in a variety of different ways to express and satisfy this need, including the following (McClelland, 1975; Winter, 1973):

1. Reading books or watching films with an emphasis on violence, explicit sexuality, or competitive sports.
2. Collecting prestige possessions as symbols of influence and status.
3. Engaging in competitive sports, especially those with a "one-on-one" situation where a player tries to outwit or dominate a particular opponent.
4. Taking alcohol or drugs, or participating in mystical-religious rituals to heighten experience of personal strength and influence over events.
5. Helping others or giving advice in a way that demonstrates personal superiority and the weakness or dependence of others.
6. Joining organizations and assuming a leadership role in them.

People with a strong need for power prefer occupations that entail the exercise of influence, such as executive, politician, labor leader, police officer, military officer, and lawyer.

When a person's stories indicate he thinks a lot about establishing or restoring close, friendly relationships, joining groups, participating in pleasant social activities, and enjoying shared experiences with family or friends, the person probably has a high need for affiliation.

Such a person receives great satisfaction from being liked and accepted by others, including the people with whom he works. Effective performance is sometimes instrumental for attaining acceptance by coworkers, but concern for the task can also impede coworker acceptance, such as when there is disagreement over work procedures or standards. The person with a dominant need for affiliation is usually unwilling to allow the work to interfere with harmonious relationships (Litwin & Stringer, 1966; McClelland, 1975).

Motivational Patterns in Entrepreneurial Managers

Research by McClelland and others indicates need for achievement is an essential attribute for managers who are entrepreneurs. A person who is the top executive of a business he started himself is likely to have a strong need for achievement together with a strong need for independence (Collins, Moore & Unwalla, 1964). The need for independence includes a desire to avoid submission to authority figures, as well as a preference to do things in one's own way.

Studies of small firms in Finland (Kock, 1965, reported in McClelland & Winter, 1969), India (Hundal, 1971), and the United States (Wainer & Rubin, 1969) find that the achievement motivation of owner-managers and other top executives correlated significantly with measures of growth rate for these firms. Results were not as clear for other needs, but there was some indication that successful entrepreneurial managers in small firms had only a moderate power need and a relatively low need for affiliation. Thus, the dominant motive for successful entrepreneurial managers appears to be need for achievement. Of course, success depends on the manager's ability as well as his motivation; the person needs relevant expertise as an inventor, product designer, promoter, financier, and so on.

Motive Patterns of Organizational Managers

The optimal motive pattern for middle and top executives in large, established organizations is somewhat different from that of entrepreneurial managers, since success is much more dependent on influencing and motivating subordinates. Research indicates that the dominant motive of most successful organizational managers is need for power (McClelland, 1975; McClelland & Burnham, 1976; Winter, 1973). People who are low in need for power seem to lack the assertiveness and self-confidence necessary to organize and direct group activities effectively. If a manager has much greater need for affiliation than need for power, he avoids making unpopular decisions, even when these decisions are necessary for effective group performance. Moreover, such managers show favoritism to personal friends in dispensing rewards and favors, or in permitting exceptions to rules. The tendency of these managers to disregard procedures and rules "leaves employees feeling weak, irresponsible, and without a sense of what might happen next, of where they stand in relation to their manager, or even of what they ought to be doing" (McClelland & Burnham, 1976; p. 104).

It is desirable for organizational managers to have a dominant need for power, but a manager's effectiveness also depends on how this power need finds expression. McClelland (1975) finds that persons with a high need for power tend to have either a "personalized power concern" or a "socialized power concern." People with a personalized power concern have little inhibition or self-control, and they exercise power impulsively. According to McClelland and Burnham (1976, p. 103), "They are more rude to other people, they drink too much, they try to exploit others sexually, and they collect symbols of personal prestige such as fancy cars or big offices." Such managers are sometimes able to inspire loyalty and team spirit, but organizational role clarity suffers. Moreover, any subordinate loyalty is to the leader rather than to the organization, and when the leader departs there is likely to be disorder and a breakdown in team spirit.

A person with a socialized power concern is more emotionally mature. He exercises power more for the benefit of others, is more hesitant about using power in a manipulative manner, is less egoistic and defensive, accumulates fewer material possessions, has a longer-range view, and is more willing to take advice from experts. The strong need for power is expressed by exercising influence to build up the organization and make it successful. The person with a socialized power concern is more willing to sacrifice his own self-interest for the welfare of the organization. Because of his orientation toward building organizational commitment, this kind of leader is more likely to use a participative, coaching style of managerial behavior and is less likely to be coercive and autocratic. Such leaders "help make their subordinates feel strong and responsible, bind them less with petty rules, help produce a clear organizational structure, and create pride in belonging to the unit" (McClelland, 1975; p. 302). Thus, the combination of emotional maturity plus a strong need for power usually results in more effective leadership.

A study by McClelland and Burnham (1976) provides a good example of the consequences of different motive patterns in one large company. In 16 sales districts, increase in sales over the prior year was related to team spirit and organizational role clarity within the unit, as reported by subordinates. These intervening variables were related in turn to the motive pattern of the sales managers. Sales managers with higher need for power than for affiliation, and with emotional maturity, had subordinates with greater team spirit, a stronger sense of personal responsibility, and a clearer understanding of organizational procedures. In other words, these managers were able to create a more effective work climate, which resulted in better group performance.

Even though achievement motivation is not the most essential motive for managers in large organizations, it is still important. A study by Cummin (1967) found that managers who were successful in terms of career advancement usually had high need for achievement as well as high need for power. Donley and Winter (1970) analyzed the inaugural addresses made by several American presidents to determine if the motive patterns reflected in a President's speech related to his administrative style and record of accomplishment. The most dynamic, innovative presidents, such as Theodore Roosevelt, Franklin Roosevelt, John Kennedy, Harry Truman, and Lyndon Johnson, appeared to have a strong need for both power and achievement.

The evidence from these correlational studies on the importance of achievement motivation is consistent with the results found in a training experiment by Aronoff and Litwin (1971). A group of managers in a large company participated in a five-day training program designed to enhance their achievement motivation. The rate of advancement of each manager during the two years following the training was compared to the advancement rate of a similar group of managers who participated in the company's regular four-week training course. Managers in the experimental training program had a faster rate of advancement than managers in the control group, even though the latter group had higher "visibility" as a result of the prestige associated with attending the regular company course. The difference in managerial success was attributed to the increased achievement motivation of managers in the experimental program.

An organizational manager is most likely to be effective if his need for achievement is subordinated to a strong power need, so that it will be expressed in efforts to facilitate team performance rather than in the pursuit of individual success. If achievement is the dominant need, a manager tries to accomplish everything by himself. He is reluctant to delegate and fails to develop a strong sense of responsibility and commitment among his subordinates (McClelland & Burnham, 1976).

Need for affiliation is less relevant than power and achievement needs, but it is likely that a moderate degree of affiliation motivation is also beneficial for a manager. A person who is very low in need for affiliation tends to be a "loner" who doesn't like to socialize with others, except perhaps the immediate family or a few close friends. Such a person is likely to lack the motivation to engage in the many social and public relations activities that are essential for a manager, including those involved in establishing effective interpersonal relationships with subordinates, superiors, peers, and outsiders (e.g., clients, customers, suppliers, government officials). As Litwin and Stringer (1966) point out , some basic concern for the needs and feelings of other people seems critical as a source of motivation to build and maintain effective working relationships.

MANAGERIAL INTERESTS AND VALUES

Another source of information about managerial motivation is research on interests and values. Some studies compare managers and nonmanagers with respect to their interests and values. Other studies relate a manager's interests and values to measures of managerial effectiveness.

Interests

Interests indicate the extent to which a person likes to engage in a particular kind of activity. Interests have been found to be a predictor of occupational choice and success in an occupation. It is reasonable to assume that a person who enjoys activities typically associated with a managerial role is more likely to select this role as a career and to be successful at it. Nash (1965, 1966) reviewed research on the vocational interests of managers and found limited evidence for this premise. Successful managers tend to be interested in verbal and persuasive activities, and they have a strong interest in interacting with people, especially in relationships where the manager is dominant. In addition, successful managers prefer activities that involve independent thought, initiative, and risk. The pattern of results for interests appears consistent with the findings for managerial motivation discussed earlier.

Values

Values are defined by Gordon (1975, p. 2) as "constructs representing generalized behaviors or states of affairs that are considered by the individual to be important." Unlike needs, values may be satisfied by a large variety of behaviors, and they do not dominate behavior in such a compelling manner. Values are important because they influence a person's perception of situations and problems, and they influence his preferences, aspirations, and choices (England, 1967; Gordon, 1975). In addition, a person's satisfaction depends in part on how well his values find expression in his daily life style. The most widely used measures of values in managerial research are the All-port–Vernon Study of Values (Allport, et al., 1960) and the Gordon (1976) Survey of Interpersonal Values (SIV). The separate values measured by the SIV are labeled and defined as follows (Gordon, 1975, pp. 22–25):

SUPPORT: Being treated with understanding, receiving encouragement from other people, being treated with kindness and consideration.

CONFORMITY: Doing what is socially correct, following regulations closely, doing what is accepted and proper, being a conformist.

RECOGNITION: Being looked up to and admired, being considered important, attracting favorable notice, achieving recognition.

INDEPENDENCE: Having the right to do whatever one wants to do, being free to make one's own decisions, being able to do things in one's own way.

BENEVOLENCE: Doing things for other people, sharing with others, helping the unfortunate, being generous.

LEADERSHIP: Being in charge of other people, having authority over others, being in a position of leadership or power.

Research on the relationship between values and managerial effectiveness has yielded different results depending on the nature of the administrative position (Nash, 1965; Gordon, 1975, 1976). Several studies using the survey of interpersonal values found that the Leadership scale tends to be positively correlated with managerial effectiveness, and the Benevolence, Support, and Conformity scales tend to be negatively related to effectiveness (Gordon, 1976). Gordon also reports results comparing leaders and nonleaders on the SIV. The relatively high Leadership scores and low Support scores found for managers and military officers indicates these leaders place a high value on influencing others and a low value on receiving supportive attention.

A different approach for investigating managerial values was used by England (1967). He conducted a descriptive study of the personal values of 1,072 American managers in 1966, and this study was essentially replicated several years later by Lusk and Oliver (1974). These two studies asked managers to rate the importance of different concepts, and the extent to which each concept is perceived to be pleasant, ethical–moral, and instrumental for success. The results indicated that for American managers in general, the primary value orientation is pragmatic rather than moralistic or hedonistic. Managers tended to consider personal qualities such as skill, ambition, achievement, and creativity to be both important and instrumental for success. Loyalty, trust, honor, tolerance, dignity, rationality, and individuality were seen as important but not instrumental for success. Rated low in importance but highly instrumental were qualities such as risk, force, power, and aggressiveness.

The Managerial Mind

The value orientation and attitudes of managers and administrators have also been studied by analysis of case histories, biographies, and autobiographies of distinguished executives. Ewing (1964) found that successful managers tend to have the following orientation:

1. The successful manager's primary commitment is to the organization, and though he may criticize certain policies and practices, he remains loyal to the organization as long as he is a member of it.
2. The processes of supervising and coordinating are foremost in the successful manager's thinking. However, he recognizes that an attempt to control people is partly self-defeating, because it restricts their spirit and creativity. Thus, he tolerates some forms of tension and disagreement as an essential requirement for creativity, innovation, and adaptation to external change.
3. The successful manager is hesitant about manipulating subordinates or controlling them closely. His preference is to assign tasks and objectives to subordinates and allow substantial autonomy and self-control in performing the tasks.
4. The successful manager considers it important to establish a climate that encourages subordinates to enlarge their horizons, set high aspirations, be flexible in their behavior, and have less anxiety about mistakes.
5. The successful manager deemphasizes personal values such as kindness, gentleness, and sympathy. His emphasis is on what people can accomplish and on getting desired results.

Ewing (1964, p. 209) concludes with the following commentary about the kind of persons who flourish in an administrative role:

As for the administrator himself, I suspect his future is about the same in any organization, in any place. His efforts can never be completely successful; the dilemmas of management and control will always be with him. He has the gift of being able to be absorbed in his work, however, to immerse himself into turning suffering into growth, argument into creativity, defeat into progress. People may say that he "seems to take a beating," but he does not resist the daily give and take. He belongs to it and it to him.

White (1965, p. 366) in writing about American presidents, provides a similar perspective of the kind of person most likely to be successful as a leader:

Whether a man is burdened by power or enjoys power; whether he is trapped by responsibility or made free by it; whether he is moved by other people and outer forces or moves them—this is of the essence of leadership.

MANAGERIAL SKILLS

It is not enough to have the appropriate motivational pattern; a person also needs considerable skill to be an effective leader. The early trait studies uncovered a variety of abilities likely to be important, including general intelligence, conceptual skills, creativity, judgment, persuasive ability, speech fluency, tact, social sensitivity, and task-related knowledge. In this section, we will review efforts to develop a skill typology with similar skills grouped into broader categories. Research on the relationship between managerial skills and effectiveness will also be examined.

Three-Skill Typology

The most widely accepted approach for classifying managerial skills is in terms of a three-skill typology. This typology was initially proposed by Katz (1955), and a similar three-skill typology was later proposed by Mann (1965). The skill categories were defined as follows:

1. TECHNICAL SKILLS: knowledge about methods, processes, procedures, and techniques for conducting a specialized activity, and the ability to use tools and operate equipment related to that activity.

2. HUMAN RELATIONS SKILLS: knowledge about human behavior and interpersonal processes, ability to understand the feelings, attitudes, and motives of others from what they say and do (empathy, social sensitivity), ability to communicate clearly and effectively (speech fluency, persuasiveness), and ability to establish effective and cooperative relationships (tact, diplomacy, knowledge about acceptable social behavior).

3. CONCEPTUAL SKILLS: general analytical ability, logical thinking, proficiency in concept formation and conceptualization of complex and ambiguous relationships, creativity in idea generation and problem solving, ability to analyze events and perceive trends, anticipate changes, and recognize opportunities and potential problems.

It is evident that technical skills are primarily concerned with things, human relations skills are primarily concerned with people, and conceptual skills are primarily concerned with ideas and concepts. Each of the three skill categories is relevant to the role requirements of managers and administrators.

The technical skills are necessary for a manager to train and direct subordinates with specialized activities. This type of skill is the most concrete and easiest to understand. Technical skills are learned during formal education in specialized subjects (e.g., accounting, finance, marketing, engineering, business law, computer programming, etc.) and through on-the-job training and experience.

Human relations skills are important for establishing effective relationships with subordinates, superiors, peers, and outsiders. Unless a manager is sensitive to the attitudes, feelings, and needs of people, he cannot estimate accurately how they will react to what he says and does. As Katz (1955, p. 34) points out:

> Real skill in working with others must become a natural, continuous activity, since it involves sensitivity not only at times of decision making but also in the day-by-day behavior of the individual. . . . Because everything a leader says and does (or leaves unsaid or undone) has an effect on his associates, his true self will, in time, show through. Thus, to be effective, this skill must be naturally developed and unconsciously, as well as consistently, demonstrated in the individual's every action.

Conceptual skills are essential for effective planning, organizing, coordinating, policy formation, problem solving, and program development. A major administrative responsibility is coordination of the separate, specialized parts of the organization. In order to accomplish effective coordination and make necessary modifications in organization structure, a manager needs to understand how the various parts of the organization relate to each other, and how changes in one part of the system affect the other parts. An administrator should also be sensitive to the external environment and be able to comprehend how changes in it will affect the organization. The importance of this "external perspective" is explained by Katz and Kahn (1978, p. 541):

The decision to merge or resist merger, to make a major change in location or to maintain a present position, to launch an entirely new line of products or to stay with the traditional items, to be the first with a new manufacturing process or to wait until others attempt it—these are the kinds of issues that demand the greatest understanding of the environment on the part of management. They are also the kinds of issues that will make the difference between successful and unsuccessful competition, between growth and stagnation, survival and failure.

Skill Importance and the Situation

Leaders need all three kinds of skills to fulfill their role requirements, but the relative importance of the skills and the specific types of skills within each category depends on the leadership situation. Katz (1955) and Mann (1965) have proposed that the appropriate skill mix depends in part on a manager's position in the authority hierarchy of the organization, and this proposition is supported by research (Mann, 1965; Misshauk, 1971; Porter & Henry, 1964). Human relations skills are needed at all levels of management, but they are relatively less important for top-level managers than for lower-level managers. Technical skills are usually more important than conceptual skills for low-level managers, who are mainly responsible for implementing policy and maintaining the workflow within the existing organization structure. Katz and Kahn (1978) describe the role of middle managers as primarily one of supplementing existing structure and developing ways to implement policies and goals established at higher levels. This role requires a roughly equal mix of technical, human relations, and conceptual skills. For top-level managers, conceptual skills are most important. The major responsibility of top executives is making strategic decisions. Some technical knowledge is necessary to make these decisions, and human relations skills are helpful for obtaining information and influencing subordinates to implement decisions enthusiastically. However, the quality of strategic decisions ultimately depends on the conceptual skills of the decision makers (Katz & Kahn, 1978).

Some research indicates the absolute skill requirements for top-level managers will vary somewhat from organization to organization, depending on the type of organization, its size, and the degree of centralization of authority (McLennan, 1967). For example, in some organizations where operating decisions are highly decentralized, technical skills are of minimal importance for top-level managers. A greater degree of relevant technical skill is needed by executives in organizations where operating decisions are highly centralized, and in organizations where the top executives have functionally special-ized roles (e.g., selling to key customers, product design) in addition to general administrative responsibilities.

Mann (1965) reminds us that the relative priority of different skills probably changes from time to time, depending on the develop-mental stage of an organization. Technical skills become relatively more important in periods of rapid change, such as when there is a reorganization or when new technology is introduced into the organi-zation. Early in a period of transition, technical problems are most salient, and a great deal of technical and conceptual skill is required. Later, when the major technical problems have been solved, the re-maining problems in completing the change are usually of the inter-personal variety, and human relations skills are essential. Mann (1965) found that the changeover to a new computer in the accounting de-partment of a large corporation affected skill priorities differently, depending on how involved in the change a manager was. For most of the 22 groups centrally involved in the change, subordinates reported technical skills were of primary importance for their supervisors, whereas in 12 groups only marginally involved in the change, most subordinates reported that human relations skills were of primary im-portance.

One interesting question about managerial skills is the extent to which they are transferable from one situation to another. Writers generally agree that lower-level managers cannot easily transfer to a different functional specialty (e.g., from sales manager to engineering manager) because the technical skills at this level of management are so vital and so different across functions. However, there is much less agreement about the transferability of managerial skills at the execu-tive level. Katz (1955) proposed that top-level managers with ample human relations and conceptual skills can be shifted from one indus-try to another with great ease and no loss of effectiveness. Other writ-ers contend that the transferability of skills for top executives is very limited (Dale, 1960; McLennan, 1967; Shetty & Peery, 1976). These writers point out that, even between companies in the same industry, there are unique requirements due to variations in ownership, tradi-tions, organizational climate, and internal functioning characteris-tics. For different industries with unique economic, market, and technological characteristics, skill requirements are even more di-verse. Familiarity with technical matters, products, personalities, and tradition is a type of knowledge that is acquired only through long experience in the organization. Thus, only the general ability compo-nents of conceptual and human relations skills can be transferred to a different situation; the situation-specific knowledge component of these skills must be relearned. The greater the difference between situations and the more technical expertise required in the new position, the harder it will be to make the transition. The case against transferability of skills is supported by results from a study by Shetty and Peery (1976) of 270 chief executives. Only 10 percent of the firms in their sample went outside the organization to find a chief executive, as opposed to promotion from within, and firms with a newly promoted chief executive had higher subsequent performance than firms with a chief executive recruited from another organization.

PRACTICAL APPLICATIONS OF TRAIT RESEARCH

Findings from research on leader traits and skills have the greatest potential application to the selection and promotion of managers and administrators in large organizations. Intensive measurement procedures such as those used in most assessment centers provide moderately accurate information about managerial motivation, personality traits, interpersonal skills, and cognitive skills. When analyzed together with information about the prior experience and performance of candidates, these assessments can be used to make reasonably good predictions about likely success in a higher managerial position. The accuracy of prediction is increased when the skills, traits, and knowledge especially relevant for a position are determined in advance. The varying requirements of different kinds of managerial positions are discussed in more detail in Chapter 7.

Information about the managerial skills of employees in an organization is very useful for identifying training needs and planning management development activities. Such information also facilitates manpower planning when the skill requirements for each administrative position are determined and considered in relation to the existing skills of current employees.

Knowledge about managerial traits and skills is also useful for career planning. Some people in an organization who aspire to move into a particular kind of management position lack the appropriate pattern of skills and/or motivation to be successful in that position. Assessment data can be used in advising an employee to undertake relevant training. In the event of a serious deficiency in qualifications, the information makes it easier to provide adequate counseling.

Summary

The early trait studies attempted to identify physical characteristics, personality traits, and abilities of "natural leaders." Hundreds of trait studies were conducted, but individual traits failed to correlate in a strong and consistent manner with leadership effectiveness. The early trait research suffered from several methodological deficiencies, and not much attention was paid to the situation as a determinant of the relevance and priority of various traits. Also neglected was the question of how traits interact as an integrator of personality and behavior.

In recent years, the investigation of leader traits has been more productive. Greater progress can be attributed to the inclusion of more relevant traits, use of better measures of traits, examination of trait patterns rather than looking only at individual correlations, and use of longitudinal research. Research carried out in assessment centers has shown that advancement and success of managers in large organizations can be predicted to a considerable extent from managerial traits and skills measured by a combination of methods. Although the situation largely determines the kinds of specific knowledge necessary for effective leadership, the general pattern of skills, motives, and other traits appears to be much the same for most successful administrators in large organizations.

Managerial motivation has been especially useful as a predictor of leadership effectiveness. Miner found that his projective measure of managerial motivation was correlated with leader success in 21 samples of leaders in large, hierarchical organizations. The most relevant components of managerial motivation were desire for power, desire to compete with peers, and positive attitude toward authority figures. McClelland and his colleagues found that effective managers in large organizations have a stronger need for power than for affiliation. In addition, the most effective managers have a socialized power orientation and are more interested in building up the organization than in personal aggrandizement or domination of others for its own sake. Although high need for achievement is more essential for entrepreneurial managers than for managers in large organizations, it remains an important component of managerial motivation. Successful managers are likely to have a strong desire for their group to achieve challenging goals, but they develop a strong sense of responsibility and commitment among subordinates rather than trying to accomplish everything by themselves. Finally, successful managers are more likely to have values and interests consistent with the requirements of their jobs. They tend to be very pragmatic and results-oriented, and to enjoy oral, persuasive activities requiring initiative and risk taking.

In order to be successful, a leader needs to have considerable ability as well as motivation. Three general categories of skills relevant to all managerial leaders are human relations skills, technical skills, and conceptual skills. The relative priority of the three types of skills depends on the level of management, type of organization, and developmental stage of the leader's organizational unit. The relative importance of specific skills within each of the three general skill categories also depends on the situation. Much of a leader's specialized knowledge is applicable only to his present position and cannot be readily transferred to another organization. However, skills like persuasiveness, empathy, creativity, analytical ability, speaking ability, acting ability, memory for details, and so on are applicable in almost any position of leadership in which a person finds himself.

REVIEW AND DISCUSSION QUESTIONS

1. Some writers have asserted that the trait approach is "dead and buried." Evaluate this assertion.

2. Why is it important to consider the situation when trying to identify essential leadership traits and skills?

3. What does the assessment center research tell us about the traits and skills associated with managerial success in large organizations?

4. What did Miner find to be the most consistently important aspects of managerial motivation?

5. How are need for achievement, power, and affiliation related to the effectiveness of managers in large organizations?

6. What has been learned about interests, values, and attitudes of successful managers?

7. How are technical skills, conceptual skills, and human relations skills related to managerial effectiveness?

8. How transferable are leadership skills from one situation to another?

9. Define and explain each of the following terms: projective test, situational test, In-Basket test, Leaderless Group Discussion, need for achievement, need for power, need for affiliation, personalized power concern, socialized power concern, technical skills, conceptual skills, human relations skills.

5

Leadership Behavior and Managerial Activities

As mentioned in Chapter 1, an especially useful way of studying leadership is examination of leader behavior and comparison of behavior patterns for effective and ineffective leaders. Leadership behavior can be conceptualized in a variety of ways and at different levels of abstraction. The actions of a leader may be described in terms of "activity patterns," "managerial roles," or "behavior categories." In this chapter, different varieties of research on leadership behavior will be reviewed. One objective of the chapter is to provide an overview of different methods of studying leadership behavior. A second objective is to provide the reader with a better understanding of what managers and administrators typically do in their jobs. A third objective is to review the results of research on behavior patterns associated with effective leadership.

METHODS FOR STUDYING LEADERSHIP BEHAVIOR

A variety of different methods have been used to describe the activities and behavior of managers and other kinds of leaders. The methods most commonly used will be described briefly. Each method has unique advantages and limitations, and the best research strategy is to use a combination of methods rather than continuing the single-method strategy predominant up to now (McCall, Morrison & Hannan, 1978).

Diary

Managers are given pads of sheets with specified response categories to describe what they do, when they do it, and where they do it (Carlson, 1951). The use of predetermined categories is usually necessary to enable the managers to record their activities during the day without disrupting their work. However, even with a simple recording form, the researcher is dependent on the manager to record his own behavior diligently and accurately, and it is difficult to obtain the required cooperation for extended periods of time. The diary method will be reasonably accurate if used properly, but it suffers from one major limitation. The predetermined categories must be clearly defined so that respondents are able to determine the appropriate category in which to classify each of their activities. Since the researcher typically uses only a small number of mutually exclusive activity categories, it is likely that much highly relevant information about the manager's behavior will be lost (Mintzberg, 1973).

Continuous Observation

Managers are observed continuously over a period of several work days by a behavioral scientist who records the managers' activities. The observer may use predetermined categories to aid in classifying activities ("structured observation"), or the observer may simply record a description of any activity that appears to be relevant, without reference to predetermined activity categories ("unstructured observation"). Observation is believed to be more effective and reliable than the diary method, but it is a costly method for the researcher, who must spend long hours observing the managers. A potential problem is that the presence of the observer may cause the manager to act differently than usual. A variation of the method is to have subordinates themselves observe the behavior of their leader and record these observations by writing descriptions of behavior episodes on a form provided by the researcher. Of course, subordinates are not trained, unbiased observers, and they are not always diligent about recording their observations.

Activity Sampling

Managers are observed repeatedly for brief intervals of time on randomly selected occasions by a behavioral scientist (Kelly, 1964). The assumption of activity sampling is that several random observations will provide a representative picture of the total activities of the managers being studied. The advantage of activity sampling over continuous observation is that fewer observer hours are needed to conduct the study. A disadvantage of activity sampling is the difficulty of interpreting activities not observed in their entirety. In addition, the method requires the use of predetermined descriptive categories to facilitate rapid recording. As with structured observation and other methods that rely on predetermined categories, much useful information may be lost.

Retrospective Self-Reports

Managers are asked to describe their usual activities or their past behavior by answering questions in an interview or on a questionnaire. The managers may be asked to indicate how much time is typically spent in each of several activities and how often each activity occurs. This method of measuring behavior is usually quite unreliable, because managers are unable to remember much detailed information about their past activities and behavior. Moreover, they typically give themselves inflated scores on types of behavior perceived to be desirable, and they understate their use of undesirable behavior (Smith, 1975).

Questionnaires

Most leadership questionnaires are highly structured and contain questions on a set of specific leadership behaviors with predetermined response choices for the questions. For example, respondents (subordinates, peers, superiors) may be asked to indicate how often a leader consults subordinates before making decisions. Typical response choices for this kind of item are "always," "usually," "sometimes," "seldom," and "never." The method relies on the assumption that respondents have been in a position to observe the behavior and can remember it accurately. Unfortunately, these assumptions are frequently not met. Descriptions of leadership behavior are often biased by selective memory, stereotypes, and judgmental errors (Eden & Leviatan, 1975; Rush, et al., 1977; Schriesheim, et al., 1979). Nevertheless, under favorable conditions, questionnaires are capable of providing useful information about leadership behavior. The method is economical, it allows respondents to remain anonymous, and it is especially useful in research with large samples of managers where more time-consuming methods would not be feasible.

Critical Incidents

Critical incidents are concrete examples of especially effective or especially ineffective behavior (Flanagan, 1951). They can be collected from leaders themselves or from subordinates, peers, and superiors. It is commonplace to compare incidents from different respondents in order to identify behaviors that respondents agree are important. It is also a common procedure to group similar incidents into broader behavior categories. The method differs from most of the others in that the selection of relevant leader behavior is made by respondents themselves rather than by the researchers. Critical incidents are especially useful in exploratory research designed to examine very specific, situationally relevant aspects of managerial behavior.

MANAGERIAL ACTIVITIES AND ROLES

Activities are defined here as observable events. They can be described most easily at a very concrete level, such as what the leader is doing (e.g., reads memos or reports, tours facility, attends meeting, talks on telephone, writes memo), where the activity is taking place (e.g., in the leader's office, in a subordinate's office, in the plant, in the cafeteria, etc.), and whom the leader is interacting with (e.g., boss, subordinate, peer, customer, etc.). Studies of this type usually try to determine how much time a leader spends in each activity and how frequently each activity occurs.

Activities can also be defined at a more abstract level in terms of the content of the behavior. For example, the activity may be classified as "getting information," "giving information," "making decisions," and so forth. This kind of description provides a better understanding of the purpose of the activity, but it requires a set of meaningful and unambiguous categories for classifying activity content. Unfortunately, behavioral scientists have been unable to agree about what categories are most meaningful.

Distinguishing Characteristics of Managerial Activities

Empirical studies on managerial work activities have been limited in number and scope. The methods commonly used to collect data in this research are observations and diaries. The most systematic studies of this type are listed and described briefly in Table 5–1 (McCall, et al., 1978). Mintzberg (1973) reviewed the results from much of this research, including the findings from his own study on activities of executives. He concluded that managerial work appears to have several distinguishing characteristics:

1. Pace of Work

The typical manager performs his work at "an unrelenting pace." There is seldom a break in the workload during the day, and higher-

TABLE 5-1
Empirical Studies of Managerial Activities

Author(s)	Method	N	Levels	Organization(s)
Carlson (1951)	Diary & Observation	10	Chief Executives	10 Different Organizations
Burns (1954)	Diary	4	4 Levels (low to middle)	1 Manufacturing Plant
Blau (1954)	Observation	16	Mid-Level Agents	1 Gov't Law Enforcement Agency
Guest (1956)	Observation	56	Foremen	1 Assembly Plant
Jasinski (1956)	Observation	56	Foremen	1 Assembly Plant
Burns (1957)	Diary	76	Top-Level Managers	8 Different Firms
Ponder (1957)	Observation	24	Foremen	1 Manufacturing Plant
Dale & Urwick (1960)	Diary & Observation	10	Chief Executives	10 Different Organizations
Landsberger (1961)	Observation	?	Mid-Level Managers	2 Engineering Plants
Brewer & Tomlinson (1964)	Diary	6	Mid-Level Managers	6 Different Firms
Dubin & Spray (1964)	Diary	8	Senior & Junior Executives	2 Manufacturing & 1 Savings & Loan Association
Kelly (1964)	Observation	4	Foremen	1 Manufacturing Plant
Hinrichs (1964)	Diary	232	Nonsupervisory to Middle Management	1 Company (?)
Horne & Lupton (1965)	Diary	66	Middle Managers	10 Different Organizations
Thomason (1966)	Diary & Observation	30	Low–Middle-Level Managers	7 Different Organizations
Thomason (1967)	Diary & Observation	26	Low–Upper-Middle-Level Managers	4 Different Organizations
Marples (1968)	Diary	8	Low–Middle-Level Managers	1 Industrial Organization
Lawler, Porter & Tennenbaum (1968)	Diary	105	Low–Middle-Level Managers	1 Manufacturing Organization & 4 Social Service
Mintzberg (1973)	Observation	5	Chief Executives	5 Different Organizations
Cohen & March (1974)	Observation	42	College Presidents	42 Different Colleges
Dahl & Lewis (1975)	Diary	12	Mid–High-Level Administrators	1 College
Stewart (1976)	Diary & Observation	16	Low–High-Level Managers	9 Different Organizations
Hinrichs (1976)	Diary	142	Low–Middle-Level Managers	1 Chemical Research Plant

SOURCE: M. W. McCall, Jr., A. M. Morrison and R. L. Hannan, *Studies of Managerial Work: Results and Methods*. Greensboro: Center For Creative Leadership, Technical Report #9, 1978.

level managers often take work home with them. In part, the pace can be attributed to the manager's own preferences. Having trained their minds to search for and analyze new information continually, managers do this automatically and find it difficult to forget about their job.

2. Activity Duration and Variety

Managers typically engage in a great variety of activities during a work day, and they tend to spend only a brief amount of time on each activity. In Mintzberg's (1973, p. 33) observations of chief executives, "half of the activities were completed in less than nine minutes, and only one-tenth took more than an hour." Interruptions occur frequently, and important activities are interspersed with trivial ones, requiring rapid shifts of mood. The brevity and fragmentation of activities are even more pronounced at lower levels of management.

3. Action Versus Reflection

Managers tend to gravitate toward active aspects of their jobs, and they prefer activities that are nonroutine but well defined. Current information is given much more attention than old information. The focus of interest is on specific issues rather than on general ones. Contrary to the common image of a manager as a reflective planner, managers were seldom found to engage in general planning or abstract discussion. Mintzberg (1973) suggests that managerial effectiveness can be improved by reducing the superficiality of their activities and spending more time on important but neglected functions (e.g., planning and organizing, subordinate development, team building).

4. Use of Communication Media

Managers have five principal ways to obtain information, including written messages (e.g., memos, letters, reports, work orders, etc.), telephone messages, scheduled meetings, unscheduled meetings, and observational tours. Each medium is used for somewhat different purposes. Managers show a strong preference for use of the oral media. Every study of managerial activities has found that managers spend from 57 percent to 89 percent of their time engaged in oral communication. In Mintzberg's (1973) study of chief executives (see Figure 5–1), two-thirds of the oral contacts were accounted for by telephone calls and unscheduled meetings, although these contacts were usually of short duration.

FIGURE 5-1
Distribution of Time and Activities for a Sample of Five Chief Executives

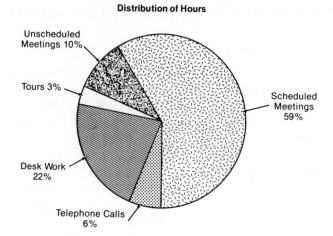

Distribution of Hours

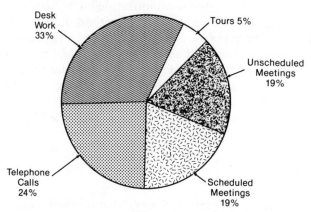

Distribution of Number of Activities

SOURCE: Figure 4 (p. 39) from *The Nature of Managerial Work* by Henry Mintzberg. Copyright © 1973 by Henry Mintzberg. Reprinted by permission of Harper & Row, Publishers, Inc.

5. Interaction Patterns

Managers spend considerable time in lateral communication and contacts with persons outside of the immediate organization subunit. These interactions typically account for one-third to one-half of the managers' contact time. Managers also spend considerable time with their subordinates. Interactions with subordinates account for one-third to one-half a manager's contact time. A relatively small proportion of a manager's time is spent communicating with the manager's boss.

Mintzberg's Ten Managerial Roles

After reviewing earlier studies of managerial activities, Mintzberg (1973) came to the conclusion that the studies failed to provide much insight into what a manager does. The focus of these studies was usually on activities defined at a concrete level rather than in terms of activity content. The few studies that examined activity content used predetermined content categories that provide only an incomplete picture of a manager's job.

Mintzberg conducted a study designed to overcome these limitations. He used unstructured observation and developed new content categories during and after the initial observations. The meaning of the activities was interpreted by identifying a set of ten underlying managerial roles that accounted for all of the activities observed by Mintzberg. Each activity can be explained in terms of at least one role, although many activities involved more than one of the ten roles. Three of the managerial roles ("figurehead," "leader," "liaison") deal with interpersonal behavior. Three other roles ("monitor," "disseminator," "spokesman") deal with information processing behavior. The remaining four roles ("entrepreneur," "disturbance handler," "resource allocator," "negotiator") deal with the decision-making behavior of managers. All of the roles are relevant for any manager or administrator, although their relative importance may vary from one kind of manager to another. A manager's roles are largely predetermined for him by the nature of his position, but he can interpret them in different ways while carrying them out. Each of the roles will be described briefly.

1. Figurehead Role

As a consequence of their formal authority as the head of an organization or one of its subunits, managers are obliged to perform certain symbolic duties of a legal and social nature. These duties include signing documents (e.g., contracts, expense authorizations), presiding at certain meetings and ceremonial events (e.g., retirement dinner for a subordinate), participating in other rituals or ceremonies, and receiving official visitors. The manager must participate in these activities, even though they are usually of marginal relevance to the job of managing.

2. Leader Role

Managers are responsible for making their organizational sub-unit function as an integrated whole in the pursuit of its basic purpose. Consequently, the manager must provide guidance to subordinates, insure that they are motivated, and create favorable conditions for doing the work. A number of managerial activities are expressly concerned with the leader role, including hiring, training, directing, praising, promoting, criticizing, and dismissing. However, the leader role pervades all of a manager's activities, even those with some other basic purpose.

3. Liaison Role

The liaison role includes behavior intended to establish and maintain a web of relationships with persons and groups outside of a manager's organizational subunit. These relationships are vital as a source of information and favors. Development of such contacts and relationships is part of a chief executive's responsibility for linking his organization to the external environment. Horizontal relationships are also essential for middle- and lower-level managers in order to obtain information and provide some influence over suppliers, clients, service units, and regulators. The essence of the liaison role is in "making new contacts," "keeping in touch," and "doing favors" that will allow the manager to ask for favors in return. Some examples of activities involving the liaison role include attending social events or professional conferences, joining outside boards, clubs, or associations, writing to congratulate a colleague, and calling another manager to provide some helpful information or offer assistance.

4. Monitor Role

Managers continually seek information from a variety of sources. Some examples of activities with this purpose include reading reports and memos, attending meetings and briefings, and conducting observational tours. Some of the information obtained is passed on to subordinates ("disseminator role") or to outsiders ("spokesman role"). Most of the information is analyzed to discover problems and opportunities, and to develop an understanding of outside events and of the internal processes within the manager's organizational subunit.

5. Disseminator Role

Managers have special access to sources of information not available to subordinates. Some of this information is factual in nature, and some of it concerns the stated preferences of individuals and organizations desiring to influence the manager, including persons at high levels of authority. Some of the factual information must be passed on to subordinates, either in its original form or after interpretation and editing by the manager. The information about preferences must be assimilated according to the influence of the source, and it is then expressed to subordinates either in the form of value statements (e.g., rules, goals, policies, standards) or as specific responses to subordinates' questions.

6. Spokesman Role

Managers are obliged to transmit information and express value statements to persons outside their organizational subunit as well as to subordinates. Middle-and lower-level managers must report to their superiors; a chief executive must report to his board of directors. Each of these managers is also expected to serve as a lobbyist and public relations representative for his organizational subunit when dealing with superiors and persons outside of the organization (e.g., suppliers, clients, government agencies, the press). As Mintzberg (1973, p. 76) points out, "To speak effectively for his organization and to gain the respect of outsiders, the manager must demonstrate an up-to-the-minute knowledge of his organization and its environment."

7. Entrepreneur Role

The manager of an organization or one of its subunits acts as an initiator and designer of controlled change to exploit opportunities for improving the existing situation. Such change takes place in the form of "improvement projects" such as development of a new product, purchase of new equipment, or reorganization of formal structure. Some of the improvement projects are supervised directly by the manager, and some are delegated to subordinates. Mintzberg (1973, p. 81) offers the following description of the way a manager deals with improvement projects:

> The manager as a supervisor of improvement projects may be likened to a juggler. At any one point in time he has a number of balls in the air. Periodically, one comes down, receives a short burst of energy, and goes up again. Meanwhile, new balls wait on the sidelines and, at random intervals, old balls are discarded and new ones added.

8. Disturbance Handler Role

In the disturbance handler role, a manager deals with sudden crises that cannot be ignored, as distinguished from problems that are voluntarily solved by the manager to exploit opportunities ("entrepreneur role"). The crises are caused by unforeseen events, such as conflict among subordinates, the loss of a key subordinate, a fire or accident, a strike, and so on. A manager typically gives this role priority over all of the others. Since managers usually spend much of their time reacting to sudden disturbances, little time is left for reflective planning or general strategy formation.

9. Resource Allocator Role

Managers exercise their authority to allocate resources such as money, manpower, material, equipment, facilities, and services. Resource allocation is involved in managerial decisions about what is to be done, in the manager's authorization of subordinates' decisions, in the preparation of budgets, and in the manager's scheduling of his own time. By retaining the power to allocate resources, the manager maintains control over strategy formation and acts to coordinate and integrate subordinate actions in support of strategic objectives.

10. Negotiator Role

Any negotiations requiring a substantial commitment of resources will be facilitated by the presence of a manager having the authority to make this commitment. The manager may also aid negotiations by serving as an expert spokesman for his organizational subunit. Finally, the manager's participation as the figurehead for his subunit adds credibility to the negotiations. Thus, when a manager serves as the chief representative of his unit during negotiations, his activities are likely to involve the resource allocator, spokesman, and figurehead roles in addition to the negotiator role. A chief executive is likely to participate in several different types of negotiations, including labor–management negotiations with unions, contract negotiations with important customers, suppliers, or consultants, employment negotiations with key personnel, and other nonroutine negotiations (e.g., acquisition of another firm, application for a large loan). Middle-level and lower-level managers also perform a negotiator role, but the negotiations are more likely to occur between different subunits of the organization and are more informal.

Managerial Activities and Effectiveness

Studies of managers' activities provide insight into the nature of a manager's job, but most of this research has not proven very helpful for understanding what makes a manager effective. As Campbell, et al. (1970, p. 76) point out, "The studies suffer from being strictly descriptive at the expense of developing more general categories or of differentiating between more and less important parts of managerial behavior." Only a few of the studies have attempted to relate activity patterns to measures of subunit performance, and these studies were not very successful. For example, O'Neil and Kubany (1959) studied 85 foremen over twenty weeks and failed to find any consistent relationship between observed job activities and measures of leader effectiveness.

A more promising approach than looking at activity frequency and duration is to compare the content of managerial activities for effective and ineffective managers. As yet, only a few studies of this type have been conducted (Kay & Meyer, 1962; Morse & Wagner, 1978; Ponder, 1958). In the study by Morse and Wagner, a questionnaire was developed with behavior items representing each of Mintzberg's ten managerial roles. The questionnaire included examples of effective and ineffective role behavior provided by a sample of managers. The questionnaire was administered to subordinates and peers of managers in a manufacturing company and a data processing firm. Managerial effectiveness was found to be significantly correlated with activity content based on the questionnaire descriptions of the managers. The most essential managerial roles were found to differ for the two companies. The implication of this study is that, although none of the managerial roles should be neglected, a manager's effectiveness depends on how well he carries out the particular roles that are most important for his situation. A manager will be more effective if he correctly decides which roles to emphasize and has the skills needed to perform these roles successfully.

CRITICAL INCIDENTS AND MANAGERIAL EFFECTIVENESS

A number of studies have used the critical incidents method to discover what managers do in order to be effective (see Table 5–2). As explained earlier in this chapter, the critical incidents method obtains examples of effective and ineffective behavior from managers and/or other respondents. Some examples of critical incidents for production foremen are provided by Kay (1959, p. 26):

1. "A foreman repeatedly allowed empty trucks, on their way back to the plant, to pass by materials he had been told needed to be picked up."

2. "A foreman failed to notify the relief shift foreman that a machine was in need of repair before it could be operated again."

3. "Observing a man engaged in horseplay while riding on a fork lift truck, a foreman stopped the truck and warned the man not to repeat such behavior."

4. "Aware that a change in set-up was scheduled for the next day, a foreman checked a machine, noted a missing part, and ordered it."

The first two examples are of ineffective behavior, and the second two examples are of effective behavior, as perceived by the respondents.

In most critical incidents studies, similar behaviors are grouped into categories, either by the researchers or by some of the respondents. The categories have differed considerably from study to study, due in part to the variety of leaders studied. The differences in categories also reflect the arbitrary and subjective nature of the classification process used in the critical incidents research. Despite the differences, close examination of the results reveals a moderate degree of similarity across studies. The following types of leader behavior were considered important by respondents in most of the studies:

1. Planning, coordinating, and organizing operations.
2. Establishing and maintaining good relations with subordinates.
3. Supervising subordinates (directing, instructing, monitoring performance).
4. Establishing effective relations with superiors, associates, and outsiders.
5. Assuming responsibility for observing organizational policies, carrying out required duties, and making necessary decisions.

TABLE 5–2

Studies of Critical Effective and Ineffective Leader Behaviors

Investigators	Type of Leader Studied
Anderson & Nilsson (1964)	Grocery Store Managers
Borman (1973)	First-Line Insurance Supervisors
Borman, Dunnette & Johnson (1974)	Naval Officers
Campbell, Dunnette, Arvey & Hellervik (1973)	Department Managers in Retail Stores
Gellerman (1976)	Production Supervisors
Heckman, Groner, Dunnette & Johnson (1972)	Police Sergeants & Commanders
Heizer (1972)	Line & Staff Production Supervisors
Hellervik, Dunnette & Arvey (1971)	Production Foremen
Kay (1959)	Production Foremen
Latham, Fay & Saari (1978)	Foremen
Latham & Wexley (1977)	Logging Crew Supervisors
Van Fleet (1974)	Heterogeneous Managers & Administrators
Van Fleet, Chamberlain & Gass (1974)	ROTC Cadet Officers
Williams (1956)	Corporate Executives

The critical incidents method assumes that most respondents know what behaviors are critical. If a certain type of behavior is mentioned frequently by respondents, it is assumed to be important. However, these assumptions are not necessarily correct, and the importance of the "critical" incidents should be verified by further research whenever possible. One method of achieving verification of the relevance of a set of critical incidents for a particular sample of leaders is to conduct a questionnaire study. The questionnaire items are based on the incidents but are worded in a more concise form. The questionnaire is administered to persons familiar with the behavior of the leaders. The behavior descriptions obtained from respondents can be analyzed to check on the accuracy of classification of incidents into categories, and to determine if the critical behaviors are in fact related to independent criteria of leader effectiveness, such as subunit productivity. This follow-up approach has been successfully demonstrated by Latham and Wexley (1977) in a study of logging crew supervisors.

Studies using critical incidents reveal that effective and ineffective behavior of leaders varies greatly from one situation to another. Some critical incidents describe specific behaviors that are only applicable to a certain type of leader in a particular situation, such as sales managers in a retail store. Other critical incidents describe specific behaviors that are relevant for most kinds of leaders (e.g., "shows appreciation when a subordinate performs a task effectively"). The "situation specific" incidents may be just as important as the "universally relevant" incidents, but they tend to be neglected by reseachers seeking a simple answer to the question of what makes a leader effective. It is useful to look for categories of leadership behavior that are widely applicable to leaders in different situations, but one should never forget that a substantial portion of critical leader behavior is likely to be situation specific. One contribution of critical incidents research is that it reveals situation specific aspects of leadership behavior that might otherwise be overlooked.

OHIO STATE LEADERSHIP STUDIES

By far the greatest number of studies on leader behavior have used questionnaires to describe what leaders do. Questionnaire research on leadership has been dominated by the influence of the Ohio State University Leadership Studies. The program of leadership research at the Ohio State University was initiated in the late 1940s. The focus of much of the research was the identification of leadership behavior that is instrumental for the attainment of group and organizational goals.

Development of Leader Behavior Questionnaires

The first phase of the research was the development of questionnaires to measure leader behavior. The researchers compiled a list of about 1,800 examples of leadership behavior. This list was then reduced to 150 items that staff members could agree were good examples of leader functions considered important in the managerial literature (e.g., organization, communication, representation, evaluation, integration, initiation, recognition, etc.). These items were used to develop a preliminary leadership questionnaire. The questionnaire was administered to samples of civilian and military personnel who were asked to describe the behavior of their supervisor. The questionnaire responses were factor analyzed to determine which behavior items were highly intercorrelated and to identify meaningful clusters of related items. The analyses indicated that subordinates perceived their leader's behavior primarily in terms of two distinct categories of leadership behavior (Fleishman, 1953, 1957; Halpin & Winer, 1957; Hemphill & Coons, 1957). The two leadership behavior categories were subsequently labeled "Consideration" and "Initiating Structure." Both were broadly defined categories containing a variety of specific behaviors. Consideration included behavior items concerned with leader supportiveness, friendliness, consideration, consultation with subordinates, representation of subordinate interests, openness of communication with subordinates, and recognition of subordinate contributions. These "relationship oriented" behaviors are all instrumental for establishing and maintaining good relationships with subordinates. Initiating Structure included behavior items concerned with directing subordinates, clarifying subordinate roles, planning, coordinating, problem solving, criticizing poor work, and pressuring subordinates to perform better. These "task-oriented" behaviors are instrumental for efficient utilization of personnel and resources in the attainment of group goals. Both Consideration and Initiating Structure involve leader influence over the motivation and behavior of subordinates.

Based on the results of the initial studies, two revised and shortened questionnaires were constructed to measure Consideration and Initiating Structure. The questionnaires were called the Leader Behavior Description Questionnaire (abbreviated LBDQ) and the Supervisory Behavior Description (SBD or SBDQ). Another questionnaire, called the Leader Opinion Questionaire (LOQ), was developed to measure a leader's attitudes about the desirability of the two behavior categories. Research using the LOQ will not be discussed in this chapter, since the questionnaire measures leader attitudes rather than actual leadership behavior. A fourth leadership questionnaire was eventually developed by some of the Ohio State University researchers who extended the LBDQ to include ten additional scales besides Consideration and Initiating Structure. The extended version was called the LBDQ-XII (Stogdill, Goode & Day, 1962), and the 12 scales are defined in Table 5–3. Some of the new scales measure aspects of leadership behavior, but others are more appropriately regarded as measures of a leader's traits or skills (e.g., Uncertainty Tolerance, Predictive Accuracy, Persuasiveness, Demand Reconciliation). The Ohio State leadership questionnaires and some modified versions of them have been used extensively in subsequent leadership research by many behavioral scientists, but until recently most of this research has been narrowly focused on Consideration and Initiating Structure.

TABLE 5–3

Definition of Leadership Scales in the LBDQ-XII

CONSIDERATION: regards the comfort, well-being, status, and contributions of followers.

INITIATION OF STRUCTURE: clearly defines own role, and lets followers know what is expected.

REPRESENTATION: speaks and acts as the representative of the group.

DEMAND RECONCILIATION: reconciles conflicting organizational demands and reduces disorder to the system.

TOLERANCE OF UNCERTAINTY: is able to tolerate uncertainty and postponement without anxiety or upset.

PERSUASIVENESS: uses persuasion and argument effectively; exhibits strong convictions.

TOLERANCE OF FREEDOM: allows followers scope for initiative, decision, and action.

ROLE RETENTION: actively exercises leadership role rather than surrendering leadership to others.

PREDICTIVE ACCURACY: exhibits foresight and ability to predict outcomes accurately.

PRODUCTION EMPHASIS: applies pressure for productive output.

INTEGRATION: maintains a closely knit organization; resolves inter-member conflicts.

INFLUENCE WITH SUPERIORS: maintains cordial relations with superiors; has influence with them; is striving for higher status.

Based on Stogdill, 1974; p. 143

Examples of Research on Consideration and Initiating Structure

The next step in the early Ohio State Leadership Studies was a series of correlational field studies to determine whether a leader's use of Consideration and Initiating Structure behavior was related to the leader's effectiveness. The primary criterion of leader effectiveness was the task performance of the leader's work unit, but supplementary criteria included such things as subordinate absenteeism, grievances, turnover, and satisfaction with the leader.

A study by Fleishman and Harris (1962) provides a good example of this research. The study was conducted in a truck manufacturing plant of the International Harvester Company. The behavior of 57 production foremen was described by subordinates who filled out the SBDQ. The criteria of leader effectiveness included the number of written grievances and the amount of voluntary turnover among subordinates during an eleven-month period. The relationship of Consideration and Initiating Structure to each criterion measure was computed, and the results for turnover are graphed in Figures 5–2 and 5–3.

FIGURE 5–2
Relation Between Consideration and Turnover Rate

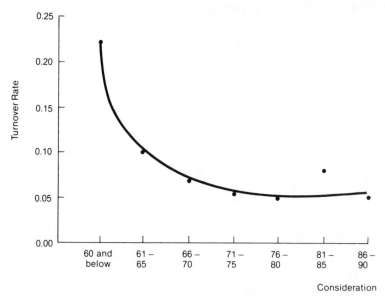

SOURCE: From E. A. Fleishman and E. F. Harris, "Patterns of Leadership Behavior Related to Employee Grievances and Turnover." *Personnel Psychology*, 1962, 15, 43–56.

FIGURE 5–3
Relation Between Initiating Structure and Turnover Rate

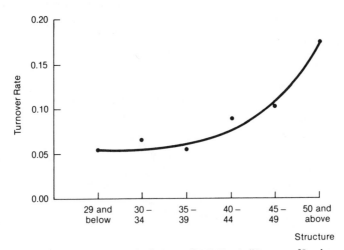

SOURCE: From E. A. Fleishman and E. F. Harris, "Patterns of Leadership Behavior Related to Employee Grievances and Turnover." *Personnel Psychology*, 1962, 15, 43–56.

Foremen who were high on Consideration had less grievances and turnover in their work units than foremen who were low on Consideration. The relationship was in the opposite direction for Initiating Structure; foremen who used a lot of structuring behavior had more turnover and grievances in their work units. Statistical analyses confirmed the existence of a significant curvilinear relationship. As noted by Fleishman and Harris (1962, p. 53), "there appear to be certain critical levels beyond which increased Consideration or decreased Initiating Structure have no effect on grievances or turnover rate."

The researchers also examined the combined effect of different amounts of the two leadership behaviors in order to obtain a better understanding of the results. The joint relationships are shown graphically in Figures 5–4 and 5–5. The results from the Fleishman and Harris study were generally corroborated by a similar study conducted with foremen in a textile firm (Skinner, 1969). The practical implications of the results are obvious. When a production foreman needs to use a substantial amount of structuring, directive behavior, he had better be very considerate as well. Otherwise, subordinates will become dissatisfied, and some of them are likely to quit their jobs or file grievances against the foreman. A high incidence of turnover, grievances, and other expressions of dissatisfaction (e.g., slowdowns, absenteeism, sabotage, theft, drugs and alcohol) could ultimately wipe

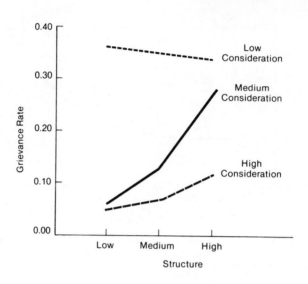

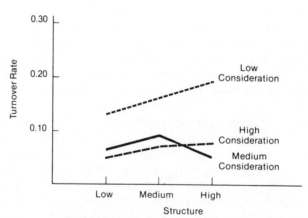

SOURCE: From E. A. Fleishman and E. F. Harris, "Patterns of Leadership Behavior Related to Employee Grievances and Turnover." *Personnel Psychology,* 1962, 15, 43–56.

out any short-term performance gains obtained by use of more structuring behavior.

The results from the two studies are impressive, but it is necessary to consider whether the findings can be generalized to other kinds of leaders besides production foremen, or to other outcomes such as subordinate performance. Since the days of the Ohio State research, many more studies have investigated the relationship of Consideration and Initiating Structure to various criteria of leader effectiveness. Several writers have reviewed this research, and the reviews show that neither behavior category is related consistently to subordinate performance (Kerr & Schriesheim, 1974; Korman, 1966; Stogdill, 1974; Yukl, 1971).

Results from studies testing the relationship between leader behavior and subordinate satisfaction with the leader are also mixed. Sometimes subordinates are more satisfied with a leader who is high on Initiating Structure and sometimes they are less satisfied or unaffected. The results for Consideration are somewhat more consistent, but not entirely so. Subordinates usually report greater satisfaction with a leader who is considerate than with a leader who is inconsiderate.

Problems in Determining Causality

A serious deficiency of research on the effects of leadership behavior is overreliance on "static correlational" research methods (Korman, 1966). Most studies have measured leadership behavior with a questionnaire administered to subordinates, and the behavior scores have been correlated with a measure of leader effectiveness or subordinate satisfaction obtained at the same point in time. When a significant correlation is found, there is no way to determine the direction of causality. For example, when a positive correlation is found between Consideration and subordinate performance for a sample of leaders, there are a variety of possible interpretations. Researchers have usually assumed that considerate leaders cause their subordinates to be more motivated and productive. An equally plausible interpretation is that leader Consideration is influenced by subordinate performance, and leaders will act in a more considerate manner toward subordinates who perform effectively. Another possibility is that subordinate descriptions of their leader's behavior are systematically influenced by the subordinates' awareness of how well the group is performing, with high-performance groups giving their leaders higher Consideration scores on the questionnaire (Lord, et al., 1978; Mitchell, et al., 1977).

A fourth interpretation is that somehow leader Consideration and subordinate performance are both affected in the same way by some other variable, which would cause Consideration and subordinate performance to be correlated, even though there was no causal relationship between them. This possibility is not too likely for studies in which leader effectiveness is measured in an objective manner, but it is a distinct possibility in studies correlating subordinate descriptions of leader behavior with subordinate reports of their own satisfaction with the leader, their own motivation, or their own evaluation of group performance.

The best way to determine causality in research on the effects of leader behavior is to conduct an experiment in which leader behavior is manipulated by the researcher rather than measured in its existing state. Several experiments of this type have been conducted in a laboratory setting with university students acting as the leaders and subordinates (Day, 1971; Day & Hamblin, 1964; Herold, 1977; Lowin & Craig, 1968; Misumi & Sharakashi, 1966; Misumi & Seki, 1971). These studies found that leader behavior comparable to Consideration and Initiating Structure affected subordinate performance, but the nature of the relationships varied from study to study. Some laboratory experiments have also tested the possibility of reverse causality by manipulating subordinate performance and seeing how leaders adapt their behavior to differences in subordinate performance (see Chapter 7). These studies demonstrate that causality usually operates in both directions.

The results from laboratory experiments are interesting, but they should be regarded as suggestive rather than conclusive. Laboratory experiments are usually of short duration, with an artificial task and no opportunity to develop deep interpersonal relationships. It is questionable whether the complex, emotional interactions characteristic of real relationships between leaders and followers can be accurately simulated in this kind of study. More dependable evidence for the consequences of leader behavior can be obtained either from longer and more realistic laboratory studies or from field experiments.

Field experiments are difficult to conduct, and only a handful have been done on effects of task-oriented and considerate leadership behavior. Leader behavior has been manipulated in two different ways in field experiments. One approach is to have leaders act in a predetermined way for a period of time to determine the effects on subordinates. Among four studies of this type, two were carried out with persons hired in a temporary job in a simulated organization (Gilmore, et al., 1970; Lowin, et al., 1969), one was with supervisors instructed to act either considerate or inconsiderate toward regular workers (Schachter, et al., 1961), and one examined effects of varying the leadership behavior of classroom instructors (Dawson, et al., 1972). In two other studies, leader behavior was manipulated by providing managerial training to steel plant managers (Hand & Slocum, 1972) and hospital supervisors (Wexley & Nemeroff, 1975). The success of the behavior manipulation was verified by having subordinates describe the behavior of their manager before and after training to see if it changed in the intended manner. The effects on subordinates from altering leader behavior were determined by comparing trained leaders to untrained ones.

Five of the six experiments found that considerate leaders had higher subordinate performance and/or satisfaction. The results for Initiating Structure were less consistent, in part because it was not manipulated in some of the studies and was only weakly manipulated in the other studies. These field experiments, together with laboratory experiments and some longitudinal field studies (Greene, 1975, 1979a, 1979b) show that considerate and directive-structuring leader behavior does indeed affect subordinate satisfaction and performance under some conditions. However, the different results from study to study also remind us that the effects of leader behavior on subordinate satisfaction and performance depend to a great extent on the nature of the situation.

MICHIGAN LEADERSHIP STUDIES

A second major program of research on leadership behavior was carried out by researchers at the University of Michigan at approximately the same time as the Ohio State Leadership Studies. The focus of the Michigan research was identification of relationships among leader behavior, group processes, and measures of group performance. As in the Ohio State Leadership Studies, one primary objective was to discover what pattern of leadership behavior leads to effective group performance.

Early Studies of Managers

The initial research was a series of field studies, each conducted with a sample of similar organizational subunits. Objective measures of group productivity were used to classify the managers as relatively effective or ineffective leaders. In the earliest studies, supervisors and their subordinates were interviewed; in later studies, questionnaires were used also. Descriptions of managerial behavior were analyzed to see how effective managers differed from ineffective managers. Studies of this type were carried out with section managers of an insurance company (Katz, Maccoby & Morse, 1950), supervisors in a manufacturing company (Katz & Kahn, 1952), supervisors in a large public utility (Mann & Dent, 1954), and foremen of railroad section gangs (Katz, et al., 1951).

Some interesting results were found in these studies. One finding was that effective leaders did not spend their time and effort doing the same kind of work as their subordinates. Instead, effective leaders concentrated on supervisory functions such as planning and scheduling the work, coordinating subordinate activities, and providing necessary supplies, equipment, or technical assistance. However, this production-oriented behavior did not occur at the expense of concern for human relations. The effective supervisors were more considerate, supportive, and helpful with subordinates. Moreover, effective supervisors tended to use general supervision rather than close supervision. That is, after establishing goals and general guidelines, the leaders allowed subordinates some autonomy in deciding how to do the work and how to pace themselves (see Figure 5–6).

FIGURE 5–6
Relationship Between Two Aspects of Leadership Behavior and Leader Effectiveness

NUMBER OF FIRST-LINE SUPERVISORS WHO ARE:

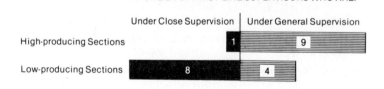

FOREMEN'S REACTION TO A POOR JOB
(as reported by their men)

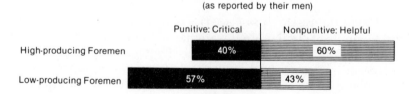

SOURCE: R. Likert, *New Patterns of Management.* New York: McGraw-Hill, 1961.

Studies of Participative Leadership

Another series of studies by researchers at the University of Michigan was concerned about the way leaders interact with subordinates in making decisions. A number of field experiments were conducted to test the hypothesis that leaders will be more effective if they allow subordinates to participate in making decisions (Coch & French, 1948; French, 1950; French, Israel & As, 1960; Morse & Reimer, 1956; Tannenbaum & Allport, 1956). The results from these studies were mixed, but they showed that in some situations participative leadership results in greater subordinate satisfaction and performance. The subject of participation will be discussed in greater detail in Chapter 8.

Likert's Contributions

Likert (1961), in his book entitled *New Patterns of Management*, attempted to integrate the findings of the Michigan studies and provide a theoretical framework to explain them. A refinement and elaboration of his theory was presented in a second book several years later (Likert, 1967). Likert proposed that the Michigan studies demonstrate the general effectiveness of certain managerial practices.

1. Supportive Behavior

A manager should treat each subordinate in such a way that the subordinate "will view the experience as supportive and one which builds and maintains his sense of personal worth and importance" (Likert, 1961; p. 103). Supportive behavior includes such things as showing trust and confidence, trying to understand and handle subordinate problems, helping to develop subordinates and further their careers, keeping subordinates informed, being friendly and considerate, showing appreciation for subordinate ideas and contributions, and providing recognition for subordinate accomplishments rather than trying to take all the credit for them.

2. Group Method of Supervision

Instead of supervising each subordinate separately, a manager should rely heavily on group meetings. The group method of supervision facilitates subordinate participation in decision making, improves communication, promotes cooperation, and facilitates resolution of conflicts. The role of the manager in group meetings should be primarily to guide the discussion and keep it supportive, constructive, and oriented toward problem solving. The leader should also make sure that subordinates receive instruction in group interaction processes as well as technical training so that they are able to work together effectively as a group. Asking subordinates to make group decisions doesn't imply that a manager abdicates his responsibilities for decision making. Likert emphasizes that a leader should assume responsibility for all decisions and their results. If there are differences of opinion between the manager and subordinates, and the quality of the decision is important," the superior may feel that he has no choice but to do what his experience indicates is best" (Likert, 1961; p. 112).

3. High-Performance Goals

One especially important type of group decision is the formulation of specific performance goals and quality standards for the group and/or for individual subordinates. The leader should guide the group in setting performance goals that are high but realistic.

4. Linking Pin Functions

Since decisions and goals should be compatible with the policies and objectives of the larger organization, it is essential for a lower-level or middle-level manager to act as an intermediary between his group and higher management. In order for the manager to represent the interests of his group effectively and obtain necessary resources and benefits for them, the manager needs to have a substantial degree of upward influence with his own superiors. Likert proposed structuring the organization as a series of overlapping groups. Each manager would be a member of his own group, a member of the group of managers reporting to his boss, and in some cases a member of some other organizational subunit with whom he serves in a lateral liaison capacity. Like Mintzberg (1973), Likert viewed a manager as a central informational link between his work unit and its outside environment.

According to Likert, the recommended managerial practices in combination with appropriate technical functions (e.g., planning, coordination) will result in attainment of a high level of group performance. The positive effects of the recommended managerial practices were explained with a model of causal processes. In his explanatory model, Likert differentiated between "causal variables," "intervening variables," and "end-result variables." Causal variables include managerial behavior and skills, as well as any aspects of organization structure that may be changed by a manager (e.g., reward systems, rules and policies). "The intervening variables reflect the internal state and health of the organization, e.g., the loyalties, attitudes, motivations, performance goals, and perceptions of all members and their collective capacity for effective interaction, communication, and decision making" (Likert, 1967; p. 29). The end-result variables are indicators of group or organizational effectiveness, such as profits, costs, productivity, quality of products or services, absenteeism, and turnover.

The hypothesized causal processess are depicted in Figure 5–7. The end-result variables are determined by the intervening variables, which are determined in turn by the causal variables, including managerial behavior. When a manager alters his behavior, the initial effect will be a change in one or more intervening variables. Only after a fairly long period of time will these effects work their way through to the end-result variables.

FIGURE 5–7
Causal Relationships Proposed by Likert

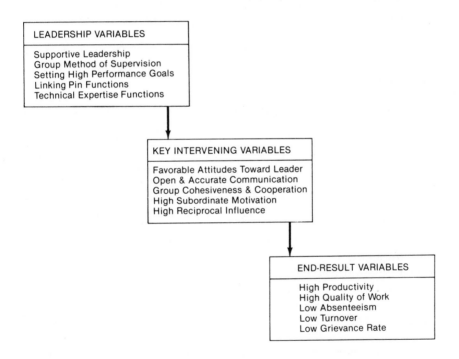

LEADERSHIP VARIABLES

Supportive Leadership
Group Method of Supervision
Setting High Performance Goals
Linking Pin Functions
Technical Expertise Functions

KEY INTERVENING VARIABLES

Favorable Attitudes Toward Leader
Open & Accurate Communication
Group Cohesiveness & Cooperation
High Subordinate Motivation
High Reciprocal Influence

END-RESULT VARIABLES

High Productivity
High Quality of Work
Low Absenteeism
Low Turnover
Low Grievance Rate

Likert (1967) describes an unpublished field experiment by Mann that demonstrates the delayed effects of changes in the causal variables. The study was conducted with four similar departments in a service company. One department served as the experimental group, and the supervisors in this department were given training to increase their skills in using the recommended managerial practices. Measurements taken six months after the start of the study indicated improvement in the intervening variables was beginning to occur, but one and a half years elapsed before there was a significant improvement in productivity. "The increase in productivity of the experimental department in comparison to the three other (control) departments proved, nevertheless, to be both substantial (cost savings of over $60,000 per year) and enduring. There was also an impressive improvement in union–management relationships in the experimental department" (Likert, 1967; p. 80). A comparable lagged effect of causal variables was also found in a correlational field study by Taylor and Bowers (1972).

Bowers and Seashore Four-Factor Theory

In 1966, Bowers and Seashore proposed a theory to explain managerial effectiveness in terms of four categories of leadership behavior. The theory was based on a reconceptualization of the findings in the early Michigan studies and the Ohio State studies. The proposed categories of leadership behavior were labeled and defined as follows (Bowers & Seashore, 1966; p. 247):

1. Support. Behavior that enhances someone else's feeling of personal worth and importance.

2. Interaction facilitation. Behavior that encourages members of the group to develop close, mutually satisfying relationships.

3. Goal emphasis. Behavior that stimulates an enthusiasm for meeting the group's goal or achieving excellent performance.

4. Work facilitation. Behavior that helps achieve goal attainment by such activities as scheduling, coordinating, planning, and by providing resources such as tools, materials, and technical knowledge.

One consequence of describing leadership in terms of behavior rather than leader traits and skills is that this definition allows for the possibility that someone in the group besides the designated leader may share in the leadership process. A manager may ask subordinates to share in performing certain leadership functions, and in some cases subordinates may carry out these functions on their own initiative. Since leadership functions need not be carried out solely by the designated group leader, the effectiveness of a group may depend more on the overall quality of leadership than on who performs the leadership functions. However, the possibility of shared leadership does not imply that it is unnecessary to have a designated leader. Bowers and Seashore (1966, p. 249) point out that "there are both common sense and theoretical reasons for believing that a formally acknowledged leader through his supervisory leadership behavior sets the pattern of the mutual leadership which subordinates supply each other."

Bowers and Seashore were the first to emphasize the need to measure subordinate leadership behavior as well as a manager's behavior. They developed parallel sets of questionnaire scales for subordinates to use in describing the leadership behavior of their supervisor and the leadership behavior of their peers (i.e., other subordinates in the same work unit). These scales are part of a larger standardized questionnaire called the Survey of Organizations (Taylor & Bowers, 1972). The questionnaire has been used extensively in a large variety of organizations by researchers at the University of Michigan.

One example of research on the Four-Factor Theory of Leadership is a correlational study conducted in 40 agencies of a life insurance company (Bowers & Seashore, 1966). The research was conducted to determine the extent to which the four categories of leadership behavior exhibited by managers and subordinates was associated with agency effectiveness. The questionnaire was administered to subordinates of the manager in each agency, and the responses were correlated with measures of intervening and end-result variables. The results revealed that agencies with a high dollar volume of sales had managers who used more Goal Emphasis behavior. Business costs were lower for agencies with managers who engaged in a great deal of Work Facilitation behavior. Business costs were also lower when subordinates had high scores on Work Facilitation, Goal Emphasis, and Interaction Facilitation. The results provide limited support for the importance of the four leadership behavior categories as determinants of group effectiveness. As with other correlational studies, it was not possible to demonstrate that leadership behavior actually causes group performance.

Research on the four leadership factors, like research on Consideration and Initiating Structure, has yielded different results from one study to another. One likely reason is the importance of the situation in determining what aspects of leadership behavior will be essential. It is unlikely that the four categories of leadership behavior proposed by Bowers and Seashore are all essential in every situation. Bowers (1975) has reviewed the results of research on 1,683 work groups from 21 organizations. There was ample evidence that leadership behavior was related to subordinate satisfaction and group processes, but the pattern of results varied, depending on the kind of industry and the authority level of the manager. Thus, once again, the behavior research demonstrates the need to examine situational variables more closely in order to understand leadership effectiveness.

CATEGORIES OF LEADERSHIP BEHAVIOR

The various kinds of research on leadership behavior have led to the proposal of many different behavior taxonomies. Earlier in this chapter we saw how the two categories from the early Ohio State Leadership Studies evolved into Stogdill's twelve-category taxonomy, and how the task- and employee-oriented behavior dichotomy in the early Michigan leadership studies evolved into Bowers and Seashore's four factors. Leadership research at the University of Southern California in the early 1950s (Comrey, Pfiffner & High, 1954) produced yet another taxonomy of leadership behavior with many more separate categories. Since the decade of the 1950s, research on classification of leadership behavior has continued, and several other taxonomies have been proposed. Recent examples include the three categories found by House and Dessler (1974), the five categories found by Bass and Valenzi (1974), the six categories found by Morse and Wagner (1978), and the four categories found by Schriesheim (1978).

It is obvious that there has been little agreement across studies. The widely discrepant results are disturbing, because research on the consequences of leader behavior is impeded by absence of a widely accepted taxonomy. It is very difficult to compare results from studies using different categories and measures of leadership behavior. The most widely used categories are Consideration and Initiating Structure, but it is now apparent that these broadly defined categories provide too general and simplistic a picture of leadership. They fail to capture the great diversity of behavior required by most kinds of managers and administrators. The more elaborate taxonomies that have been proposed are better, but even they fail to include some of the most relevant aspects of leadership behavior, such as providing praise and recognition, setting specific performance goals, providing tangible rewards for effective performance, providing necessary training and coaching, and inspiring subordinate confidence and commitment.

The more general a behavior category is, the more likely it is relevant to many different kinds of leaders, but the less useful it is for determining what makes a leader effective in a particular situation. The most desirable solution to this dilemma would seem to be a set of behavior categories at an intermediate level of abstraction. They should be more specific than Consideration and Initiating Structure, but less specific than critical incidents, many of which are relevant only for a particular kind of leader. The behavior categories should be applicable to a variety of measurement techniques, particularly questionnaires, diaries, observations, and classification of critical incidents.

In order to fill the conceptual void, Yukl and his colleagues recently completed a four-year program of research to identify meaningful and measurable categories of leadership behavior. A preliminary report on studies with six samples of leaders showed that substantial progress had been made toward attainment of this objective (Yukl & Nemeroff, 1979). Fourteen behavior categories were identified in the early research, and five additional categories have been isolated in the follow-up research. The nineteen behavior categories in the taxonomy are labeled and defined below. After each definition are examples based on behavior incidents observed by subordinates in one study.

1. PERFORMANCE EMPHASIS: the extent to which a leader emphasizes the importance of subordinate performance, tries to improve productivity and efficiency, tries to keep subordinates working up to their capacity, and checks on their performance.

My supervisor made the rounds to check on the status of the work and make sure everyone was working fast enough.

My supervisor urged us to be careful not to let any orders go out with defective components.

2. CONSIDERATION: the extent to which a leader is friendly, supportive, and considerate in his or her behavior toward subordinates and tries to be fair and objective.

On the day of the big snowstorm, my supervisor told subordinates they could leave early so they wouldn't get caught in the traffic jams.

When a subordinate was upset about something, the supervisor was very sympathetic and tried to console her.

3. INSPIRATION: the extent to which a leader stimulates enthusiasm among subordinates for the work of the group and says things to build subordinate confidence in their ability to perform assignments successfully and attain group objectives.

My supervisor held a meeting to talk about how vital the new contract is for the company and said he was confident we could handle it if we all did our part.

My boss told us we were the best design group he had ever worked with and he was sure that this new product was going to break every sales record in the company.

4. PRAISE–RECOGNITION: the extent to which a leader provides praise and recognition to subordinates with effective performance, shows appreciation for their special efforts and contributions, and makes sure they get credit for their helpful ideas and suggestions.

My boss complimented me on the professional manner in which I handled a difficult situation and said I am developing well in my new position.

In a meeting the supervisor told us she is very satisfied with our work and said she appreciated the extra effort we made this month.

5. STRUCTURING REWARD CONTINGENCIES: the extent to which a leader rewards effective subordinate performance with tangible benefits such as a pay increase, promotion, more desirable assignments, a better work schedule, more time off, and so on.

My supervisor established a new policy that any subordinate who brought in a new client would earn 10 percent of the contracted fee.

My supervisor recommended a promotion for a subordinate with the best performance record in the group.

6. DECISION PARTICIPATION: the extent to which a leader consults with subordinates and otherwise allows them to influence his or her decisions.

The supervisor held a meeting with subordinates to get their ideas and suggestions about the best way to deal with some operational problems.

My supervisor asked me to attend a meeting with him and his boss to develop a new production schedule, and he was very receptive to my ideas on the subject.

7. AUTONOMY–DELEGATION: the extent to which a leader delegates authority and responsibility to subordinates and allows them to determine how to do their work.

My boss gave me a new project and encouraged me to handle it any way I think is best.

My supervisor delegated a lot more authority to me, because she is frequently out of the office and is leaving me in charge of operations.

8. ROLE CLARIFICATION: the extent to which a leader informs subordinates about their duties and responsibilities, specifies the rules and policies that must be observed, and lets subordinates know what is expected of them.

The supervisor gave a new employee a written job description and a manual containing rules and regulations for the department, then explained the most important things the employee should know about the job.

My boss called me in to inform me about a rush project that must be given top priority, and he gave me some specific assignments related to this project.

9. GOAL SETTING: the extent to which a leader emphasizes the importance of setting specific performance goals for each important aspect of a subordinate's job, measures progress toward the goals, and provides concrete feedback.

The supervisor held a meeting to discuss the sales quota for next month.

My supervisor met with me for two hours to establish performance goals for the coming year and develop action plans.

10. TRAINING–COACHING: the extent to which a leader determines training needs for subordinates, and provides any necessary training and coaching.

The sales manager went out on sales calls with a new salesman last week to provide instruction and advice.

My boss asked me to attend an outside course at the company's expense and said I could leave early on the days it was to be held.

11. INFORMATION DISSEMINATION: the extent to which a leader keeps subordinates informed about developments that affect their work, including events in other work units or outside the organization, decisions made by higher management, and progress in meetings with superiors or outsiders.

My supervisor held a meeting to tell us when the new machines would arrive and how they would affect our operations.

The supervisor briefed us about some high-level changes in policy.

12. PROBLEM SOLVING: the extent to which a leader takes the initiative in proposing solutions to serious work-related problems and acts decisively to deal with such problems when a prompt solution is needed.

The supervisor held a meeting to let us know that we were behind sched-
ule on a critical project; after we identified the source of the problem,
he suggested a procedure to eliminate unnecessary delays.

The unit was short-handed due to illness, and we had an important
deadline to meet; my supervisor arranged to borrow two people from
other units so we could finish the job today.

13. PLANNING: the extent to which a leader plans how to efficiently organize and schedule the work in advance, plans how to attain work unit objectives, and makes contingency plans for potential problems.

The supervisor anticipated that we will be swamped with work next week
and has rearranged the work schedule so that everyone in the depart-
ment will be available to help out.

My supervisor devised a short cut that allows us to prepare our financial
statements in three days instead of the four days it used to take.

14. COORDINATING: the extent to which a leader coordinates the work of subordinates, emphasizes the importance of coordination, and encourages subordinates to coordinate their activities.

My supervisor asked me to meet with another subordinate working on a
similar project so that we won't waste time doing the same preparations
separately.

My supervisor had subordinates who were ahead in their work help
those who were behind so that the different parts of the project would
be ready at the same time.

15. WORK FACILITATION: the extent to which a leader obtains for subordinates any necessary supplies, equipment, support services, or other resources, eliminates problems in the work environment, and removes other obstacles that interfere with the work.

I asked my boss to order some supplies, and he arranged to get them
right away.

A typewriter in our office was not working properly; the supervisor put
in a requisition for a new one and persuaded her boss to approve it.

16. REPRESENTATION: the extent to which a leader establishes contacts with other groups and important people in the organization, persuades them to appreciate and support his work unit, and uses his influence with superiors and outsiders to promote and defend the interests of the work unit.

My supervisor met with the data processing manager to get some revisions made in the computer programs so they will be better suited to our needs.

Top management is planning a reorganization, and my supervisor has been lobbying hard in meetings to keep control over key operations for our department.

17. INTERACTION FACILITATION: the extent to which a leader tries to get subordinates to be friendly with each other, cooperate, share information and ideas, and help each other.

The sales manager took the group out to lunch to give everybody a chance to get to know the new sales representative.

My supervisor set up a "buddy system" in the department so that members could help each other with questions and problems.

18. CONFLICT MANAGEMENT: the extent to which a leader restrains subordinates from fighting and arguing, encourages them to resolve conflicts in a constructive manner, and helps to settle conflicts and disagreements between subordinates.

The supervisor asked two subordinates to settle their differences in a professional manner without so much bickering and name calling.

Two members of the department who were working together on a project were having a dispute about it: the manager met with them to help resolve the matter.

19. CRITICISM–DISCIPLINE: the extent to which a leader criticizes or disciplines a subordinate who shows consistently poor performance, violates a rule, or disobeys an order; disciplinary actions include an official warning, reprimand, suspension, or dismissal.

The supervisor was annoyed that a subordinate kept making the same kind of errors and warned him to make a more concerted effort.

The supervisor called me in to tell me that I had neglected to include two items of information in an important report.

TABLE 5–4

Approximate Correspondence Among Leadership Categories in Different Questionnaires

MBS Categories	Halpin & Winer (1957)	Fleishman (1953)	Stogdill et al. (1962)	Bowers & Seashore (1966)	House & Dessler (1974)	Bass & Valenzi (1974)	Comrey et al. (1954)
Planning						Direction	Planning, Advance Planning, Organizing
Coordinating	Initiating Structure	Initiating Structure	Initiating Structure		Instrumental Leadership	Direction	Formalization
Role Clarification							
Goal Setting							
Performance Emphasis	Production Emphasis		Production Emphasis	Goal Emphasis			Production Pressure
Criticism–Discipline	(Initiating Structure)						Discipline
Autonomy–Delegation			Tolerance of Freedom			Delegation	
Problem Solving			Role Assumption				
Training–Coaching				Work Facilitation			
Work Facilitation							

Consideration

Consideration

Consideration

Consideration

Supervisor Support

Supportive Leadership
Participative Leadership

Consultation, Participation

Manipulation

Helpfulness, Sympathy
Lack of Arbitrariness

Influence on Superiors

Communication Down

Representation
Infl. on Superiors

Integration

Interaction Facilitation

Persuasiveness

Consideration
Decision Participation
Structuring Rewards
Praise–Recognition
Representation
Interaction Facilitation
Conflict Management
Information Dissemination
Inspiration

The new taxonomy provides a means of reconciling the discrepancies among most of the earlier studies on leadership behavior categories. Most of the nineteen categories in the Yukl taxonomy are components of more broadly defined categories found in earlier research. Some of the new categories have direct counterparts in earlier research, and others do not. The approximate correspondence with behavior categories in other taxonomies is shown in Table 5–4. The advantage of the new taxonomy is that it has a larger number of more specific behavior categories than earlier ones, and it includes most behaviors found to be important in leadership research.

The method used to measure the new behaviors is administration of a questionnaire called the Managerial Behavior Survey (MBS) to a leader's subordinates. However, the behavior categories have also proven useful for classifying observations and critical incidents. The behavior categories are separate and distinct, but in practice they are not entirely independent, and actual behavior incidents often involve more than a single behavior category. The situations in which each type of behavior is especially relevant will be summarized in Chapter 7, after we first review situational theories and research in Chapters 6 and 7.

Summary

A popular approach for studying leadership is examination of leader behavior. Methods used to conduct this research include observation, activity sampling, self-report diary, interviews, questionnaires, and critical incidents. Each method has certain advantages and disadvantages.

One important type of behavioral research is the observation of typical behavior exhibited by managers and administrators. Managerial work typically involves a large variety of activities, most of which entail interaction with other people. The activities are usually characterized by brevity and fragmentation. Mintzberg proposed a ten-category typology of managerial roles to describe the content of managerial activities. The ten roles were grouped into three general categories: interpersonal behavior, information processing, and decision making.

Studies of effective and ineffective leadership behavior using the critical incidents method yield highly divergent results, due mainly to the prevalence of situation-specific behaviors. However, when the behavior incidents are grouped into broader categories of leadership behavior, more consistency of findings is evident across studies. The most commonly found categories of critical leadership behavior were planning and coordinating, supervising subordinates, carrying out position responsibilities, and maintaining good relations with subordinates, peers, and superiors.

Questionnaire research on leadership behavior has been dominated by the concepts and methods that came out of the leadership research at Ohio State University in the early 1950s. Since those days, questionnaire scales measuring Consideration and Initiating Structure have been used in hundreds of studies to determine if these broadly defined aspects of leadership behavior are related to leader effectiveness. The results have been inconsistent except for the finding that subordinates are usually more satisfied with a leader who is highly considerate, which is hardly a momentous discovery. Lack of stronger, more consistent results in the questionnaire research has been attributed to inadequate conceptualization of leadership behavior, lack of accurate measures, effects of situational variables, and problems in determining causality and separating feedback effects from forward-acting effects.

At the University of Michigan, another influential series of studies on leadership behavior was carried out in the 1950s. Comparison of the behavior patterns for effective and ineffective managers revealed that effective managers usually concentrated on administrative functions like planning, coordinating, and facilitating work. These task-oriented aspects of leadership behavior were carried out without neglecting interpersonal relations with subordinates. Effective supervisors were more likely to treat subordinates in a considerate, supportive manner and allow them some autonomy in deciding how to do the work and how to pace themselves. Likert (1961) emphasized the importance of investigating the leader's impact on intervening variables such as subordinate attitudes and motivation. He concluded that effective leaders are more likely to act supportive, set high-performance goals, use group methods of supervision, serve as a "linking pin," and carry out appropriate administrative activities. Bowers and Seashore (1966) found that subordinates themselves may engage in leadership behavior, with implications for leadership effectiveness.

Another important line of behavioral research is the continuing effort to develop a more acceptable taxonomy of leadership behavior, with behavior categories that are neither situation-specific nor overly broad and abstract. Some recent research by Yukl and his colleagues has generated a behavior taxonomy that appears to reconcile the diverse findings from most earlier studies.

REVIEW AND DISCUSSION QUESTIONS

1. Briefly describe the nature of managerial work.

2. What methods have been used to study leadership activities and behavior, and what are the advantages and disadvantages of each method?

3. Briefly describe Mintzberg's ten managerial roles.

4. What do critical incidents studies tell us about the behavior of effective leaders?

5. What problems have impeded research on leadership behavior?

6. What did we learn about leadership effectiveness from the Ohio State Leadership Studies in the 1950s?

7. What did the research at the University of Michigan discover about leadership effectiveness?

8. To what extent can leadership be shared with subordinates? Does shared leadership imply that a designated leader is unnecessary?

9. Briefly identify the leadership behaviors in Yukl's taxonomy. How do these behaviors correspond to other leadership behaviors discussed in this chapter?

10. Define and explain each of the following terms: diary, activity sampling, structured and unstructured observation, critical incidents, managerial activities, Consideration, Initiating Structure, LBDQ, LBDQ-XII, linking pin functions, intervening and end-result variables, Four-Factor Theory.

6

Situational Theories of Leadership Effectiveness

In Chapters 4 and 5 we saw that different traits and behaviors are important for leaders in different situations. This discovery fostered a situational approach to leadership. One variation of the situational approach has been concerned with identifying aspects of the situation that determine what traits, skills, and behaviors are required for a leader to be effective in a given situation. Aspects of the situation that enhance or nullify the influence of a leader's traits or behavior are called "moderator variables." In this chapter, we will review six situational theories of leadership effectiveness. Each of the theories is referred to as a "contingency theory," because a leader's effects on subordinates are postulated to be contingent on particular situational moderator variables.

FIEDLER'S CONTINGENCY MODEL OF LEADERSHIP

The earliest and best known of the situational theories of leadership is the one proposed by Fiedler (1964, 1967). In 1953, at the University of Illinois, Fiedler began a program of research on a large variety of leaders, including bomber crew commanders, artillery crew commanders, tank commanders, ROTC cadet officers, supervisors in a steel plant, general managers of farm supply cooperatives, and captains of high school basketball teams. Fiedler's early research was an example of the trait approach. That is, he attempted to predict leader effectiveness using a measure of leader attitudes called the LPC score. When he found different results for different kinds of leaders, Fiedler developed a situational theory to explain the discrepant results. His Contingency Model specifies the kind of situation in which a leader with a high LPC score will be more effective than a leader with a low LPC score, and vice versa.

Measurement and Interpretation of LPC

The letters "LPC" refer to "least preferred coworker." A leader's LPC score is obtained from his responses to a semantic differential scale, which is a type of questionnaire composed of bipolar items (see Figure 6–1). The leader is asked to think of all past and present coworkers, and he is instructed to select the one with whom he could work least well. Then the leader rates this least preferred coworker on each bipolar item. The rating for each item is coded in terms of a number ranging from 1 to 8, and the item scores are added together to compute the leader's LPC score. A leader who is critical in rating his least preferred coworker will obtain a low LPC score, whereas a leader who is lenient in his ratings will obtain a high LPC score.

The interpretation of LPC scores has changed several times over the years since they were first used by Fiedler in leadership research. Fiedler's (1971, 1972) most recent interpretation is in terms of a leader's motive hierarchy. The primary motive of a high LPC leader is to have close, interpersonal relationships with other persons, including subordinates. This kind of leader will emphasize socializing with subordinates and will act in a considerate, supportive manner if relations need to be improved. Achievement of task objectives is a secondary motive, which will become important only if the leader's primary affiliation motive is already satisfied by close personal relationships with subordinates and peers. The primary motive of a low LPC leader is achievement of task objectives. This kind of leader is very concerned about doing a good job and will emphasize task-oriented behavior in dealing with subordinates whenever there are task problems. The secondary motive of establishing good relations with subordinates will be pursued only if the group is performing well and there are no serious task problems. According to Fiedler, a high LPC score does not necessarily imply that a leader will be generally more considerate or less directive in his behavior toward subordinates. High and low LPC leaders act differently, but the precise pattern of behavior varies depending on the situation.

Rice (1978) has reviewed twenty-five years of research on the meaning of LPC scores, and he finds considerable support for a value–attitude interpretation. Low LPC leaders value task success, whereas high LPC leaders value interpersonal success. This interpretation is basically in accord with Fiedler's motive hierarchy interpretation, but is more parsimonious and better supported by diverse kinds of research on LPC scores.

FIGURE 6–1
Example of an LPC Scale

Instructions:

People differ in the ways they think about those with whom they work. On the scale below are pairs of words which are opposite in meaning. You are asked to describe someone with whom you have worked by placing an "X" in one of the eight spaces on the line between the two words. Each space represents how well the adjective fits the person you are describing, as in the following example:

Very neat: _____ : _____ : _____ : _____ : _____ : _____ : _____ : _____ : Not neat

	8	7	6	5	4	3	2	1
	Very neat	Quite neat	Some-what neat	Slight-ly neat	Slight-ly untidy	Some-what untidy	Quite untidy	Very untidy

Now, think of the person with whom you can work least well. He may be someone you work with now, or he may be someone you knew in the past. He does not have to be the person you like least well, but should be the person with whom you had the most difficulty in getting a job done. Describe this person as he appears to you.

Pleasant	:___:___:___:___|___:___:___:___: Unpleasant
Friendly	:___:___:___:___|___:___:___:___: Unfriendly
Rejecting	:___:___:___:___|___:___:___:___: Accepting
Helpful	:___:___:___:___|___:___:___:___: Frustrating
Unenthusiastic	:___:___:___:___|___:___:___:___: Enthusiastic
Tense	:___:___:___:___|___:___:___:___: Relaxed
Distant	:___:___:___:___|___:___:___:___: Close
Cold	:___:___:___:___|___:___:___:___: Warm
Cooperative	:___:___:___:___|___:___:___:___: Uncooperative
Supportive	:___:___:___:___|___:___:___:___: Hostile
Boring	:___:___:___:___|___:___:___:___: Interesting
Quarrelsome	:___:___:___:___|___:___:___:___: Harmonious
Self-assured	:___:___:___:___|___:___:___:___: Hesitant
Efficient	:___:___:___:___|___:___:___:___: Inefficient
Gloomy	:___:___:___:___|___:___:___:___: Cheerful
Open	:___:___:___:___|___:___:___:___: Guarded

SOURCE: Adapted from F. E. Fiedler, *A Theory of Leadership Effectiveness*. New York: McGraw-Hill, 1967.

Situational Moderator Variables

In Fiedler's model, the relationship between leader LPC scores and leader effectiveness depends on a complex situational variable with multiple components. This situational variable is called either "situational favorability" or "situational control." It is defined as the extent to which the situation gives a leader influence over subordinate performance. Situational control is usually measured in terms of the following three aspects of the situation:

1. Leader–Member Relations. A leader who has the loyalty and support of subordinates can depend on them to comply enthusiastically with his directions. On the other hand, a leader whose subordinates dislike him has no referent power and must be careful that they do not ignore his directions or subvert his policies.

2. Position Power. When a leader has substantial position power, he is able to administer rewards and punishments to increase subordinate compliance with his directions and policies. Leaders with little or no position power must rely on other sources of influence over subordinates.

3. Task Structure. A task is highly structured when there is a detailed description of the finished product or service, there are standard operating procedures that guarantee successful completion of the task, and it is easy for the leader to determine how well the work has been performed. With a highly structured task, it is easier for the leader to monitor and influence subordinate task behavior. The leader can give subordinates detailed directions, and can easily determine if these directions are being followed. On the other hand, when the task is unstructured, the leader does not know the best way to do it and cannot easily determine how well subordinates are performing. Subordinates are more likely to disagree with the leader about the best task procedures to use, and they can more easily circumvent the leader's directions.

Fiedler has found that leader–member relations are the most important of the three determinants of situational control, followed next by task structure and finally position power. By combining and weighting ratings of these three aspects of the situation, Fiedler obtains his index of situational control. The ratings are made by the leaders being studied or by observers who are familiar with the leadership situation for that kind of leader. Situational control is greatest when leader–member relations are good, the task is highly structured, and the leader has substantial position power. Some examples of leaders in this kind of situation include the well liked commander of an artillery crew and the foreman of an open-hearth steel shop who has loyal subordinates. Situational control is lowest when leader–member relations are poor, the task is unstructured, and the leader has little position power. Some examples of leaders in this kind of situation include the unpopular chairperson of a volunteer committee with a vague problem-solving task, and the disliked chairperson of the board of directors in a small farm-supply cooperative. Examples of an intermediate favorability situation include the well liked leader of a research team who has limited position power and an unstructured task, and the unpopular new supervisor of a crew of assembly-line workers with a highly structured task.

Hypotheses Regarding Leader Effectiveness

According to Fiedler, when the situation is either very high or very low in situational control, leaders with low LPC scores will be more effective than leaders with high LPC scores. When there is intermediate situational control, leaders with high LPC scores will be more effective. The proposed causal relationships in Fiedler's model are depicted in Figure 6–2. It is important to note the absence of intervening variables in the model. Without intervening variables, the model is unable to explain why low LPC leaders are more effective in some situations and high LPC leaders are more effective in other situations. Fiedler (1978) has recently proposed a tentative explanation saying, in effect, that the particular motive hierarchy of some leaders makes them more likely to use the kind of leadership behavior that is appropriate for that situation, whereas leaders with a different motive hierarchy will tend to use an inappropriate behavior pattern. The details of the explanation are too involved to review here. As yet, the proposed explanation is still speculative and requires further empirical verification.

Validation Evidence for the Model

The relationships between leader LPC, situational control, and group performance were hypothesized by Fiedler after examination of the results from a number of his earlier studies. These early leadership studies cannot be regarded as proof for the model, since it was based on them. Fiedler (1978) has recently reviewed the evidence from sev-

FIGURE 6–2
Causal Relationships in Fiedler's Contingency Theory

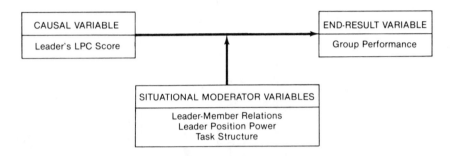

eral studies conducted since his model was originally proposed in 1964. The results from the early studies and those from the subsequent validation studies are summarized graphically in Figure 6–3. The pattern of correlations between leader LPC scores and group performance across situations is depicted as a line graph. It is obvious from this figure that the curve for the validation studies is roughly similar to the curve based on the original set of studies. The correspondence between the two curves provides moderately strong support for the model.

The results from one study by Chemers and Skrzypek (1972) are graphed separately in the figure, because this study is regarded by Fiedler (1978) as an especially appropriate validation study. Unlike most studies testing the model, this study was an experiment in which leader LPC and situational variables were manipulated. The study was conducted with 128 cadets at the United States Military Academy at West Point. The LPC scale was administered to the cadet sample three weeks before the groups performed their tasks to insure that the LPC scores would not be affected by group performance. Leaders were selected from among cadets with either very high or very low LPC scores. Sociometric preferences were also measured to determine which cadets liked each other, and this information was used to form groups of cadets in which leader–member relations were either good or poor. Each group of cadets was given both a structured task and an unstructured task to perform. Position power was manipulated by giving the leader in one condition (high power) the responsibility for evaluating the performance of his group members and assigning a score to be entered in each cadet's permanent service record. In the low power condition, the leaders had no position power except the authority of their designated role as chairperson of the group. All eight octants along the situational control continuum were represented in the study, unlike most of the earlier studies, which excluded some octants

FIGURE 6-3

Relationship Between LPC and Group Performance

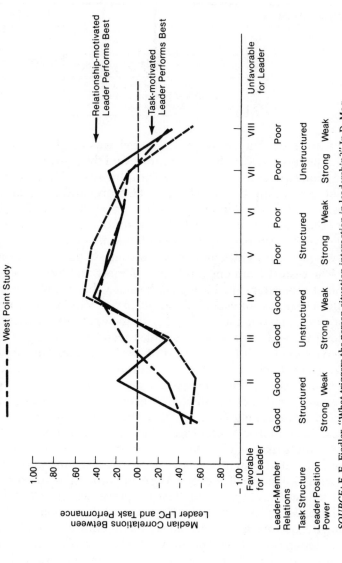

SOURCE: F. E. Fiedler, "What triggers the person-situation interaction in leadership?" In D. Magnusson & N. S. Endler (Eds.). *Personality at the Crossroads: Current Issues in Interactional Psychology.* Hillsdale, New Jersey: Lawrence Erlbaum Associates, 1977.

due to the difficulty of finding enough similar leaders. The results from the West Point study supported the predicted curvilinear relationship between LPC and group performance, and the curve was similar to that found in the other validation studies.

Criticisms of Fiedler's Model

Fiedler's model and the methodology of the validation studies have been severely criticized in the last few years. The major criticisms are as follows:

1. The LPC score is a "measure in search of a meaning" (Schriesheim & Kerr, 1976; p. 23). Its interpretation has been changed in an arbitrary fashion, and the current interpretation is speculative and inadequately supported.
2. The model is not really a theory, since it doesn't explain how a leader's LPC score has a causal effect on group performance. The model makes predictions without explaining the reason for the prediction (Ashour, 1973).
3. The supporting results for the model are weak and inconsistent. In most cases the correlational results, although in the predicted direction, are not statistically significant (Graen, Alvares, Orris & Martella, 1970; McMahon, 1972).
4. The weights assigned to the three situational variables used to compute the index of situational control were determined in an arbitrary manner, and no explicit rationale for these weights has been presented (Shiflett, 1973). The model doesn't explain why three different aspects of the situation should be combined and treated as a single unitary continuum.
5. The situational measures may not be entirely independent of the leader's LPC score (Kerr & Harlan, 1973). In most of the studies testing the model, the measure of LPC and the measure of leader–member relations were both obtained from the leaders, and various kinds of response tendencies on the part of the leaders could have confounded the results.
6. Since a leader is usually able to alter leader–member relations by acting more or less considerate toward subordinates, leader–member relations should be treated as an intervening variable rather than as a situational variable.

Fiedler (1971, 1973, 1977) has replied to most of the criticisms, and the debate over his model is still continuing. As further research is conducted, many of the questions about the model's validity and utility will probably be resolved in the coming years.

HERSEY AND BLANCHARD'S SITUATIONAL LEADERSHIP THEORY

We saw in Chapter 5 that measures of Consideration and Initiating Structure are not consistently related to leader effectiveness. In an attempt to explain the inconsistencies, Hersey and Blanchard (1972, 1977) formulated a contingency theory of leadership. It was originally called the "Life Cycle Theory of Leadership," and in its revised form it is referred to as the "Situational Leadership Theory." This theory is an extension of Blake and Mouton's (1964) Managerial Grid model and Reddin's (1967) 3–D Management Style Theory.

Leader Behavior

The theory is concerned with two broad categories of leadership behavior (Hersey & Blanchard, 1977; p. 104):

TASK BEHAVIOR: The extent to which leaders are likely to organize and define the roles of members of their group (followers); to explain what activities each is to do and when, where, and how tasks are to be accomplished; characterized by endeavoring to establish well-defined patterns of organization, channels of communication, and ways of getting jobs accomplished.

RELATIONSHIP BEHAVIOR: The extent to which leaders are likely to maintain personal relationships between themselves and members of their group (followers) by opening up channels of communication, providing socioemotional support, "psychological strokes," and facilitating behavior.

Task behavior corresponds approximately to Initiating Structure in the Ohio State Leadership Studies, and relationship behavior corresponds approximately to Consideration.

Situational Moderator Variable

Hersey and Blanchard's model deals explicitly with only one situational moderator variable, called follower "maturity." It is defined as "the capacity to set high but attainable goals (achievement motivation), willingness to take responsibility, and education and/or experience." (p. 161). Maturity of a subordinate is measured only in relation to a particular task that the subordinate is to perform. Thus, a subordinate may be quite mature in relation to one task but very immature in relation to another aspect of the job. Hersey and Blanchard (1977, p. 161) provide the following example: "A saleswoman may be very responsible in securing new sales but very casual about completing the paperwork necessary to close on a sale." Maturity is likely to differ from one subordinate to another, as well as from task to task.

According to Hersey and Blanchard, follower maturity involves two related components: "job maturity" and "psychological maturity." Job maturity is a subordinate's task-relevant skills and technical knowledge. Psychological maturity is a feeling of self-confidence and self-respect. A "high maturity" subordinate has the ability to do a particular task and also has a high degree of self-confidence about the task. A "low maturity" subordinate lacks both ability and confidence.

Hersey and Blanchard recognize that other situational variables such as the expectations of the leader's boss, the nature of the task, and time pressures are sometimes as important as follower maturity. However, they have chosen to exclude these other kinds of situational variables in order to have a more narrowly focused model of leader effectiveness.

Behavior Prescriptions for Leader Effectiveness

According to Situational Leadership Theory, as the level of subordinate maturity increases, the leader should use more relationship-oriented behavior and less task-oriented behavior up to the point where subordinates have a moderate level of maturity. As subordinate maturity increases beyond that level, the leader should then decrease the amount of relationship-oriented behavior, while continuing to decrease the amount of task-oriented behavior. The prescriptions about the appropriate behavior combination for each level of maturity are depicted in Figure 6–4. In this figure, four degrees of subordinate maturity are distinguished, even though they are merely segments of a continuum ranging from immature to mature.

For a situation (M1) where subordinates are very immature in relation to the task, the leader should concentrate on task-oriented behavior and not engage in much relationship-oriented behavior. In other words, the leader should be very directive and autocratic in defining subordinate roles and establishing objectives, standards, and procedures.

For situations (M2 and M3) where subordinates have a moderate amount of maturity, the leader should engage in considerable relationship-oriented behavior. In other words, the leader should act very considerate and supportive, consult with subordinates in making decisions, and provide praise and attention. At the same time, a moder-

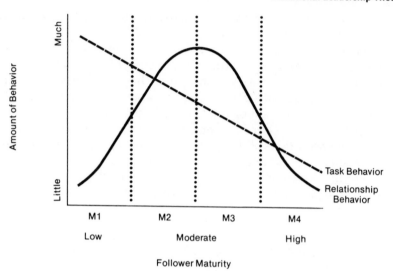

Follower Maturity

ate degree of directing subordinates and organizing of the work is desirable, especially in the M3 quadrant.

For a situation (M4) where subordinates are very mature, the leader should delegate responsibility for deciding how the work is done to subordinates and allow them to have considerable autonomy. Since the subordinates are mature, they will be self-motivated by their achievement needs and will have the ability to do the work without much direction. Mature subordinates will not need much supportive behavior from the leader, because they are self-confident and feel good about themselves.

The causal relationships implied by the theory are shown in Figure 6-5. In addition to the relationships already described between leader behavior and effectiveness (arrows 1 and 2), there is a more delayed causal effect of the leader's behavior on subordinate maturity (arrow 3). According to Hersey and Blanchard, the leader can alter the maturity level of subordinates by use of "developmental interventions." At the simplest level, a developmental intervention for an immature subordinate would consist of relaxing the amount of directive behavior and delegating more responsibility for a specific task. If the subordinate responds positively, the leader should reinforce him by providing praise and emotional support. A more complex developmental intervention is referred to as "contingency contracting." Here

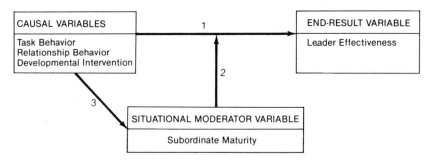

the leader and subordinate negotiate an agreement regarding the objectives and duties of the subordinate and the leader's role in helping the subordinate to accomplish the objectives. How long it takes to "mature" a subordinate depends on the complexity of the task and the characteristics of the subordinate. There is no set formula, and it may take as little as a few days or as long as a few years to advance a subordinate from low to high maturity on a given task. After maturity increases, the leader should adapt his task- and relationship-oriented behavior to fit the new situation he has created.

Hersey and Blanchard also point out the possibility of a regression in subordinate maturity, which again calls for a flexible adjustment of the leader's behavior. For example, a highly motivated and responsible subordinate may have a personal tragedy that leaves him apathetic about his work. This person would then require closer supervision and leader behavior designed to boost his maturity back to former levels, if possible.

Evaluation of the Theory

Hersey and Blanchard provide little evidence in support of their theory. Unlike Fiedler, they have not published validation studies testing their theory. They claim that it is able to explain the results of earlier studies on the consequences of task- and relationship-oriented behavior, but even this assertion seems questionable. Hardly any of the earlier studies attempted to measure maturity as they define it, and none of these studies used the kind of analysis needed to evaluate properly the complex relationships proposed in their theory.

The conceptual basis of the theory is weak, because Hersey and Blanchard have neglected to provide a coherent, explicit rationale for the hypothesized relationships. Moreover, a number of important situational variables are ignored, as the authors themselves admit. This omission is serious, because the other situational variables are pertinent to the determination of appropriate leader behavior. By continuing to look only at two broadly defined categories of leader behavior, many important distinctions between different aspects of each kind of behavior are overlooked. Maturity is also defined too broadly. It is a kind of a composite situational variable containing diverse elements, and no guidance is provided for weighting and combining these elements. For example, a confident subordinate with a difficult task is not equivalent to an insecure subordinate with an easy task, or to a moderately secure subordinate with a moderately difficult task. Yet the theory does not distinguish between these three conditions; they all fall into the medium maturity classification.

Despite its deficiencies, Situational Leadership Theory makes some positive contributions. Perhaps the greatest of these is the emphasis on flexible, adaptable leader behavior. Hersey and Blanchard remind us that it is essential to treat different subordinates differently, and to treat the same subordinate differently as the situation changes. They also advance the rather innovative proposition that leaders have another option besides just adapting to the present situation, namely, changing the situation by building the skills and confidence of subordinates. A final contribution of the theory, and its predecessor by Reddin (1967), is the recognition that leader behavior can be exhibited in a more or less skillful fashion. Even though a particular style of leadership is appropriate in a given situation, it will not be effective unless the leader has sufficient skill in using that style of leadership.

HOUSE'S PATH-GOAL THEORY OF LEADERSHIP

The Path-Goal Theory of Leadership was developed to explain how the behavior of a leader influences the motivation and satisfaction of subordinates. After an early, non-situational version of the theory was proposed by Evans (1970), House (1971) formulated a more elaborate version of the theory that includes situational variables. The theory has been further refined and extended in the last few years (House & Dessler, 1974; House & Mitchell, 1974; Stinson & Johnson, 1975).

According to House (1971, p. 324), "the motivational function of the leader consists of increasing personal payoffs to subordinates for work-goal attainment, and making the path to these pay-offs easier to travel by clarifying it, reducing roadblocks and pitfalls, and increasing the opportunities for personal satisfaction en route." The leader's motivational functions are supplemental ones. A leader should provide subordinates with essential coaching, guidance, and performance incentives that are not otherwise provided by the organization or the work group.

In addition to its effect on subordinate motivation, a leader's behavior will also effect subordinates' job satisfaction, especially their satisfaction with the leader. According to House and Dessler (1974, p. 31), "the theory asserts that leader behavior will be viewed as acceptable to subordinates to the extent that the subordinates see such behavior as either an immediate source of satisfaction or as instrumental to future satisfaction." The effect of the leader's actions on subordinate satisfaction is not necessarily the same as the effect on subordinate motivation. Depending on the situation, a certain pattern of leader behavior may increase satisfaction but lower motivation, or vice versa. In other situations, the same behavior may increase both satisfaction and motivation, or increase one without affecting the other.

Intervening Variables

The intervening variables in Path-Goal Theory explain how a leader's behavior affects subordinate motivation and satisfaction. These intervening variables were borrowed from a motivation theory called "expectancy theory" (Georgopolous, Mahoney & Jones, 1957; Vroom, 1964). There are several versions of expectancy theory, but they all explain work motivation in terms of a rational choice process in which the worker decides how much effort to devote to the job, at a given point in time. In choosing between a maximal effort and a minimal (or moderate) effort, a worker considers the likelihood that a given level of effort will lead to successful completion of the task and attainment of task goals. The perceived likelihood or probability is referred to as the worker's "effort–performance expectancy." The worker also considers the likelihood that successful task completion will lead to desirable outcomes (e.g., higher pay, promotion, recognition by superiors and coworkers) and undesirable outcomes (e.g., layoffs, accidents, coworker rejection, dismissal, suspension, reprimand). The desirability of each outcome is called its "valence," and the perceived likelihood or probability of each outcome is called its "performance–reward expectancy." There are also benefits and costs experienced by a worker directly while performing the work, and their desirability is called the "intrinsic valence" of goal-directed behavior and task accomplishment (House, Shapiro & Wahba, 1974). Intrinsic benefits refer to the enjoyment and fulfillment that are experienced when the work is interesting, meaningful, and pleasant. Intrinsic costs refer to the psychological stress and physical discomfort experienced when the work is tedious, boring, dangerous, or frustrating.

Whether a worker will ultimately choose to exert a maximal effort or a minimal effort in his job depends on all of these expectations and valences. The precise manner in which they jointly effect employee effort is still a matter of speculation and controversy (Mitchell, 1974). A more detailed discussion of expectancy theory is beyond the scope of this book. This brief description was intended merely to acquaint the reader with the motivational concepts used as the foundations of the Path-Goal Theory of Leadership.

Leadership Behavior

In House's (1971) initial formulation of Path-Goal Theory, he attempted to reconcile the inconsistent findings from research on the effects of leader Consideration and Initiating Structure. In the revision of the theory made by House and Dessler (1974), leader behavior was described in terms of three categories: Supportive Leadership (similar to Consideration), Instrumental Leadership (similar to Initiating Structure), and Participative Leadership. The latest version of the theory includes four categories of leader behavior (House & Mitchell, 1974), and these were labeled and defined in the following manner.

1. SUPPORTIVE LEADERSHIP: behavior that includes giving consideration to the needs of subordinates, displaying concern for their well-being, and creating a friendly climate in the work unit.

2. DIRECTIVE LEADERSHIP: letting subordinates know what they are expected to do, giving specific guidance, asking subordinates to follow rules and procedures, scheduling and coordinating the work (same as Instrumental Leadership).

3. PARTICIPATIVE LEADERSHIP: consulting with subordinates and taking their opinions and suggestions into account when making decisions.

4. ACHIEVEMENT-ORIENTED LEADERSHIP: setting challenging goals, seeking performance improvements, emphasizing excellence in performance, and showing confidence that subordinates will attain high standards.

Situational Moderator Variables

One general type of situational variable in Path-Goal Theory is the nature of the subordinates, and another general type of situational variable is the nature of the group task and work environment. Specific subordinate characteristics that are considered important include a subordinate's needs (e.g., need for achievement, affiliation, autonomy), a subordinate's ability to do the task (e.g., job skills, knowledge, and experience), and a subordinate's personality traits (e.g., self-esteem). Specific characteristics of the task that are considered important include task structure (defined the same as in Fiedler's theory), the extent to which the job is mechanized, and the degree of formalization imposed by the organization for the subordinate's job (i.e., detailed formal descriptions of job duties, rules, standard procedures, and performance standards).

As a situational theory of leadership, Path-Goal Theory says that the effect of leader behavior on subordinate motivation and satisfaction depends on the leadership situation. Characteristics of the subordinates and characteristics of the task determine both the potential for increased subordinate motivation and the manner in which the leader must act to improve motivation. Situational variables also determine subordinate preferences for a particular pattern of leadership behavior, thereby influencing the impact of the leader on subordinate satisfaction and acceptance of the leader. These general causal relationships in the theory are illustrated in Figure 6–6. In the following sections, the propositions of Path-Goal Theory dealing with four aspects of leadership behavior will be examined.

FIGURE 6–6
Causal Relationships in Path-Goal Theory of Leadership

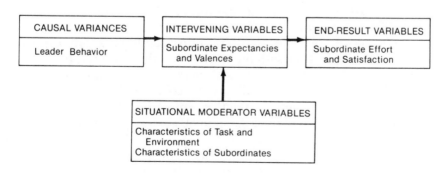

Effects of Directive Leadership

According to Path-Goal Theory, directive leadership will increase subordinate effort and satisfaction when there is role ambiguity, but not when there is role clarity. Role ambiguity is likely to occur when the task is unstructured, there is little formalization, and subordinates are inexperienced in doing the task. It is assumed that role ambiguity causes subordinates to have a low expectancy of being able to perform their tasks effectively, even with a maximum effort. In other words, since subordinates do not know what is expected of them, they are pessimistic about doing their work effectively. Directive leadership behavior that clarifies each subordinate's role is likely to increase the effort–performance expectancy and thereby to increase subordinate effort. This hypothesized causal relationship is depicted in Figure 6–7.

FIGURE 6–7

Causal Relationships for Effects of Directive Leadership Behavior on Subordinate Effort

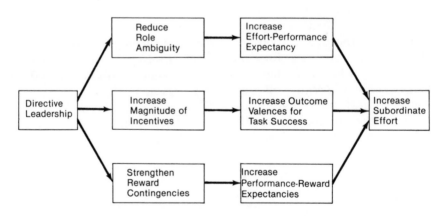

Path-Goal Theory assumes that role ambiguity is dissatisfying to subordinates in most cases. When role ambiguity is dissatisfying, directive leadership behavior that reduces role ambiguity will increase subordinate satisfaction with the work and with the leader. If there is already role clarity and subordinates know what to do and how to do it, then directive leadership will have no effect on their expectancies and is likely to lower their satisfaction, especially when subordinates perceive close, directive supervision to be an unnecessary imposition of leader control.

Figure 6–7 shows that there is more than one way in which directive leadership can affect subordinate motivation. In addition to clarifying subordinate roles, the leader may also try to increase subordinate motivation by making rewards more closely contingent upon subordinate performance and by increasing the magnitude of performance rewards. These two behavior strategies were proposed in the initial formulations of Path-Goal Theory by Evans (1970) and House (1971), but they have been neglected in most subsequent restatements of the theory and in most of the validation studies. Leaders who insure that effective performance by subordinates is consistently recognized and rewarded will increase the performance–reward expectancies of subordinates. Leaders who can provide new and larger rewards for effective performance will increase their subordinates' perceived outcome valences. These higher expectancies and valences will increase the desirability for subordinates of making a maximum effort in their job, and this will tend to result in higher subordinate effort. Once again, however, the strength of the relationship depends on the situation. Leadership behavior that involves strengthening reward contingencies will have the greatest effect on subordinate motivation when the leader has substantial power over rewards and the subordinates are not already highly motivated.

Effects of Supportive Leadership

When subordinates have a task that is stressful, tedious, boring, dangerous, frustrating, or otherwise unpleasant, the leader can make performance of necessary work more tolerable by acting considerate and supportive, and by trying to minimize the negative aspects of the work environment. In the language of expectancy theory, supportive leadership will tend to increase the intrinsic valence of necessary task behavior, thereby increasing subordinate effort. This causal relationship is depicted in Figure 6–8. In addition to increasing subordinate effort, supportive leadership in this situation will also increase subordinate satisfaction. However, in the situation where the task is interesting and enjoyable, supportive leadership will have little or no effect on either subordinate effort or satisfaction.

There is yet another way that supportive leadership can affect subordinate effort (Wexley & Yukl, 1977). If the task is difficult and a subordinate lacks self-esteem or has a high fear of failure, supportive leadership may reduce the subordinate's anxiety and increase his confidence and determination. In the language of expectancy theory, supportive leadership will tend to increase the effort–performance expectancy of the subordinate, thereby increasing his effort and persistence in doing the task. This causal relationship is also depicted in Figure 6–8. On the other hand, in a situation where subordinates have

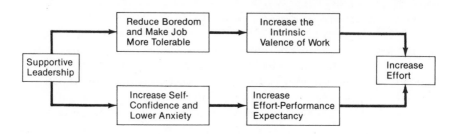

high self-esteem and a low fear of failure, supportive leadership will have little or no effect on the effort–performance expectancy of the subordinates.

Effects of Achievement-Oriented and Participative Leadership

House and Mitchell (1974) proposed that achievement-oriented leadership will cause subordinates to have more confidence in their ability to achieve challenging goals. In the terminology of expectancy theory, leaders who set challenging goals and show confidence in subordinates attaining the goals will increase the effort–performance expectancy of subordinates. According to House and Mitchell, this relationship will only occur in the situation where subordinates have ambiguous and nonrepetitive tasks ("unstructured tasks"). In the situation where subordinates have repetitive, highly structured tasks, achievement-oriented leadership will have little or no effect on subordinate expectancies or effort.

Participative leadership is hypothesized to increase subordinate effort in the situation where subordinates have an unstructured task. While participating in decision making about task goals, plans, and procedures, subordinates learn more about the task and their expected role. Thus, role clarity will be increased and subordinates will have a higher effort–performance expectancy. If the role ambiguity associated with an unstructured task is something that subordinates dislike and prefer to avoid, then participative leadership may also result in higher subordinate satisfaction. In the situation where subordinates have a highly structured task and a clear understanding of their job, participative leadership will have little or no effect on the effort–performance expectancy of subordinates.

There is another way in which participative leadership may affect subordinate motivation and satisfaction. In the situation where subordinates have a high need for autonomy and achievement, participation in decision making will tend to increase the intrinsic valence of the work for these subordinates, resulting in greater effort and higher satisfaction. When subordinates have a low need for autonomy and achievement, participative leadership will not increase subordinate effort, and it may decrease subordinate satisfaction if the subordinate finds participation to be an unpleasant, threatening experience.

Validation and Evaluation of Path-Goal Theory

Research conducted to test Path-Goal Theory has yielded mixed results. Reviews of this research (Filley, House & Kerr, 1976; House & Mitchell, 1974; Schriesheim & Von Glinow, 1977) find that some studies support the theory but other studies do not. More support is found for the hypotheses about the effects of leader behavior on subordinate satisfaction than for the hypotheses about the effects on subordinate motivation and performance. The validation research is not very conclusive, in part because of methodological deficiencies in many of the studies attempting to test the theory (Schriesheim & Kerr, 1976). One common deficiency is failure to measure subordinate expectancies and valences. Many of the studies measured leader behavior and subordinate satisfaction or performance, without checking to see if any relationships found were due to the proposed motivational processes. Another deficiency of the validation research is that most studies have tested only a few of the theory's propositions, while the remaining propositions have been ignored. When all of these limitations of the validation research are considered together, it becomes obvious that more and better research is needed to test the theory adequately.

Path-Goal Theory has some serious conceptual deficiencies that limit its utility. Several major criticisms of the theory are as follows:

1. Schriesheim and Kerr (1976) point out that the linkage between Path-Goal Theory and expectancy theory guarantees that the former is limited by the conceptual problems of the latter. Expectancy theory is an overly complex and seemingly unrealistic representation of human motivational processes. Research on expectancy theory indicates that conscious expectancies and valences do not provide an adequate explanation of employee effort and satisfaction (Behling & Starke, 1973; House, Shapiro & Wahba, 1974; Mitchell, 1974). As Schriesheim and Kerr (1976, p. 16) point out, "the conceptual underpinnings of Path-Goal Theory are certainly questionable."

2. There is a great deal of conceptual ambiguity in Path-Goal

Theory. The confusion is due in part to the complexity of the theory and the proliferation of different versions of the theory. The conceptual confusion stems also from failure to define variables and causal relationships clearly. Leader behavior is defined in terms of broad behavior categories when it is obvious that only certain aspects of the behavior account for the hypothesized effects. For example, instead of looking at directive leadership, we should examine the separate effects of more specific behaviors such as clarifying roles, providing instruction, structuring reward contingencies, providing praise and recognition, planning, coordinating, and facilitating work.

3. The manner in which different situational variables interact has not been specified, and it is not clear whether different aspects of the situation have a different moderating influence on the effects of leader behavior (Osborn, 1974).

4. Major hypotheses rest on assumptions that are only valid in some cases. For example, it is assumed that role ambiguity is unpleasant to an employee. However, some people seem to like a job in which duties and procedures are not specified in great detail. People with the desire to provide their own role definition and clarify their own path relationships will prefer a leader who allows considerable autonomy and who does not supervise closely (Stinson & Johnson, 1975). Another assumption is that role ambiguity will cause effort–performance expectancies to be unrealistically low and that clarifying roles will increase them. However, as House (1971) himself recognized, clarifying roles sometimes just makes it clear that the subordinate has little chance of obtaining task goals and rewards, in which case lower expectancies will result in lower subordinate motivation.

5. The theory focuses on the motivational functions of leaders, but does not deal explicitly with other ways in which the leader affects subordinate performance, such as training subordinates to increase task skills, which has a direct effect on performance beyond any indirect effect through increased motivation. In the same way, the leader's planning, organizing, and coordinating behavior may increase group performance by utilizing personnel and equipment more efficiently, aside from any improvement in subordinate motivation that may also occur.

Despite its limitations, Path-Goal Theory has already made an important contribution to the study of leadership by providing a conceptual framework to guide researchers in identifying potentially important situational moderator variables. The proponents of the theory intended it to be only a tentative explanation of the effect of leadership on subordinate motivation and satisfaction. No attempt was made to include all situational variables that may be relevant. The general way in which the theory is stated makes it easy to include additional variables as new knowledge is acquired. In coming years, it is likely that the theory will continue to be refined and extended to make it less ambiguous and more comprehensive.

YUKL'S MULTIPLE LINKAGE MODEL OF LEADER EFFECTIVENESS

Prior to 1970, there were no leadership theories that used both situational moderator variables and intervening variables at the same time to explain leader effectiveness. Likert (1961, 1967) pointed out the desirability of using intervening variables to explain the delayed effects of a manager's behavior on the productivity and profits of the organizational subunit. However, Likert did not systematically incorporate situational moderator variables into his management theory, which he regards as applicable to all types of leaders regardless of the situation. Early situational theories such as Fiedler's (1964) contingency theory did not include explicit intervening variables.

In order to encourage progress toward more comprehensive theories of leader effectiveness, Yukl (1971) proposed a metatheory called the "Multiple Linkage Model" of leader effectiveness. The initial version of the Multiple Linkage Model was too simplistic, and it has subsequently been refined and extended. The present version incorporates a larger number of intervening variables and deals with a broader range of more specific leadership behaviors. In addition to a leader's short-term influence on the intervening variables, the model also recognizes the leader's longer term capacity to modify situational variables as a means of improving group performance.

Intervening Variables

The intervening variables in the model are group characteristics and individual subordinate characteristics that influence group performance. The model explains any short-term effect of the leader's behavior on group performance by showing how the effect is mediated by the intervening variables. In other words, the leader's behavior influences the intervening variables, and they in turn affect group performance. The list of intervening variables in the model is not meant to be exhaustive, but an attempt was made to include those most likely to be important for formal leaders in task groups. The intervening variables are labeled and defined as follows:

SUBORDINATE EFFORT: the extent to which subordinates make an effort to attain a high level of performance and show a high degree of personal responsibility and commitment toward achieving the work unit's goals and objectives.

SUBORDINATE ROLE CLARITY: the extent to which subordinates understand their job duties and responsibilities and know what is expect of them.

SUBORDINATE TASK SKILLS: the extent to which subordinates have the experience, training, and skills necessary to perform all aspects of their jobs effectively.

RESOURCES AND SUPPORT SERVICES: the extent to which subordinates are able to obtain the tools, equipment, supplies, and support services needed to do their jobs.

TASK-ROLE ORGANIZATION: the extent to which the work unit is effectively organized to ensure efficient utilization of personnel, equipment, and facilities and the avoidance of delays, duplication of effort, and wasted effort.

GROUP COHESIVENESS AND TEAMWORK: the extent to which subordinates get along well with each other, share information and ideas, and are friendly, helpful, considerate, and cooperative.

LEADER–SUBORDINATE RELATIONS: the extent to which subordinates get along well with their leader, are friendly toward him (her), are comfortable working for him (her), and are satisfied with him (her).

An individual subordinate's performance is determined primarily by his effort, role clarity, and task ability. However, even if a subordinate is highly motivated, highly skilled in the work, and understands his current role requirements, he will achieve less than maximum potential productivity if necessary supplies, equipment, and support services are lacking.

The collective performance of a group of subordinates will depend upon other factors beyond those determining each individual's performance. Task-role organization and group cohesiveness are two characteristics of the work unit that determine the collective performance of its members. Task-role organization involves the efficiency of resource utilization. When the tasks for which the group is responsible require different skills, and subordinates differ in the extent to which each person possesses these skills, then the productivity of the group will depend in part on how the tasks are assigned to subordinates. If the assignment achieves a good match between task requirements and subordinate skills, group performance is likely to be higher. Efficiency of resource utilization also depends on other aspects of group organization, such as the design of work procedures to avoid wasted effort and costly errors, and the careful scheduling of activities to avoid delays, "bottlenecks," and duplication of effort.

Group cohesiveness and teamwork involve the interpersonal relationships among subordinates. It is important to distinguish between these personal relationships and the more formal workflow relationships represented by task-role organization. When the personal relationships are good and there is a high degree of group cohesiveness, there will be more cooperation and mutual support among subordinates. Cohesiveness is an important determinant of group performance whenever subordinates have interdependent work roles and performance depends on teamwork and cooperation.

Leader–subordinate relations involve the dyadic relationship between the leader and each subordinate. The quality of these dyadic relationships has implications for group performance as well as for individual performance. If leader–subordinate relations are poor, subordinates are likely to react in one of the following ways: (1) restrict upward communication to the leader by withholding useful information and covering up mistakes; (2) withdraw from the job by quitting, being absent frequently, or escaping with alcohol or drugs; (3) act out hostility toward the leader by sabotaging the work, stealing, filing formal grievances, or complaining to higher management about the leader; (4) reduce the amount of task effort by working slower or less carefully. The effect of leader–subordinate relations on group performance is often indirect and is not always certain to occur. In some cases, the effect of poor relations on subordinate performance is itself mediated by other intervening variables in the model, such as subordinate effort.

Situational Moderator Variables

Situational variables in the Multiple Linkage Model are divided into three types, according to the kind of influence they exert. The first type of situational variable directly affects one or more of the intervening variables in the model, thereby indirectly influencing group performance. Two situational influences on subordinate effort are the formal reward system in the organization and the intrinsic motivating potential of the subordinate tasks. If the organization has a reward system that makes rewards and punishments automatically contingent upon objective measures of subordinate performance, subordinate effort will tend to be greater than if rewards and punishments are administered without regard for performance. If the task is one in which skill variety, autonomy, task identity, task significance, and internal feedback are all present to a large degree, then subordinates will tend to be motivated by the work itself, regardless of the leader's actions (Hackman & Lawler, 1971; Hackman & Oldham, 1975). Subordinates may also be internally motivated if they have a strong work ethic, professional ethics, or other work values such as the strong loyalty to the organization found in many Japanese companies.

As in Path-Goal Theory, the primary situational determinants of role clarity in the Multiple Linkage Model are task structure and role formalization. If the task is highly structured, with obvious "best" procedures, clear objectives, routine or repetitive operations, and indicators of performance adequacy, it will usually be apparent to subordinates what they are supposed to do and how they should do it. Similarly, if job duties are specified in detail and there are elaborate formal rules, procedures, and standards, then the work roles of subordinates will tend to be clear and unambiguous.

Task skills usually vary greatly from subordinate to subordinate, and differences in the combined skills of group members are usually found when work groups are compared. At the time when a new leader assumes his position as head of a work unit, the existing skill level can be regarded as an aspect of the leadership situation that influences group performance. If selection of subordinates into the work unit is not under the control of the leader, then the adequacy of the organizational selection-placement process is another situational determinant of subordinate skill level. Even when the leader has some control over subordinate selection, there may be situational factors such as salary schedules, geographical location of work unit, and so forth that make it easier to attract skilled employees to some work units than to other work units. A final situational determinant of skill level is the extent to which the subordinates receive adequate training by the organization prior to joining the leader's work group.

A situational determinant of task-role organization, as with role clarity, is the imposition of formal role prescriptions, rules, and standard operating procedures on the work group by the larger organization of which it is a part. The manner in which the work is organized may also be influenced by staff experts, the whims of higher management, and informal practices that have evolved over time among subordinates. Aside from the actions of the leader, these situational influences contribute to the creation of an efficient or inefficient task-role organization in a work unit. Of course, in some newly formed work units, there are no predetermined constraints on how personnel and equipment are used to do the work. Here the influence of situational factors is minimal, and the leader has primary responsibility for organizing the work.

The extent to which a work unit has adequate supplies, equipment, and support services is partly determined by higher-level budgetary decisions, procurement systems, inventory control systems, procurement policies, and a host of other factors, including availability of needed supplies and services outside of the work unit, and the extent to which subordinates have direct access to these sources. In some situations, organizational practices largely guarantee an adequate level of resources and support for the work unit, whereas in other organizations, the responsibility for determining resource needs and obtaining resources is vested in the leader.

Groups tend to be more cohesive if they are small, if the members have similar attitudes, values, and interests, and if the membership is relatively stable without much turnover. Cohesiveness is likely to be greater if subordinates have a group incentive or some other common goal with important consequences, and if there are no conditions fostering intense competition among subordinates.

Leader–subordinate relations depend primarily on the skill and behavior of the leader, but some aspects of the situation make it more difficult for a leader to establish and maintain good relations with subordinates. One aspect of the situation that may be important is the underlying climate of relations between employees and the organization. A leader who becomes a middle- or lower-level manager in an organization where there has been previous hostility and strife between employees and top management is likely to face some initial coolness and distrust by subordinates. Another reason why there is sometimes initial hostility and suspicion by subordinates is an obvious difference between them and the leader in age, race, sex, religion, or ethnic background.

The second type of situational variable found in the Multiple Linkage Model is any aspect of the situation that determines the relative importance of the intervening variables as determinants of group performance. Some of the intervening variables have a greater effect on group performance than others, and the relative importance of each intervening variable changes from situation to situation. The relative importance of subordinate effort is reduced in situations where technology replaces human energy and control with mechanical energy and control. The relative importance of subordinate task skill is reduced in situations where the technology and design of the job simplify the work, reduce skill requirements, and minimize the adverse consequences of subordinate errors. The relative importance of role clarity is reduced in situations where the technology or task insure that subordinates receive immediate, automatic feedback if they are doing something wrong or have not performed a required duty. The relative importance of task-role organization is reduced in situations where the technology automatically insures coordination and efficient resource utilization, or where the nature of the work requires subordinates to assume identical roles without any difference in skill requirements. The relative importance of group cohesiveness is reduced in situations where there is little or no role interdependence among subordinates and thus no need for cooperation and teamwork. The relative importance of supplies, equipment, and support services is reduced in situations where the task does not require much of these kinds of resources and the work is not disrupted by a shortage of supplies or a breakdown of equipment.

The third type of situational variable in the Multiple Linkage Model includes any organizational constraints on leader actions to directly alter the intervening variables. The extent to which a leader is capable of doing something in the short run to improve any of the intervening variables is limited by the leader's position power and authority. Some leaders occupy a managerial position in which they have a great deal of control over rewards and punishments for subordinates, whereas other leaders find themselves in a position with little or no control over rewards and punishments and no possibility of using them to increase subordinate effort. In some situations a leader will have a great deal of discretion over work assignments and work procedures, whereas in other situations a leader will be unable to change assignments and procedures to improve task-role organization, due to a restrictive union contract or inflexible organizational policies and prescriptions. Some leaders have considerable authority to requisition supplies, support services, and equipment, whereas other leaders can only request these without any assurance that the request will be filled.

Leadership Behavior

There are several action strategies a leader can use to increase subordinate effort. Two approaches that have been demonstrated to be effective are goal setting (Locke, 1968; Latham & Yukl, 1975) and positive reinforcement (Hamner & Hamner, 1976; Schneier, 1974). Positive reinforcement is the use of praise, recognition, and tangible benefits (e.g., pay increase, promotion) as a reward for effective performance by a subordinate. Other strategies for improving subordinate effort include job enrichment (Aldag & Brief, 1979; Hackman & Oldham, 1976; Paul, Robertson & Herzberg, 1969), delegation, and decision partipation (see Chapter 8).

Subordinate role clarity and task skills can be increased by a leader who meets individually with subordinates to agree jointly on their duties and responsibilities, provides coaching and instruction, and arranges for subordinates to receive any necessary off-the-job training. The leader can also clarify subordinate roles by assigning specific goals, standards, and deadlines.

The leader is usually able to affect task-role organization through his planning and coordinating activities. These activities include immediate problem solving (Mintzberg's "disturbance handling" role) and advance planning to schedule subordinate tasks, allocate resources efficiently, and prepare to deal with possible problems and emergencies.

The quality and availability of supplies, equipment, and support services for subordinates can be influenced by the leader through careful planning, together with actions designed to obtain needed resources from superiors and other work units. These external activities involve the leader's role as a representative, negotiator, and spokesperson for the group.

A leader may utilize a number of specific actions to improve group cohesiveness. These actions include using rewards based on group performance rather than individual performance to encourage cooperation, "team building" activities to improve interpersonal relations and develop identification with the group (Dyer, 1977), and conflict management activities designed to help subordinates resolve their disagreements in a constructive manner.

Leader–subordinate relations are determined primarily by the extent of leader consideration and representation of subordinate interests. A leader is more likely to have good relations with subordinates if he is considerate, supportive, and honest with them, looks out for their welfare, and does not act in an arrogant, insulting, demeaning, hostile, sarcastic, rejecting, callous, or excessively critical manner.

General Propositions

A basic, general proposition of the Multiple Linkage Model is that a leader's effectiveness in the short run depends on the extent to which he acts skillfully to correct any deficiencies in the intervening variables for his work unit. The situation determines which intervening variables are most important, which ones are in need of improvement, and what potential corrective actions are available to the leader. The causal relationships are depicted in Figure 6–9. A leader will be less than optimally effective if he fails to recognize opportunities to correct deficiencies in intervening variables, if he recognizes the opportunities but fails to act, or if he acts but is not skillful enough to achieve the desired results. The effectiveness of a leader will also be reduced by inappropriate behavior that creates deficiencies in intervening variables or makes them worse instead of better. The Multiple Linkage Model does not necessarily imply that only one particular pattern of leader behavior is optimal in any given situation. Alternative ways of acting to correct a deficiency are recognized, and the model allows for the possibility of different sequences of actions when there are several deficient intervening variables, as long as the leader does not neglect important deficiencies in favor of dealing with minor ones. Finally, it is important to note that the Multiple Linkage Model recognizes the potential short-term influence of the leader on group performance is much greater in some situations than in others. In the situation where there are no serious deficiencies in any intervening variables, and in the situation where there are deficiencies but situational constraints prevent the leader from acting to correct the deficiencies, short-term leadership behavior will have little impact on subordinate performance.

A second basic proposition of the revised Multiple Linkage Model is that, over a longer time period, leaders can act to change some of the situational variables and create a more favorable situation. These potential actions by a leader are represented by the dotted lines in Figure 6–9. Much less is known about these longer-range actions than about the short-term actions described earlier. Leader behavior affecting situational variables involves strategic planning, policy formation, program development, organizational change, and political activities with superiors and other important persons outside of the work unit. Some examples of possible strategies to improve the leadership situation include (1) developing better relations with superiors to increase their trust and support and persuade them to provide more authority to deal decisively with work unit problems; (2) gaining more control over input acquisition and output disposal for the work unit by cultivating relationships with suppliers and clients, finding alternative sources of supplies and resources, and reducing dependence on unreliable suppliers or customers; (3) initiating new and more profitable activities, products, or services for the work unit to improve utilization of existing personnel, equipment, and facilities; (4) initiating long-term improvement programs to upgrade personnel, equipment, and facilities; (5) changing the organization structure of the work unit (e.g., redefining authority relationships, increasing delegation or centralization of decision making, modifying communication patterns and information systems, creating or eliminating subunits) in order to solve chronic problems and reduce demands on the leader for short-

FIGURE 6–9

Causal Relationships in the Multiple Linkage Model of Leadership Effectiveness

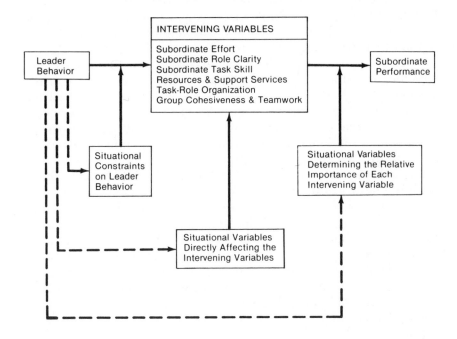

term "trouble shooting" and "disturbance handling" activities. By successfully pursuing these kinds of changes over a period of months and years, a leader is often able to do as much, if not more, to improve group performance than is possible by short-term responses to immediate deficiencies in the intervening variables. The long-range actions may be directed at changing any of the three types of situational variables. The leader may change the situation in order to alter the relative importance of some intervening variables, to correct deficiencies in intervening variables attributable to the existing situation, or to eliminate situational constraints on his future reactions to short-term deficiencies. Although the Multiple Linkage Model recognizes the importance of long-range actions by the leader, at this stage in the development of the model, the long-range actions are described in a more general manner than the short-term actions. No attempt is made to prescribe specific leader actions for a particular kind of leader in a particular situation. The theory will be extended to include more detailed, specific propositions about long-range leader behavior as more knowledge about such behavior is accumulated in ongoing research.

Evaluation and Validation

Although developed independently around the same time as Path-Goal Theory, the Multiple Linkage Model shares certain features in common with Path-Goal Theory. One common feature is the conception that the primary short-term function of a formal leader is a supplementary one in which he acts to correct any deficiencies in intervening variables in order to maintain subordinate performance at adequate levels. However, unlike Path-Goal Theory, the Multiple Linkage Model takes into account deficiencies in several intervening variables besides subordinate motivation. The two theories have some of the same situational variables, but the Multiple Linkage Model includes a broader range of situational variables. Both theories treat leader behavior as a causal variable, but the Multiple Linkage Model considers a larger number of more specifically defined aspects of leader behavior, and it takes into account long-range behavior as well as short-term behavior. Both theories consider the effects of leader behavior on subordinate performance in different situations, but revisions of Path-Goal Theory have emphasized leader effects on subordinate satisfaction and motivation rather than on performance. The Multiple Linkage Model emphasizes the explanation of subordinate performance and treats subordinate motivation and satisfaction with the leader as intervening variables rather than as an end-result variable.

The Multiple Linkage Model incorporates findings of previous research on goal setting, positive reinforcement, group dynamics, conflict management, training, personnel administration, and organizational administration, as well as research on leadership per se. However, the previous research provides only indirect support for the model; no direct tests of the model have yet been completed. Research on the model is now in progress, but it will be a while before enough evidence is accumulated to assess its validity and utility. It is likely that the model will require modification and refinement as more data is collected, but even in its present imprecise form the model has been useful in guiding the design of research on leadership effectiveness.

SUBSTITUTES FOR HIERARCHICAL LEADERSHIP

The situational leadership theories described in this chapter have dealt with the effects of leaders on subordinate satisfaction, motivation, and performance. The theories imply that leadership is always important, even though some kinds of leadership behavior may be inappropriate or redundant in particular situations. Kerr and Jermier (1978) present a more radical viewpoint, namely, that there are situations in which hierarchical leadership has no substantial impact on subordinate satisfaction, motivation, or performance. They have formulated a leadership model identifying aspects of the situation that reduce the importance of managerial leadership.

The model makes a distinction between two kinds of situational variables: "substitutes" and "neutralizers." Substitutes for leadership make leader behavior unnecessary and redundant. Substitutes are any characteristics of the subordinates, the task, or the organization that insure subordinates will clearly understand their roles, know how to do their work, be highly motivated to perform effectively, and be satisfied with their jobs. A preliminary set of substitutes for supportive and instrumental leader behavior is shown in Table 6-1.

Neutralizers are any characteristics of the task or the organization that prevent the leader from acting in a specified way or that counteract the effects of his behavior. For example, lack of control over

TABLE 6-1

Specific Substitutes and Neutralizers:
Supportive and Instrumental Leadership

Substitute or Neutralizer	Supportive Leadership	Instrumental Leadership
A. *Subordinate Characteristics:*		
1. Experience, Ability, Training		Substitute
2. "Professional" Orientation	Substitute	Substitute
3. Indifference Toward Rewards Offered by Organization	Neutralizer	Neutralizer
B. *Task Characteristics:*		
1. Structured, Routine, Unambiguous Task		Substitute
2. Feedback Provided by Task		Substitute
3. Intrinsically Satisfying Task	Substitute	
C. *Organization Characteristics:*		
1. Cohesive Work Group	Substitute	Substitute
2. Low Position Power (leader lacks control over organizational rewards)	Neutralizer	Neutralizer
3. Formalization (explicit plans, goals, areas of responsibility)		Substitute
4. Inflexibility (rigid, unyielding rules and procedures)		Neutralizer
5. Leader Located Apart from Subordinates with Only Limited Communication Possible	Neutralizer	Neutralizer

Based on Kerr and Jermier, 1978

rewards prevents the leader from using them as an incentive for exceptional performance. Lack of subordinate desire for the rewards controlled by a leader counteracts the motivating potential otherwise provided by such rewards. In the first example, the behavior (offering incentives) is impossible; in the second example, it is possible but pointless. Other conditions that will serve as neutralizers for supportive leader behavior and instrumental leader behavior are listed in Table 6–1.

Subordinate Characteristics

A number of subordinate characteristics appear to serve as substitutes and/or neutralizers. Subordinates with extensive training and experience already possess the skills and knowledge necessary to know what to do and how to do it. For example, a medical doctor, airline pilot, electrician, accountant, and other professionals and craftsmen do not require close supervision. Their skill serves as a substitute for instrumental leadership by their boss. Similarly, most professionals are internally motivated by their values, needs, and ethics, and they do not need a leader to influence them to do high-quality work. A professional orientation serves as a neutralizer as well as a substitute for instrumental leadership and supportive leadership if subordinates look primarily to similar professionals rather than to their boss for approval, recognition, and standards of performance. Examples of such professionals include university professors, research scientists, medical doctors, attorneys, journalists, musicians, and others who belong to active professional associations.

Task Characteristics

Various task attributes serve as substitutes for instrumental leadership. If the task is simple and repetitive, subordinates are able to learn the appropriate skills quickly without extensive training and direction. If the task automatically provides internal feedback to the worker, the supervisor does not need to tell the worker how he is doing. If the task is interesting and enjoyable, the supervisor does not need to provide supportive leadership that might otherwise be required to make the job situation tolerable to subordinates.

Organizational Characteristics

Like prior experience and simple tasks, organizational formalization can serve as a substitute for directive behavior by the leader. In organizations with detailed written rules, plans, procedures, standards, and regulations, the supervisor does not need to tell subordinates how to do their jobs. Rules and policies can serve as a neutralizer as well as a substitute if they are so inflexible that the leader is prevented from making any changes to facilitate subordinate effort. As noted earlier, when the leader has little position power, the situation tends to neutralize his use of rewards and punishments to influence subordinates. When subordinates work apart from their supervisor and have little contact with him, both instrumental and supportive leadership behavior are substantially neutralized. Finally, the existence of a highly cohesive group can serve as a substitute for supportive leadership, because subordinates can obtain any necessary psychological support from each other rather than from the leader.

Validation and Evaluation

Kerr and Jermier's ideas about substitutes and neutralizers serve to remind us that the potential impact of the leader on subordinate motivation and satisfaction may be greatly limited by the leadership situation. As these authors point out, the absence of a substantial effect of leader behavior on subordinate satisfaction and performance in many studies may be due to the presence of substitutes and neutralizers. The possibility that the situation makes some kinds of leader behavior unnecessary, or that it limits the leader from acting in certain ways, is implicit in earlier situational theories of leadership. In Path-Goal Theory and the Multiple Linkage Model, some of the substitutes and neutralizers appear as situational variables or intervening variables. The contribution of Kerr and Jermier has been to emphasize explicitly the possibility that leaders are sometimes redundant and to initiate a systematic investigation of the aspects of the situation that may serve as substitutes or neutralizers. Since the model was only recently formulated, not much research has been conducted to verify the propositions about specific substitutes and neutralizers. Thus, it is still too early to assess the validity and utility of the model.

GENERAL EVALUATION OF SITUATIONAL LEADERSHIP THEORIES

The five situational leadership theories described in this chapter are summarized in Table 6-2. Included with them is the situational theory proposed by Vroom and Yetton (1973), which is discussed in Chapter 8. Although other contingency models and theories have been proposed (Bass & Valenzi, 1974; Hunt & Osborn, 1978; Reddin, 1967), these six are the best known and/or most promising. Table 6-2 facili-

TABLE 6–2
Summary of Situational Models

Situational Theory of Leadership	Variables Included in Models				Validation	
	Leader Traits	Leader Behavior	Situational Variables	Intervening Variables	Empirical Tests	Results
Fiedler's Contingency Theory	LPC	None	Task Structure L–M Relations Position Power	None Explicit	Many Studies	Inconclusive
House's Path-Goal Theory	None	Instrumental, Supportive, Participative	Many Aspects	Subordinate Motivation	Many Studies	Inconclusive
Yukl's Multiple Linkage Model	None	Many Aspects	Many Aspects	Many Aspects	No Direct Tests	
Vroom & Yetton Normative Theory	None	Decision Styles	Aspects Related to Decision Making	Decision Acceptance (Subordinate Commitment), Decision Quality	Few Direct Tests	Inconclusive
Hersey & Blanchard Situational Leadership Theory	None	Task-Oriented, Person-Oriented	Subordinate Maturity	None	No Direct Tests	
Kerr & Jermier Substitutes for Leadership	None	Instrumental, Supportive	Many Aspects	None	Few Direct Tests	Inconclusive

tates comparison among the theories with respect to content and validation. All but Fiedler's theory focus on leader behavior as the primary determinant of leader effectiveness in a given situation. Only three of the theories contain intervening variables to explain how leader behavior impacts on group performance. Of course, all of the theories contain situational variables, but there are differences in the variety of situational variables taken into account. It seems desirable to consider many different aspects of the situation, but to do so makes a theory very complex and difficult to test. Only the theories by Fiedler and House have been extensively tested so far, and the results for these theories are inconclusive.

It is difficult to design a study that will provide a clear test of the complex causal relationships among variables in the situational theories. The deficiencies of most previous research on situational theories have been pointed out by critics (Korman, 1973; Korman & Tanofsky, 1975). The research suffers from problems such as lack of comparable situational measures from study to study, lack of accurate measures of leader behavior and intervening variables, and reliance on correlational studies that do not permit strong inferences about the direction of causality in relationships among variables. The lack of conclusive results in research on situational theories is also due to conceptual deficiencies in the theories themselves. Most situational leadership theories are stated so ambiguously that it is difficult to derive specific, testable hypotheses.

It should be noted that not all behavioral scientists agree about the utility of situational leadership theories. For example, McCall (1977) questions the usefulness of complex situational theories of leader behavior for improving managerial effectiveness. These theories can be applied by a manager only if he has enough time to analyze his situation and select an appropriate style. McCall contends that the hectic, fragmented pace of managerial work and the relative lack of control over it by managers prohibit their deliberate, systematic use of situational theories. Managers are so busy making decisions and responding to crises that they do not have time to stop and analyze the situation with a complicated model. McCall also criticizes the common assumption that there is a single "best way" for the leader to act in a given situation. Leaders face an immense variety of rapidly changing situations, and several different patterns of behavior may be equally effective for a leader in a given situation. The greater the number and variety of distinct leadership situations that may exist, and the smaller the percentage of situations for which there is a single "best" pattern of leader behavior, the less useful a situational theory will be.

Summary

Contingency theories of leadership are concerned with the moderating influence of situational variables on the relationship between leader behavior or traits and end-result variables such as group performance. These theories assume that different situations require different patterns of traits and behavior for a leader to be effective.

Fiedler's Contingency Model of Leadership Effectiveness deals with the moderating influence of three situational variables on the relationship between a leader trait (LPC score) and subordinate performance. According to the model, leaders with high LPC scores are more effective in moderately favorable situations, whereas leaders with low LPC scores are more effective in situations that are either very favorable or very unfavorable.

Hersey and Blanchard's Situational Leadership Theory examines how the effectiveness of task-oriented and relationship-oriented leader behavior is contingent on the maturity of the subordinate. The theory prescribes different combinations of these two behaviors, depending on a subordinate's confidence and skill in relation to the immediate task to be performed. The theory emphasizes flexible, adaptive leadership that is responsive to changing conditions. The possibility of altering subordinate maturity to make the situation more favorable is also considered.

The Path-Goal Theory of Leadership examines the leader's influence on subordinate satisfaction and motivation. Aspects of the situation such as the nature of the task, the work environment, and subordinate characteristics determine the potential for increasing subordinate satisfaction and motivation. These situational moderator variables determine what type of leader behavior is necessary to have satisfied and motivated subordinates in a given situation.

Yukl's Multiple Linkage Model of Leadership is another situational theory dealing with the moderating influence of situational variables on the relationships between leader behavior and leader effectiveness. Several intervening variables are postulated. The relative importance of each intervening variable depends on the situation, and aspects of the situation directly affect the level of each intervening variable, aside from any influence of the leader. Aspects of the situation also moderate the influence of the leader's actions on the intervening variables. Thus, the situation determines in the short run what the leader needs to do in order to maximize group performance, but it also limits the short-term corrective actions available to the leader. In the longer run, the leader can reduce constraints and increase opportunities for improving things by altering relevant aspects of the situation through political activity.

Kerr and Jermier (1978) developed a leadership model identifying aspects of the situation that make leadership behavior redundant or irrelevant. Various characteristics of the subordinates, the task, and the organization serve as substitutes and/or neutralizers for leadership behavior.

In general, the situational theories are complex, imprecisely formulated, and difficult to test. Adequate empirical verification has not been achieved yet for any of these theories. At present, they are more useful for suggesting potentially important variables to investigate than as a source of definitive explanations about leadership effectiveness.

REVIEW AND DISCUSSION QUESTIONS

1. What is a situational moderator variable, and what part do such variables play in contingency theories of leadership effectiveness?

2. What problems are there in trying to test situational theories of leader effectiveness, especially those described in this chapter?

3. Briefly explain Fiedler's Contingency Model of Leadership.

4. Briefly explain the Path-Goal Theory of Leadership.

5. Briefly explain Yukl's Multiple Linkage Model of Leadership.

6. Briefly explain Hersey and Blanchard's Situational Leadership Theory.

7. Compare and contrast Path-Goal Theory and the Multiple Linkage Model.

8. Explain what substitutes for leadership are, and give some examples. How are substitutes different from neutralizers?

9. Some writers have asserted that situational theories of leader effectiveness are not at all useful for managers. Evaluate this assertion.

10. Define and explain each of the following terms: LPC score, situational favorability, task structure, subordinate maturity, contingency contracting, developmental intervention, expectancies and valences, role ambiguity, directive leadership, instrumental leadership, supportive leadership, participative leadership, task-role organization, subordinate role interdependence, group cohesiveness.

7

Situational Determinants of Leader Behavior

The two preceding chapters dealt with the effects of a leader on subordinates, group processes, and alterable aspects of the situation. Leader behavior was treated as a causal force or "independent variable." However, we saw in Chapter 2 that influence processes between leaders and subordinates are reciprocal. Leaders adjust their behavior to cope with the pressures and constraints of the immediate situation, and feedback about the consequences of earlier leader actions is used to determine subsequent behavior. In the present chapter, leadership behavior will be treated as a "dependent variable," and we will examine how it is shaped by situational forces and unfolding events.

There has been far more research on the consequences of leader behavior than on its determinants. The major reason for this disparity is probably the widespread bias to perceive leaders as causal agents who shape events rather than being shaped by them. It is common for people to attribute more influence to leaders than they actually possess. Leaders usually get more than their fair share of credit for the successful accomplishments of their groups, and are blamed for group failures that were not necessarily their fault.

THEORIES OF LEADER BEHAVIOR DETERMINATION

The relative scarcity of research on determinants of leader behavior is paralleled by a lack of theory development to explain the process. Nevertheless, it is possible to use some conceptual frameworks developed in other contexts to help in explaining why a leader acts as he or she does. Two conceptual frameworks that have been used in this way are role theory and expectancy theory. In this section of the chapter, concepts from these two theories will be used to analyze the process of behavior determination for leaders. The Adaptive-Reactive Theory proposed by Osborn and Hunt (1975) is also examined to identify some often neglected situational determinants of leader behavior.

Role Theory

A model of behavior determination based on role theory concepts is shown graphically in Figure 7–1. Role expectations are the leader's perception of how other people such as superiors, peers, and subordinates want him to behave in carrying out his managerial role (Kahn, et al., 1964; Pfeffer & Salancik, 1975). These "role senders" make demands on the leader and exert pressure on him to conform with their beliefs about the proper and necessary way to behave.

FIGURE 7–1
Role Model of Leader Behavior Determinants

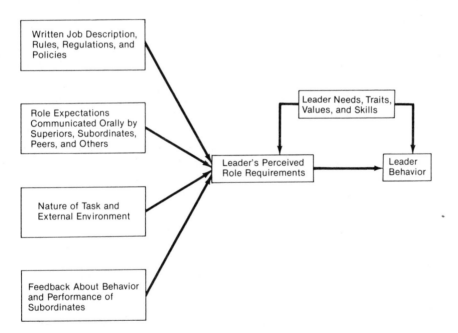

Role expectations from subordinates and peers are usually communicated orally, whereas role expectations from superiors are often conveyed by written communication as well as orally. Leaders in organizations are usually provided with a written job description and other documents enumerating the duties, responsibilities, authority, policies, and regulations applying to someone in their administrative position. A leader's perception of role requirements is influenced by these prescriptions and prohibitions, as well as by day-to-day requests, orders, and directions from superiors. Role expectations from subordinates are communicated in a more subtle manner, but a socially sensitive leader quickly learns to recognize and consider them.

At times, different people make incompatible demands on the leader, creating "role conflicts." For example, first-line supervisors often find themselves beset by conflicting demands from superiors and subordinates. Supervisors try to reconcile these conflicting role expectations, but they are likely to be more responsive to the expectations of superiors, since superiors wield more power over a manager than do subordinates or peers (Kahn, et al., 1964). Even so, the manner in which a role conflict is resolved depends in part on how important it is to each role sender. In a reanalysis of data from the Stouffer, et al. (1949) study of American soldiers in World War II, Salancik found that in attempting to reconcile inconsistent expectations of superiors and subordinates, noncommissioned officers were more responsive to superiors when the issue was important to them, and vice versa when the issue was more important to subordinates (Salancik, et al., 1975). Another study found that the task-oriented behavior of managers was influenced more by superiors, whereas social behavior was influenced more by subordinates (Pfeffer & Salancik, 1975). The extent to which a manager is able to reconcile successfully the divergent concerns of superiors and subordinates is related to the manager's effectiveness (Mann & Dent, 1954; Mann & Hoffman, 1960).

In addition to role expectations from other people, a leader's perception of role requirements will depend on the nature of the group's mission and tasks. Different kinds of tasks require somewhat different administrative activities by the leader. Role expectations from subordinates or superiors are sometimes inconsistent with objective task requirements, especially when the nature of the task or the external environment has changed while norms and beliefs about proper leader behavior have remained the same. Here, again, the leader has a role conflict. Should he conform to expectations from role senders and be less effective in facilitating group performance, or should he do what is necessary to accomplish the task and take a chance on being initially rejected by role senders?

Role expectations for a leader are seldom absolute or comprehensive, and a leader usually has considerable discretion to shape his own role over time. As noted in Chapter 2, leaders with a record of successful decisions and demonstrated loyalty to the organization are given more freedom to redefine their role and initiate innovations. Thus, given enough time, a skillful leader may be able to reconcile role requirements that were initially incompatible.

The way in which a leader attempts to redefine his role is largely determined by his needs, values, and interests. It has long been known that a leader's behavior is determined jointly by characteristics of the situation and characteristics of the person himself. A leader's choice of behavior is an attempt to accommodate both the pressures imposed by the situation and the person's internal needs and values (Burke, 1965; Crowe, Bochner & Clark, 1972). Occasionally, the behavior required for effective leadership will be contrary to the leader's needs and values. This situation can be viewed as still another kind of role conflict. In many cases, role senders recognize the objective task requirements and pressure the leader to act accordingly. However, whenever there is little guidance and pressure from role senders, a leader may choose to act in a manner consistent with his needs and values, even though this behavior is not appropriate for the situation confronting the leader. For example, Kipnis and Lane (1962) found that leaders with low self-confidence are likely to respond to a problem subordinate by trying to "pass the buck" to superiors, whereas leaders with high self-confidence are more likely to handle the matter themselves and discuss the problem with the subordinate.

In additon to affecting directly a leader's choice of behavior, leader personality affects the leader's perception of role requirements, thereby exerting an indirect influence on subsequent leader behavior (Kahn & Quinn, 1970; Kahn, et al., 1964). First, a leader's needs and values influence the way he attends to information and events. For example, a person with a dominant need for affiliation is likely to be especially sensitive to signs of acceptance or rejection by other people; a person with a strong achievement need is likely to be especially attuned to performance feedback. Second, a leader's interpretation of information and events is biased by his needs, values, and attitudes (Mass, 1950). For example, a leader with a negative stereotype about subordinates is more likely to attribute performance problems to subordinate incompetence and lack of motivation than to factors beyond the subordinates' control, such as deficiencies in the organization of the work. How a leader diagnoses the cause of a performance problem has obvious implications for the way he will act to deal with it (Green & Mitchell, 1979; Mitchell & Wood, 1980).

Expectancy Theory

An alternative conceptual framework for explaining why a leader acts in a particular way is expectancy theory. In the preceding chapter we saw that expectancy theory was used as the foundation for building the Path-Goal Theory of Leadership, which attempts to explain how a leader influences the behavior choices of subordinates. Expectancy theory can also be used to explain the leader's own choice of behavior.

Nebecker and Mitchell (1974) have proposed that a leader's behavior can be predicted from his expectancies about the consequences of the behavior. For example, a leader would be predicted to use a moderate amount of a behavior such as role clarification if this level of behavior was perceived to be more likely than either a high or low level to have desirable consequences for the leader (e.g., better group performance, greater subordinate satisfaction). If the same leader also perceived that desired outcomes were more likely with a high level of praise than with a low or moderate level, then the leader would be predicted to use praise frequently, and to use it more often than role clarification. If the leader perceived that a low level of some behavior such as criticism was more likely to lead to desired outcomes than greater amounts of the behavior, then the leader would be predicted to use criticism only infrequently, and less often than either praise or role clarification.

Nebecker and Mitchell conducted two studies to test predictions of leader behavior based on the leader's reported perception of expectancies and outcome desirability ("valence"). Leader behavior was measured with questionnaires filled out by subordinates and by the leaders themselves. Expectancy theory predictions received modest support, indicating that one determinant of leader behavior is the leader's perception of its likely consequences. Leaders choose a course of action that they perceive to have a high probability for attaining desired outcomes.

The greatest deficiency of expectancy theory is that it doesn't explain how leaders formulate expectancies or why they value some outcomes more than others (e.g., subordinate acceptance more than productivity). In order to understand a leader's expectancies and outcome valences, it is necessary to consider his needs, values, and prior experience.

Osborn and Hunt's Adaptive-Reactive Theory

Osborn and Hunt (1975) contend that the influence of macro variables on leader behavior has been neglected. By macro variables they mean such things as the structure of the organization, its external environment, and the technology used to produce goods and services. Macro variables are differentiated from micro variables, which include things like task characteristics and subordinate attitudes and traits. Macro variables are assumed to be constant for all of a leader's subordinates, whereas micro variables are likely to be different from subordinate to subordinate. According to Osborn and Hunt, the behavior of leaders is influenced more by macro variables than by micro variables. The theory is called adaptive-reactive because leaders are assumed to adapt to the macro variables and to react to the micro variables. However, the difference between adapting and reacting has not been satisfactorily explained.

The theory is elaborated in a subsequent paper by Hunt and Osborn (1978). Their major premise is that the organizational setting will present the leader with various opportunities and constraints. Some leaders have a great deal of discretion, whereas others are highly constrained in their behavior. Hunt and Osborn distinguish between "discretionary behavior" that is initiated by the leader and "nondiscretionary behavior" that is merely a response to overwhelming pressures from macro variables.

Leader discretion is reduced as the external environment becomes more complex and unstable. Uncertainty increases the difficulty of planning and controlling internal operations, particularly when the leader's unit is highly dependent on other organizations. This dependency forces the leader to spend more time on external affairs, and he must monitor changing conditions and accommodate the needs of important outsiders. Consider, for example, the president of a small firm with only two customers, each of whom is subject to unpredictable fluctuations in demand. This manager has less discretion than the president of a firm with many customers and a stable demand for its products.

Another type of macro variable is the structure of the organization to which the leader's unit belongs. Three important aspects of structure are centralization, formalization, and lateral interdependence. In a highly centralized structure where most of the important decisions are made by top management, middle- and lower-level managers have less discretion than in a decentralized organization. There is an even greater reduction in discretion when the top management in a centralized structure has a highly reactionary philosophy. That is, top management waits for environmental changes to occur before acting, instead of trying to anticipate and plan for such changes in advance. Here the middle- and lower-level managers must quickly adjust to the frequent, abrupt changes initiated by higher management, leaving little opportunity for systematic planning of their own. Managerial discretion is also reduced in a highly bureaucratic organization with elaborate rules, regulations, and policies that must be observed. Finally, when the structure of the organization creates a high degree of interdependence among subunits, managerial discretion is lower than when subunits are relatively independent in their operations. Managers of interdependent units must spend more time coordinating with each other and must accommodate each other's needs when making decisions.

The size of a leader's group is another macro variable affecting leader discretion. Not only is it more difficult to get everybody together for meetings in a large group, there is also less opportunity to interact with each subordinate on a one–to–one basis. The leader is forced to use more formal behavior and to deal more often with subgroups.

Even though micro variables are assumed to be less important than macro variables, Hunt and Osborn recognize that task and subordinate characteristics do indeed affect leader behavior. Some of these influences are identified in the more recent version of the Adaptive-Reactive Theory (Hunt & Osborn, 1978). Three of the micro variables are task complexity, task interdependence among subordinates, and subordinate goal orientation in combination with group cohesiveness. When the task is complex and subordinates are inexperienced, the leader needs to spend more time in one–to–one interactions providing guidance and instructions to subordinates who need it. When subordinates have interdependent tasks, less time is spent in one–to–one interactions, due to the need for overall coordination and "group leadership." When the group is cohesive and shares the leader's concern for task objectives, group leadership is feasible, whereas when the group is cohesive but hostile, one–to–one leadership is preferable.

The Adaptive-Reactive Theory proposed by Osborn and Hunt is a content theory instead of a process theory. It specifies the aspects of the situation that affect leader behavior, without actually explaining the causal processes involved. Expectancy theory does just the opposite. The version of role theory presented earlier deals with both content and process, but is primarily focused on the latter. All three theories appear compatible with each other, and they can be used together to gain a better understanding of how leader behavior is determined.

METHODS OF RESEARCH ON SITUATIONAL DETERMINANTS

A variety of research approaches have been used for investigating how leader behavior is influenced by the situation. The three most important research designs for this purpose are the comparative field study, the longitudinal field study, and the laboratory experiment. How each of these approaches is used will be briefly described.

Comparative Field Study

In a comparative field study, the researcher finds a set of leaders in one kind of situation (e.g., sales managers) and compares the behavior of these leaders with the behavior of one or more sets of leaders in different situations (e.g., production managers). Any significant differences in behavior are attributed to situational differences. Unfortunately, the explanation of the findings may be quite speculative if the researcher fails to include a rigorous and comprehensive assessment of situational variables other than the one used as the basis for selecting the samples of leaders. Unless many different aspects of the situation are examined, it is impossible to determine which situational variables really account for the observed differences in behavior. Differences attributed to one situational variable (group size) may be caused partly or entirely by some other situational variable (e.g., task complexity) that the researcher has neglected to measure and that just happens to be confounded with the situational variable he is preoccupied with. A good example of a comparative field study using a comprehensive assessment of situational variables is the research by Rosemary Stewart described later in this chapter.

Longitudinal Field Study

Comparative field studies are conducted at one point in time with different sets of leaders. Longitudinal field studies are conducted with repeated measurement over a period of time on the same set of leaders. These leaders either experience major changes in their job situation, or they move from one kind of leadership position to another. Differences in behavior from before to after the change are attributed to differences in the situation. Interpretation of behavior differences is easiest when the leaders remain in the same job, and only one aspect of the situation is changed. However, it is rare to find a situation that is static in all respects except one, even over a short time period. Usually there are multiple changes in the situation, and a comprehensive examination of situational variables is necessary to identify the real cause of the behavior change. Changes in leader behavior are often due to the joint effects of two or more situational variables, and cannot be understood if the researcher limits his attention to a single aspect of the situation.

Longitudinal field studies are better than static comparative ones in several respects. First, using the same leaders in two situations eliminates the possibility that behavior differences are due to leader characteristics rather than situational characteristics. For example, differences found between research managers and production managers may be due as much to differences in the kind of people who select these positions as to the positions themselves. Systematic measurement and comparison of leader characteristics would allow the researcher to rule out this possibility in a comparative field study, but this precaution is seldom taken. In a longitudinal study it is not necessary.

A second advantage of longitudinal studies is that they permit better inferences about causality. If behavior changes after a specific change in the situation, the results can safely be attributed to the situational change, particularly if everything else has remained constant. In a comparative study, as in any static correlational research, only weak inferences about causality can be made.

Longitudinal studies are especially useful for exploring the relative importance of leader traits and situational characteristics as determinants of leader behavior. This kind of research is rare, but a study by Stogdill and his associates (Stogdill, et al., 1956) demonstrates its potential utility. The study was conducted with navy officers who were being transferred from shipboard positions to positions ashore, or in some cases, to a different position in another ship. Descriptions of managerial behavior were obtained from the navy officers prior to the change, and again after they had been in their new positions for some time. Descriptions of managerial behavior were also obtained from the previous occupants of the new positions before they departed. Thus, it was possible to compare the consistency of behavior for a person in two different positions with the consistency of behavior for two persons occupying the same position. Since navy personnel are rotated frequently, there was no reason to expect any systematic differences in leader traits between the two sets of navy officers. The results showed that navy officers tended to act in a consistent manner across jobs with respect to interpersonal behavior such as consulting with subordinates, supervising, coordinating, organizing, negotiating, and team building. The situation had a much stronger influence on specific kinds of professional activities such as writing reports, interviewing personnel, conducting research, conducting public relations campaigns, and making speeches within the organizational unit.

Laboratory Experiment

Laboratory experiments have been a popular approach for investigating how leader behavior is determined. The effects of situational variables can be determined by systematically manipulating one or more of them while holding the others constant. The effects of leader traits can be determined by selecting as leaders people who differ on measures of personality, values, or interests. Sometimes characteristics of the leader and situation are both manipulated in the same study to explore their interacting effects on leader behavior.

A number of laboratory studies have examined differences in leader behavior caused by variations in the task. In some of these studies, the groups were rotated through each type of task, like in a longitudinal field study.

Laboratory experiments are especially useful for exploring how leaders react to information about subordinate competence and performance, since the effect of a leader on subordinates can be separated from the effect of subordinates on the leader. For example, by placing a leader in a situation where he has one competent subordinate and one incompetent subordinate, the leader's reaction to the two subordinates can be compared.

The greatest deficiency of the laboratory approach has been artificiality, due to the preference of researchers for studies lasting less than an hour, with inexperienced leaders (usually undergraduate students) and unrepresentative tasks. Since leadership processes unfold over a long period of mutual interaction among the leader, subordinate, and situation, the essence of these processes may not be captured in such short-term studies. Thus, it is essential to confirm the results from laboratory studies by showing agreement with results from other research approaches. Fortunately, for research on effects of task characteristics and subordinate competence, there seems to be considerable agreement in results from laboratory and field studies.

OVERVIEW OF RESEARCH ON SITUATIONAL DETERMINANTS

Research on situational determinants of leader behavior has been rather unsystematic, with somewhat different situational variables and aspects of leader behavior used in each study. The variety of variables, measures, and approaches makes it difficult to compare and integrate results across studies. Nevertheless, the research provides some useful insights into the manner in which leader behavior is shaped by the leadership situation. This section of the chapter reviews results of research on situational variables found to influence leader behavior substantially.

Level in the Authority Hierarchy

A number of studies have been conducted to identify differences in managerial behavior at different levels of an organization. Authority level of the manager's position appears to be one of the most important situational influences on leader activity patterns (Mintzberg, 1973; Nealey & Fiedler, 1968). Managers at higher levels make most of the policy decisions and strategic plans, whereas lower-level managers are more concerned with interpreting and implementing policies and programs (Katz & Kahn, 1978). Thus, as one moves down the authority hierarchy, managers have less discretion and freedom of action. Lower-level managers must operate within the constraints imposed by organizational structure and by policy decisions made at higher levels. As a consequence, objectives are more specific, issues are less complex and more focused, and a shorter time perspective prevails (Martin, 1956). In general, the activities of lower-level managers tend to be shorter in duration, more fragmented, and more oriented toward current problems (Mintzberg, 1973).

Since lower-level managers are more oriented toward maintaining a steady workflow, they spend more time carrying out the disturbance handler role and less time carrying out the entrepreneur and figurehead roles than higher-level managers (Mintzberg, 1973). Lower-level managers tend to be more concerned with technical matters, staffing (personnel selection and training), scheduling work, and monitoring subordinate performance (Brooks, 1955; Hemphill, 1959; Katzell, Barrett, Vann & Hogan, 1968; Mahoney, Jerdee & Carroll, 1965; Tornow & Pinto, 1976). In contrast, higher-level managers are usually more concerned with exercise of broad authority in making long-range plans, formulating policy, modifying the organization structure, and initiating new ways of doing things.

Lower-level managers tend to use less participative leadership (Blankenship & Miles, 1968; Heller & Yukl, 1969). Perhaps this is due to time pressures and the manager's perception that subordinates have less to contribute and are less concerned about being consulted. Less participation at lower levels probably also reflects the fact that lower-level managers have less authority to make important decisions, especially in highly centralized organizations.

Function of the Organizational Unit

Another important source of variation in managerial behavior is the kind of function administered by the manager. Several studies have compared managers in different functionally specialized departments of business organizations.

The research indicated that production managers tend to spend more time with subordinates, have less time alone, and have more variety and fragmentation in their work than sales managers or staff managers (Stewart, 1967). More time is spent resolving workflow problems, and the disturbance handler role is especially important (Mintzberg, 1973). Production managers spend more time engaged in directive behavior such as checking the work, giving orders, and directing the work of subordinates (Hemphill, 1959; Webber, 1972). Decisions are more often made in an autocratic manner without subordinate participation (Heller & Yukl, 1969).

Sales managers tend to emphasize the interpersonal roles (Mintzberg, 1973). The importance of external contacts with clients and customers is reflected in the preoccupation of sales managers with the liaison and figurehead roles. Considerable time is spent outside of the company in public relations, promotional activities, image building, and socializing with customers (Stewart, 1967, 1976). The leader role is also important, but it tends to involve primarily selection and training of subordinates and giving them assignments. Sales managers spend less time than many types of managers in directing subordinate activities (Hemphill, 1959; Webber, 1972).

Managers of staff specialists (e.g., legal staff, personnel department, planning department, public relations office, industrial engineering staff) function as advisors and experts to other units and to higher management, so the monitor and spokesperson roles are especially important for them (Mintzberg, 1973). Staff managers are expected to keep informed about developments in their technical specialty, and they serve as technical advisor and representative of their specialty in meetings. These managers tend to spend more time alone, are more involved with paperwork, and have less fragmentation and variety in their work than most other kinds of managers (Mintzberg, 1973; Stewart, 1967, 1976). More of their work is self-initiated than is true for sales or production managers (Stewart, 1976; Webber, 1972). In making decisions, staff managers tend to be more participative than production, sales, or finance managers, which is probably due to the complex nature of their decisions and the greater potential of subordinates to make a significant contribution to the decision (Heller & Yukl, 1969).

Task Characteristics and Technology

The characteristics of the tasks performed by subordinates have important implications for leader behavior. Task characteristics of major interest include task structure, complexity, difficulty, variability, uncertainty, and mechanization. Integration of results from this research is complicated by the proliferation of concepts and measures, but some general patterns are evident.

When subordinates have relatively structured tasks (i.e., low complexity, low variability, low uncertainty, low difficulty), leaders tend to act more directive and autocratic (Bass, 1976; Hill & Hughes, 1974; Vroom & Yetton, 1973; Yukl, 1967). In other words, the leader provides more direction to subordinates and allows them less participation in making task decisions. It is easier for a leader to be directive and autocratic when the task is highly structured, because he can easily determine the best way to do the task. When the task is unstructured, subordinates are likely to possess relevant information lacked by the leader, and the quality of task decisions can be improved by their participation in making the decisions. Furthermore, in many situations where tasks are complex, subordinates are skilled technicians, craftsmen, or professionals who do not need much direction from the leader.

The fact that it is easier to act directive and autocratic when the task is highly structured does not imply that it is desirable to do so. According to Path-Goal Theory (see Chapter 6), directive, close supervision will be considered redundant and annoying to subordinates who possess adequate skills to perform a highly structured task. Directive, structuring leader behavior is most appropriate in a situation where there is an unstructured task and unskilled, inexperienced subordinates.

The effect of technology appears to be somewhat distinct from effects of task structure, since technology involves mechanization and variability of operations sequencing in addition to the complexity and variability of individual subordinate tasks. Many different combinations of these factors are possible, and there is still much confusion about the best way to classify technology.

In a study of four kinds of firms in England, Thurley and Hamblin (1963) found that it was useful to distinguish between degree of mechanization and degree of variability in operations sequencing. When there was a high degree of mechanization, supervisors spent more time checking machinery and dealing with breakdowns. The greater the variation in operations sequencing, the more time was spent by supervisors in planning, scheduling, and facilitating the work. Yanouzas (1964) compared foremen in an assembly-line plant with foremen in a job-lot plant and found similar results to Thurley and Hamblin. Foremen in the job-lot plant spent more time planning production, scheduling and assigning work, and monitoring operations, whereas foremen in the assembly-line plant spent more time checking quality, dealing with machine breakdowns, and tending to interpersonal relations.

When increased mechanization results in making subordinate tasks more simple and repetitive, as on many mass production assembly lines, there is a greater need for supportive leadership, because the work is likely to be tedious and boring. However, as mechanization progresses to the point where the work is highly automated, task complexity and skill requirements begin to increase again. Thus, managing a highly automated process production plant (e.g., oil refinery, chemical manufacturing plant) is more similar in some respects to managing a job order plant (e.g., made-to-order test equipment or machinery) than to managing a mass production assembly line (Woodward, 1962).

Size of Organizational Unit

The implications of work unit size or "span of control" for leader behavior have been investigated in several studies. Interpretation of the results is complicated by the fact that group size is often confounded with other aspects of the situation, such as task complexity and degree of role interdependence among subordinates. For example, span of control tends to be lower when subordinates have complex and interdependent tasks, because more coordinating and directing by the manager is necessary. Nevertheless, some implications of size for leader behavior are apparent from the research.

As was mentioned earlier in this chapter, when the number of subordinates is large, it is more difficult to get all of them together for meetings, and it is less feasible to consult individually with each subordinate. Thus, leaders tend to use less participative leadership, or to limit it to an "executive committee" or to a few trusted "lieutenants." Heller and Yukl (1969) found that as span of control increased, upper-level managers made more autocratic decisions, but they also used more delegation. Both decisions styles allow a manager who is overloaded with responsibilities to reduce the amount of time needed to make decisions. Lower-level managers in this study also made more autocratic decisions as span of control increased, but they did not use more delegation, perhaps because delegation was less feasible for them. Results from a study by Blankenship and Miles (1968) are consistent. They found that span of control increased, managers relied more on subordinates to initiate action on decisions, and this trend was much more pronounced for upper-level managers than for lower-level managers.

As the size of the group increases, so does the administrative workload. Managers need to spend more time doing things like planning, coordinating, staffing, and budgeting (Cohen & March, 1974; Hemphill, 1950; Katzell, et al., 1968). The increase in coordination requirements is magnified when the subordinates have highly uncertain and interdependent tasks. Sometimes part of the increased administrative burden can be delegated to a second in command, to a coordinating committee composed of subordinates, or to new coordinating specialists who serve as staff assistants. In many cases, however, the leader is expected to assume the administrative responsibility himself and to provide more overall direction and integration of group activities. In this event, the amount of time available for one-to-one contact with individual subordinates is further reduced.

The decreased opportunity for interacting with individual subordinates in large groups has important implications for the leaders of these groups. There is less time available to provide support and encouragement to each subordinate and to engage in other interpersonal behavior necessary for maintaining effective relationships with subordinates. Good performance by individuals is less likely to be recognized and rewarded in large groups (Goodstadt & Kipnis, 1970). Problems with subordinates are likely to be handled in a more formalized, impersonal manner (Kipnis & Lane, 1962). When a subordinate has a performance problem, the leader is less likely to provide individualized instruction and coaching.

Group size also has implications for the team-building activities of a leader. As a group grows larger, separate cliques and factions are likely to emerge. These subgroups often compete for power and resources, creating conflicts and posing a threat to group cohesiveness and teamwork. Thus, the leader of a large group needs to devote more time to building group identification, promoting cooperation, and managing conflict. However, the pressure to carry out more administrative activities in a large group may cause the leader to neglect group maintenance activities until serious problems arise.

Lateral Interdependence

The extent to which a leader's subunit is dependent on other subunits in the same organization, or on external groups, will affect leader behavior to a considerable extent. Lateral interdependence represents a threat to the subunit, because its routine activities may need to be modified to accommodate the needs of other subunits, with a resulting loss in autonomy and stability (Sayles, 1979). As lateral interdependence increases, the external activities of a leader become more important. One type of lateral interdependence occurs when each subunit performs a different step in a series of related operations. Since the work of each subunit depends on the steady flow of materials, parts, or information from other subunits, there is need for close coordination between the subunit managers. Yanouzas (1964) found that foremen in an assembly-line plant spent more time in lateral communication with other foremen than did the foremen in a job order plant where work units did not have a sequential workflow. Similar results have been reported by Walker, Guest and Turner (1956).

Lateral interdependence also occurs when one subunit of an organization is responsible for providing services or advice to other units, evaluating their output, or monitoring their activities (Sayles, 1979). The leader's role in lateral relations includes functions such as gathering information from other subunits, obtaining assistance and cooperation from them, negotiating agreements, reaching joint decisions to coordinate unit activities, defending the unit's interests, promoting a favorable image for the unit, and serving as a spokesperson for subordinates. The extent to which a leader emphasizes each of these activities depends on the nature of the lateral relationship. For example, when a unit provides services on demand to other units, acting as a buffer for subordinates against these external demands is a primary concern of the leader (Sayles, 1979).

Just as the leader tries to reconcile demands from above and below, so also is he required to make compromises in seeking to reach agreements with other units. The leader is expected by subordinates to represent their interests, but he must also be responsive to the needs of other units or he will not be able to maintain an effective working relationship with them. Salancik, et al. (1975) conducted a study of managers in an insurance company to investigate this kind of role conflict. Managers with interlocking work activities tended to develop a pattern of similar behavior through a process of mutual reinforcement. They became more responsive to each other's needs in order to maintain a cooperative effort. The more departments a manager's unit had to interact with on a regular basis, the less responsive the manager was to his own subordinates' desires.

Research on the influence tactics used in lateral relations suggests that rational persuasion is commonly employed, as are appeals based on friendship and/or reciprocity for past favors (Patchen, 1974; Sayles, 1979; Strauss, 1962). Although a manager usually lacks authority over other subunit managers, legitimate requests are made by appeal to role requirements, organizational policy, or prior tradition. Direct coercion is less common, because managers seldom have much lateral coercive power. However, indirect pressure can sometimes be applied by cultivating high-level supporters and forming coalitions with other subunits. Managers are more likely to spend time in political activities of this kind when there is competition for scarce resources or jurisdictional disputes among subunits (Dalton, 1950; Dutton & Walton, 1965; Seiler, 1963).

Crisis Situations

When a group is under extreme pressure to perform a difficult task or to survive in a hostile environment, the role expectations for the leader are likely to change in a predictable manner. In this kind of situation, subordinates expect the leader to be more assertive, directive, and decisive (Halpin, 1954; Mulder & Stemerding, 1963). They look to the leader to show initiative in defining the problem, identifying a solution, and directing the group's response to the crisis. Consistent with this proposition, Halpin (1954) found that platoon members were more satisfied with a high structuring leader in combat than in training. A study conducted aboard navy ships showed that navy officers exercised more power in crisis situations and were more directive, autocratic, and goal oriented (Mulder, Ritsema van Eck & de Jong, 1970). The officers rated most effective by superiors were ones who showed initiative and exercised power in a confident and decisive manner. Research on survival of air force crews shot down over enemy territory found that a crew was more likely to survive and be rescued if the leader made a quick but adequate analysis of the situation, established a common goal orientation, and kept everybody informed about developments (Torrance, 1954).

Work groups under strong external pressure to meet deadlines or improve performance sometimes show similar but less pronounced changes in leader behavior. The leaders of such groups tend to become more goal oriented, and they display more directive–structuring behavior and less considerate–supportive behavior (Fleishman, Harris & Burtt, 1955; Guest, 1954; Pfeffer & Salancik, 1975; Yukl, 1967).

Subordinate Competence and Performance

In work organizations, one of the most important determinants of leader behavior toward subordinates is the competence and performance of the subordinates. Leaders tend to react differently toward subordinates who are performing effectively than toward subordinates whose performance is substandard. More than twenty studies have been conducted on this subject, most of them either laboratory experiments or longitudinal field studies using sophisticated correlational techniques to identify likely causal patterns. A rather consistent pattern of results emerges from these studies. Low subordinate performance usually leads to one or more of the following leader reactions:

1. Closer supervision (Farris & Lim, 1969; Lowin & Craig, 1968; Mc-Fillen, 1978).
2. More directive–structuring behavior (Greene, 1975, 1979a, 1979b; Lowin & Craig, 1968).
3. Less considerate–supportive behavior (Barrow, 1976; Dansereau, Graen & Haga, 1975; Farris & Lim, 1969; Graen & Cashman, 1975; Greene, 1975; 1979b; Herold, 1977; Lowin & Craig, 1968).
4. More critical–punitive behavior (Bankhart & Lanzetta, 1970; Barrow, 1976; Curtis, Smith & Smoll, 1979; Greene, 1979b; Herold, 1977; Sims, 1980; Szilagyi, 1979).
5. More autocratic behavior (Barrow, 1976; Farris & Lim, 1969; Greene, 1979b).
6. More performance emphasis (Barrow, 1976; Farris & Lim, 1969).
7. Less praise and positive rewards (Bankhart & Lanzetta, 1970; Curtis, Smith & Smoll, 1979; Farris & Lim, 1969; Sims, 1977; Szilagyi, 1979).

Leader behavior is also affected by judgments about the knowledge and dependability of subordinates. Leaders allow more participation to subordinates who have relevant knowledge and can be trusted to cooperate with the leader (Bass, 1976; Dansereau, Graen & Haga, 1975; Graen & Cashman, 1976; Vroom & Yetton, 1973). More responsibility and authority is delegated to subordinates who are perceived to be knowledgeable and dependable (Ashour & England, 1972; Dansereau, Graen & Haga, 1975; Graen & Cashman, 1975; Heller, 1971).

Lack of subordinate compliance has effects similar to poor performance, although this finding is based on only one study (Greene, 1979b). When a subordinate fails to comply with rules or orders, a leader is likely to act more punitive, more directive, less considerate, and less participative. These behaviors can be seen as an attempt to pressure the subordinate to comply, or failing that, to isolate and punish him. It is interesting to consider that the typical response by a leader to either poor performace or noncompliance is probably not the most effective one. As we saw in Chapter 3, coercion, pressure, and hostility are usually less effective than a firm but supportive problem-solving approach, with instruction and coaching when needed.

STEWART'S RESEARCH ON SITUATIONAL DEMANDS AND CONSTRAINTS

Most studies on situational determinants of leader behavior suffer from the lack of a broad perspective on the demands and constraints faced by a leader. In these studies, the researchers usually investigate only one aspect of the situation at a time. Other aspects are ignored, even though some of these may prove to be far more important than the aspect selected for study. Furthermore, different aspects of the situation are likely to affect leader behavior jointly, and it is not possible to understand these complex interactions unless many situational variables are examined simultaneously.

Rosemary Stewart (1974, 1976) has conducted the most comprehensive research to date on role requirements and constraints faced by different kinds of managers. The following factors were found to be important for comparing managerial jobs with respect to behavioral requirements.

Pattern of Relationships

The demands made on a manager by superiors, subordinates, peers, and persons outside of the organization will influence how the manager spends his time and will determine how much skill he needs. Demands by subordinates involve the need for coordinating due to interlocking work of subordinates, the need for frequent assignment of work to them, the importance and difficulty of monitoring subordinate performance, and the need to supplement formal authority with other forms of influence to insure subordinate compliance with orders and requests. More time and skill is needed to deal with subordinates when they have interlocking work, new assignments must be made frequently, it is important to monitor subordinate performance but difficult to do so, and automatic compliance with orders and requests is not assured by subordinate respect for legitimate authority.

Demands by superiors involve the manager's dependence on them for authority, resources, allocation of work to the manager's unit, and definition of the manager's job scope. The greater the dependence and the more unpredictable the demands made by superiors, the more time and skill is needed to deal with them.

Demands by peers involve the lateral dependence of the manager on peers for services, supplies, and cooperation, and the extent to which the manager must satisfy peers to whom he provides services, information, and advice. The more dependent the manager is on peers to provide inputs or accept his unit's outputs, the more time and skill is needed in dealing with peers.

The extent to which subordinates, peers, and superiors make incompatible demands on a manager determines how much role conflict will be experienced and has obvious implications for the difficulty of satisfying the various demands.

Demands by external contacts involve the dependence of the manager on cooperation and support by clients, customers, suppliers, subcontractors, and so on, and the extent to which it is necessary to develop personal relationships with these people, negotiate agree-ments, carry out public relations activities, create a good impression, and act discreet. The greater the dependence and the more important it is to engage in these representational activities, the more time and skill will be needed in dealing with outsiders. The difficulty of han-dling external demands is also increased by incompatible interests be-tween manager and outsider. Having to establish relationships with many people for short periods of time, as opposed to dealing with the same people repeatedly, further complicates the manager's job, espe-cially when it is necessary to impress and influence people quickly.

All managerial jobs require some mix of contacts with subordi-nates, peers, superiors, and outsiders, but for most jobs there are char-acteristic patterns of job contacts dictated by differences in the demands made by each party. Jobs with high external dependence in-clude sales manager, purchasing manager, and bank manager. Jobs with high dependence on superiors include hospital administrator and some accounting and staff unit managers. Jobs with high depen-dence on peers include product managers, production managers, training (personnel) directors, quality control managers, some service managers, and some accounting managers. Jobs with high subordi-nate demand include retail store managers and managers of other self-contained regional units.

Type of Work Pattern

Several aspects of the work pattern requirements in managerial jobs were studied. The first was the extent to which managerial activ-ities are either self-generating or a response to the requests, instruc-tions, and problems of other people. Much more initiative is required in predominantly self-generating jobs like that of product manager, research manager, and training director than for predominantly re-sponding jobs like production manager and service manager.

Need to meet deadlines is a second aspect of work pattern re-quirements. For accounting managers, staff managers, and produc-tion managers, meeting deadlines was a primary requirement of the job. For research managers and product managers, it was much less important.

A third aspect is the extent to which the work is recurrent and repetitive rather than variable and unique. For accounting managers and production managers, there was a cyclical pattern of required daily and weekly activities to be performed. For research managers, product managers, and project managers, much more flexibility and variety of activities was possible.

A fourth aspect of the work pattern requirements is uncertainty, or the extent to which a manager has to cope with unpredictable problems and workload variations beyond his control. Managers faced with frequent crises, like production managers and service managers, must do more troubleshooting and are less able to plan their time than research managers and accounting managers. However, even for a particular category of managers, the amount of uncertainty will depend on the task, technology, and external environment.

A fifth aspect is the typical duration of managerial functions, and the extent to which a manager is required to devote sustained attention to particular activities such as preparing reports, plans, and budgets. Research managers, some product managers, and some managers of staff units require this kind of sustained attention, whereas a pattern of brief, fragmented contacts is more typical of most other kinds of managers, particularly those with high demands from subordinates and peers.

Exposure

Another aspect of a managerial job that affects the required behavior and skills for the job is called "exposure." This is related to the "burden of responsibility" borne by a manager, but is not merely a question of responsibility alone. Exposure depends in part on the responsibility for making decisions with potentially serious consequences. A manager's job is more exposed if his decisions and actions have important consequences for the organization, and mistakes or poor judgment can result in loss of resources, disruption of operations, and risk to human health and life.

Another determinant of exposure is the time it takes to discover a mistake or poor decision. The longer the delay in evaluating the consequences of a manager's decisions and actions, the lower the exposure.

Exposure also depends on a manager's accountability for mistakes. Accountability is reduced when decisions are made by a group, or after consultation with others, and poor performance cannot be identified as the fault of the manager.

Product managers, project managers, and managers of profit centers have highly exposed jobs. Product managers recommend expensive marketing programs and product changes that may quickly prove to be a disaster. Project managers may fail to complete projects on schedule, or they may incur massive cost overruns. Managers of profit centers, such as division managers and regional managers, have high exposure when they are held accountable for their profit record. Exposure is relatively low for a research manager or a personnel director.

Individual Discretion versus Situational Requirements

A managerial position makes various demands on the person who occupies it, and the actions of the occupant are constrained by laws, policies, regulations, traditions, and scope of formal authority. Despite these demands and constraints, some choice of behavior remains, particularly with respect to what aspects of the job are emphasized, how much time is devoted to various activities, and how much time is spent with different people. The research showed that even for managers with similar jobs, there was considerable variability of behavior. For example, some bank managers emphasized staff supervision, whereas some others delegated much of the internal management to the assistant manager and concentrated on actively seeking out new business.

Implications for Managerial Selection

The research on core demands of managerial jobs has important implications for selection and promotion, since different jobs require somewhat different patterns of traits and skills. A person who is very energetic, resourceful, and decisive is more suited to a managerial position characterized by fragmented activities, responding work pattern, need for troubleshooting, and pressure to meet deadlines. A person who has high initiative and strong internal motivation is more suited to a managerial position characterized by self-generating activities, less fragmentation, fewer crises, and activities requiring more sustained attention. Only by first identifying the behavioral demands of a managerial position can the suitability of candidates be evaluated properly.

Stewart suggests that the work pattern associated with some kinds of managerial jobs tends to be habit forming. A person who spends a long time in one position may grow accustomed to acting in a particular way and will find it difficult to adjust to another managerial position with very different behavioral requirements. The transition appears particularly difficult from a "responding" position to a "self-generating" position, or from a position where exercise of authority over subordinates is paramount to a position where influencing peers is the primary requirement. It is important to consider these kinds of issues when a manager is being evaluated for possible promotion to a higher position.

GUIDELINES FOR DETERMINING THE RELEVANCE
OF SPECIFIC BEHAVIORS

This portion of the chapter brings us full circle back to the question of effective leadership behavior discussed in Chapter 5. As you will recall, the research on consequences of leader behavior indicated that "it all depends on the situation." The contingency theories in Chapter 6 stipulate what behavior is relevant in what situation, but we saw that these theories are inconclusive, due to conceptual deficiencies and lack of adequate validation research. The research conducted to test contingency theories has been limited by preoccupation with directive and supportive leadership. There has been little research on the moderating influence of the situation on more specific aspects of leadership behavior, such as the behaviors in the Yukl taxonomy. As for the research in the present chapter, it provides some insight into the relevance of different kinds of behavior, but this research is not directly concerned with the question of leader effectiveness. The best insights are provided by the few studies that actually examine behavioral role requirements in different situations, rather than merely comparing behavior across situations. As we saw in a couple of instances, behavior differences across situations do not necessarily indicate what leader behavior is appropriate in each situation. Sometimes the leaders in a comparative study or laboratory experiment respond to situational pressures in ways that are less than optimally effective.

Despite the limitations of research on contingency theories and situational determinants, the findings from both kinds of research permit some inferences about the relevance of particular behaviors in different situations. Drawing on this research, as well as on the research described in other chapters, some tentative propositions are made for the 19 managerial behaviors in the Yukl taxonomy presented in Chapter 5. For each type of behavior, the conditions under which the behavior is especially appropriate are listed. These conditions are not the only situations where the behavior should be used, rather, they are the conditions where the behavior is most essential, and if carried out with proper skill and timing, where it will contribute most to leader effectiveness.

Performance Emphasis

- When subordinate errors and quality deficiencies are costly and difficult to correct, or they would endanger the health and lives of people.
- When the leader's unit is in direct competition with other units or organizations, and it can only survive and prosper by being more efficient and productive than competitors.

- When the leader's unit is highly interdependent with other units in the organization, and failure to meet deadlines or achieve planned levels of output or services to these units would seriously disrupt their activities.
- When the leader is under extreme pressure from higher management, trustees, directors, or owners to increase profits, improve productivity, reduce costs, or otherwise improve unit performance.
- When subordinates are not highly motivated to do the work and are likely to "slack off" if not prodded and encouraged.

Consideration

- When the work is boring and tedious.
- When subordinates lack self-confidence, feel insecure, and depend on the leader for support and encouragement.
- When subordinates have strong affiliation needs and are concerned about acceptance by the leader.
- When the leader works in close proximity to subordinates and/or must interact frequently with them due to the nature of the task.
- When subordinates have substantial counterpower over the leader and are able to determine whether he (she) retains the leadership position.

Inspiration

- When subordinate commitment (e.g., enthusiastic effort, self-sacrifice, initiative) is essential for effective unit performance.
- When the work is difficult and frustrating, and subordinates are likely to become discouraged by temporary setbacks and lack of progress.
- When the work is dangerous, and subordinates are anxious or fearful.
- When subordinates have ideals and values that are relevant to the activities of the group and will serve as the basis for inspirational appeals.
- When the leader's unit is in competition with other units or organizations.

Praise–Recognition

- When the leader is able to obtain reliable information about subordinate performance.
- When subordinates are not able to get much direct feedback about their performance from the work itself or from clients, customers, or coworkers.
- When subordinates lack self-confidence, feel insecure, and depend on the leader for support and encouragement.

Structuring Reward Contingencies

- When the leader has substantial authority and discretion to administer tangible rewards to subordinates.
- When subordinates value the rewards controlled by the leader and are dependent on the leader for them.
- When performance outcomes are primarily determined by subordinate effort and skill rather than by events beyond the subordinate's control.
- When it is possible to measure subordinate performance accurately.
- When the work is repetitive, boring, and tedious, rather than varied, interesting, and meaningful.

Decision Participation

- When subordinates possess relevant knowledge and information needed by the leader to solve problems and make good decisions (unstructured task or inexperienced leader).
- When subordinates share the leader's concern for achieving task objectives.
- When there is adequate time available for use of participative procedures.
- When the group of subordinates is small and working in close proximity.
- When subordinates expect to be consulted about certain decisions and are unlikely to accept an autocratic decision in these matters.

Autonomy–Delegation

- When subordinates are competent professionals or craftsmen who can perform their work without much supervision.
- When subordinate performance can be measured and monitored without close supervision.
- When errors by subordinates would not be extremely costly and difficult to correct.
- When the leader is overloaded with responsibilities and cannot handle all of them effectively by himself.
- When subordinates have strong needs for achievement and independence, and they desire more responsibility, variety, and autonomy in their jobs.

Role Clarification

- When subordinates lack experience and don't know what to do or how to do it.
- When the work is complex and unstructured, and subordinates rely on the leader for guidance about objectives, procedures, and priorities.

- When the organization has elaborate rules and regulations, and subordinates are not familiar with them.
- When the unit receives many short tasks or projects to perform, and the leader must frequently give new assignments to subordinates.
- When changes in the nature of the work or the organization of activities require a redefinition of subordinate work roles.

Goal Setting

- When objective performance indicators are available for use in setting specific goals.
- When performance outcomes are highly dependent on subordinate effort and are not strongly affected by fluctuating conditions beyond the control of subordinates.
- When subordinates have at least a moderate amount of achievement motivation to be aroused by challenging goals and deadlines.

Training–Coaching

- When the work is complex and highly technical, and a long period of learning and experience is necessary for a subordinate to master all aspects of the job.
- When the nature of the work and/or technology is changing, and subordinates need to learn new skills and procedures.
- When some subordinates have skill deficiencies and need additional coaching and instruction to overcome performance problems.
- When it is frequently necessary to train new subordinates, due to a high turnover rate or to rapid expansion of the leader's unit.
- When some subordinates need special training to prepare them to assume new responsibilities and advance to higher positions of authority.

Information Dissemination

- When the work of subordinates is affected by changing policies, objectives, plans, and priorities, and subordinates are dependent on the leader to keep them informed about these changes.
- When the work of subordinates is strongly affected by developments in other parts of the organization, and subordinates are dependent on the leader to keep them informed about these developments.
- When the leader's unit deals directly with outside organizations (e.g., clients, suppliers, regulatory agencies), and the leader has exclusive access to important information about these organizations.
- When there is a crisis or emergency, and subordinates are anxious and concerned about what is happening.

Problem Solving

- When the group exists in a hostile environment, and its survival is endangered by competitors and external opponents who cause periodic crises.
- When there are serious problems that reduce the unit's effectiveness, such as inadequate equipment, inappropriate procedures, delays, excessive costs, and so on.
- When disruptions of the work are likely, due to equipment breakdowns, supply shortages, absent subordinates, and so on.
- When the leader has sufficient authority to make changes and initiate actions that will solve serious problems facing the work unit.

Planning

- When activities must be sequenced and assigned differently each time the work unit has a new task or project to do.
- When the unit has several types of tasks to perform, and group efficiency depends on organizing the work to match task requirements with subordinate skills.
- When disruptions of the work are likely, due to equipment breakdowns, supply shortages, outside interference, and so on, and ways can be found to avoid these disruptions, or by making contingency plans, to improve the group's ability to cope quickly and effectively with unavoidable disruptions.
- When there are sharp variations in the demand for the output of the leader's unit, and it is possible to anticipate the peaks and valleys and find ways to avoid them, or by preparing contingency plans, to minimize their impact.
- When the manager has sufficient authority and discretion to develop plans and carry them out.

Coordinating

- When subordinates have interdependent tasks such that each person must adjust his (her) actions to the actions of the other subordinates, and synchronization of actions is not assured by the technology.
- When subordinates work on the same task sequentially, and they depend on each other to provide the information, components, materials, or services necessary to do their work without interruptions and delays.
- When subordinates must take turns using the same equipment, facilities, materials, or support personnel.
- When activities must be sequenced and assigned differently each time the work unit has a new task or project to do.
- When there is a need for uniform practices among subordinates, such as uniform treatment of customers, use of the same materials, and so on.

- When the number of interdependent subordinates reporting to the leader is large.

Work Facilitation

- When subordinates use a large variety and amount of supplies, materials, or other inputs in their work and are dependent on the leader to obtain them.
- When subordinates are dependent on the leader to provide necessary support services such as maintenance and servicing of equipment.
- When shortages of inputs or inadequate support services would result in serious and immediate disruption of the work.
- When subordinates are dependent on the leader to obtain necessary information, approvals, cooperation, and assistance from other work units and/or outside organizations.

Representation

- When the work unit is competing with other units for scarce resources.
- When the leader's unit is highly dependent on other organizational units to provide important inputs such as supplies, services, components, or information.
- When the leader's unit is highly dependent on other organizational units to accept and/or approve its outputs.
- When the leader's unit is required to carry out joint activities with other organizational units.
- When lobbying and public relations efforts are necessary to obtain support and resources for the unit from superiors and/or outside sources.
- When the leader's unit must negotiate agreements and contracts directly with outside organizations, such as customers, suppliers, subcontractors, and so on.

Interaction Facilitation

- When subordinates work in close proximity to each other, such as in the same room, or on the same ship.
- When subordinates have highly interdependent tasks such that each person's actions affect the work of the other subordinates.
- When the organizational unit is large, and it contains competing groups or factions.
- When subordinates are highly mobile, and they are likely to feel alienated and quit the group if cohesiveness and team identification are lacking.
- When cooperation and teamwork are essential for the survival and/or prosperity of the work unit.

Conflict Management

- When subordinates are in competition with each other for resources, status, and power.
- When subordinates have interdependent jobs requiring coordination and cooperation, but have different objectives and orientations (e.g., sales and production, purchasing and engineering).
- When subordinates have different values and beliefs, and these differences are likely to cause suspicion, misunderstanding, and hostility.
- When subordinates come from different racial, ethnic, religious, or cultural backgrounds and bring external hostilities with them into the work setting.

Criticism–Discipline

- When subordinates work with dangerous substances or perform tasks in which mistakes would endanger the health and life of people.
- When subordinate compliance with rules and orders is essential for the survival and effective performance of the unit.
- When some subordinates are likely to ignore rules and orders unless strict discipline is enforced.
- When the leader has substantial authority to take disciplinary action.

Summary

Leaders adapt their behavior to the requirements, constraints, and opportunities presented by the leadership situation. Although this process of adaptation has not received the attention it deserves, the research to date does provide some valuable insight into the way leader behavior is influenced by situational variables.

Role theory has proved useful in helping to understand how the process occurs. A leader's perception of role requirements will be influenced by role senders, task characteristics, and feedback about subordinate behavior and performance. Different kinds of role conflicts are common, and research has begun to identify how these conflicts are resolved. The leader's needs, values, and interests influence perception of role requirements in addition to directly influencing the leader's preference among behavior alternatives. Expectancy theory provides further insight into the leader's choice of behavior.

Osborn and Hunt's Adaptive-Reactive Theory postulates that macro variables such as organization structure and the external environment are primary determinants of leader behavior. Leader discretion is lower in highly centralized or formalized organizations, when subunits are large or interdependent, and when there is a complex, unstable environment.

The most important research designs for studying situational determinants of leader behavior are the comparative field study, the longitudinal field study, and the laboratory experiment. Each approach has various advantages and limitations, so a combination of approaches is desirable.

Research using these approaches indicates that several aspects of the situation have important implications for leader behavior. These situational determinants include level in the authority hierarchy, function of the leader's unit, task characteristics and technology, size of organizational unit, lateral interdependence, crisis conditions, and subordinate competence.

Stewart's extensive comparative research has identified additional demands and contraints that shape a manager's behavior. The pattern of interactions with subordinates, superiors, peers, and outside persons will be affected by the demands made by each and by the difficulty of meeting these demands. The type of work pattern depends on the nature of the work—specifically, whether it is self-generating or responding, repetitive or variable, uncertain or predictable, fragmented or sustained, and subject to tight deadlines or not. Managerial exposure also affects role requirements.

Despite all of the demands and constraints a manager faces, some choice of behavior remains. Managers define their roles differently, even when they have similar positions. It is important to consider the compatibility of leader skills and habitual behavior patterns with the role requirements for a managerial position when deciding whom to select for the position.

Examination of differences in leader behavior across situations provides some insight into reasons for leadership effectiveness, especially when role requirements are examined. The research on situational determinants was considered, together with research on consequences of leader behavior in different situations, and some tentative guidelines about the relevance of 19 specific behaviors were proposed. These guidelines provide a partial integration of the findings in chapters 5, 6, and 7.

REVIEW AND DISCUSSION QUESTIONS

1. How much does a leader's behavior depend on the situation, and how much does it depend on the leader's own needs, values, and interests?

2. How can expectancy theory be used to help explain leader behavior?

3. How can role concepts be used to help explain the joint influence of leader and situational characteristics on a leader's behavior?

4. What aspects of the leadership situation are viewed by Osborn and Hunt as especially important determinants of leader behavior? Does the research reviewed in this chapter support their assertion that macro variables are more important than micro variables?

5. What are the major research methods used to study situational determinants of leader behavior, and what advantages and limitations does each method have?

6. How is leader behavior influenced by the level of the leader's position in the authority hierarchy of the organization?

7. What problems are created for leaders in large groups in comparison to small groups?

8. What kind of leader is most effective in a crisis?

9. What has the research by Rosemary Stewart contributed to our understanding of leadership?

10. Define and explain each of the following terms: role expectation, role sender, role conflict, comparative field study, longitudinal field study, technology, span of control, centralization, formalization, lateral interdependence, situational demands and constraints, self-generating activities, exposure.

8

Participation
and Delegation

Making decisions is one of the most important functions performed by leaders. Many of the activities of managers and administrators involve decision making, including planning, organizing, coordinating, solving technical problems, selecting subordinates, determining pay increases, making job assignments, and so forth. The decision making involved in strategic planning and policy formation is probably the single most important duty performed by top executives in organizations.

A leader may make a decision alone or together with other persons in the organization. It is common practice for a manager to have subordinates, peers, or superiors participate in making some of his or her decisions. Considerable research has been conducted to determine how much decision participation is desirable and when it should be used. In this chapter, we will explore these issues and review the major theories and research findings.

WHO MAKES ORGANIZATIONAL DECISIONS?

Some managers in an organization have more authority to make decisions than other managers. The higher a manager is in the authority hierarchy of an organization, the more likely it is that the manager will be responsible for making important decisions. Top leaders usually make the most important decisions, including determination of organizational objectives, planning of strategies to attain objectives, determination of general policies, design of the organization structure, and allocation of resources. As one goes down through the authority hierarchy, decisions become increasingly more specific and operational. At the lowest level of management in most organizations, the first-line supervisors have very little authority to make decisions. When there is a high degree of formalization of rules and procedures, or when there is a union contract with provisions governing work assignments, schedules, pay rates, and so on, then a first-line supervisor has practically no discretion to make task decisions and personnel decisions. During the course of this century, the authority of many first-line supervisors was drastically curtailed as more and more jobs either became unionized or came under civil service regulations (Homans, 1965; Miller, 1965). The discretion of lower-level managers was further eroded by the introduction of staff specialists who were given the authority for certain activities once performed by the managers, such as personnel selection, design of work procedures, quality control, work scheduling, training, and wage and salary administration.

Decision making in organizations often involves managers at different levels in the authority hierarchy. The person who initiates action on a decision may not be the person who makes the final choice among action alternatives. For example, a section supervisor with a problem may point out the need for a decision to his boss, the department manager. The section supervisor may or may not recommend some course of action, and the department manager may or may not ask for such a recommendation. Before the department manager makes a decision, he may consult with his own boss (the plant manager) or with managers in other departments of the organization who would be affected by the decision. Even if the plant manager is not consulted in advance, he may review the department manager's decision and decide to approve, reject, or modify it.

Blankenship and Miles (1968) studied the decision making of managers at different levels within eight companies. As might be expected, upper-level managers were found to have the most autonomy and authority. They were seldom required to consult with their superiors or with other managers at the same level before making a final decision. On the other hand, upper-level managers were less likely than managers at lower or middle levels to initiate action on a decision, and they relied more on subordinates to initiate such actions. Lower-level managers tended to have more decisions initiated for them by their superiors (middle-level managers) and were more often required to consult with superiors before making decisions or taking action on decisions (see Table 8–1).

Even when a manager is not required to consult with peers, subordinates, or superiors before making a final choice, the manager may still prefer to do so. Consultation with the boss enables a manager to draw upon the expertise of the boss, which may be greater than his own. In addition, consultation with the boss allows a manager to find out how the boss feels about a problem and how the boss is likely to react to the manager's proposed solutions. On the other hand, excessive consultation with the boss suggests a lack of self-confidence and

TABLE 8–1
Association Between Hierarchical Level and Decision Behavior

Hierarchical level	N	Final choice	Perceived influence	Autonomy from superior	Reliance on subordinates	Personal initiation
		%	%	%	%	%
Upper	54	80	67	85	70	32
Middle	93	40	51	39	49	49
Lower	43	41	29	20	34	38

SOURCE: From L. Vaughn Blankenship and Raymond E. Miles, "Organizational Structure and Managerial Decision Behavior." *Administrative Science Quarterly*, Vol. 13, #1 (June 1968), pp. 106–20.

initiative on the part of the subordinate. A manager with the authority to make a final choice in decisions is wise to avoid becoming too dependent on his boss when making these decisions.

Consultation with peers is useful when the peers have relevant information or will be affected by the decision. When other managers are involved in the implementation of a decision, consultation is a way to increase their understanding and acceptance of the decision. Lateral consultation facilitates coordination and cooperation among managers of different organizational subunits with interdependent tasks. However, such consultation should be limited to decisions for which it is appropriate, so that time is not wasted in unneccesary meetings.

VARIETIES OF SUBORDINATE PARTICIPATION

The involvement of subordinates in a manager's decisions is usually referred to by the term "participation." This term has been defined in different ways by various writers, and it is sometimes used synonymously with other terms such as consultation, joint decision making, power sharing, decentralization, and democratic management. In the United States, participation usually refers to a management style or type of decision procedure through which subordinates are allowed to influence some of the manager's decisions. Strauss (1977) points out that participation in Europe has a somewhat different meaning. The term is used to describe the practice of "industrial democracy," whereby workers through their elected representatives influence and sometimes even control decisions affecting the organization as a whole. In this chapter, we will discuss only participation by subordinates in their supervisor's decisions, since industrial democracy is a form of participation seldom used in the United States.

Decision participation is not an all-or-none process. There are a variety of different decision procedures that can be used by a manager to involve subordinates in making work unit decisions. Some procedures provide more subordinate influence over a decision than do others. Any given set of decision procedures can be ordered along an influence continuum, ranging from no subordinate influence at one end of the continuum to great subordinate influence at the other end of the continuum. Unfortunately, leadership theorists have not been able to agree on the best set of decision procedures to use in constructing an ordered typology on an influence continuum. Several different typologies have been proposed by various writers (Heller & Yukl, 1969; Tannenbaum & Schmidt, 1958; Vroom & Yetton, 1973; Strauss, 1977).

The minimum number of distinct and meaningful decision procedures is the following four:

1. AUTOCRATIC DECISION: The leader makes a decision without asking for the opinions or suggestions of subordinates, and subordinates have no direct influence.

2. CONSULTATION: The leader asks subordinates for their opinions and suggestions and then makes the decision by himself; the decision is likely to reflect limited subordinate influence.

3. JOINT DECISION: The leader meets with a subordinate or group of subordinates ("group decision") to discuss the decision problem and make a decision together; the leader has no more influence than any other subordinate over the final choice.

4. DELEGATION: The leader gives a subordinate the authority and responsibility for making a decision; limits within which the final choice must fall are usually specified, and the subordinate may or may not be required to obtain the approval of the leader before implementing the decision.

For each decision procedure, there are several possible subvarieties. Some of the more elaborate typologies that have been proposed are useful for identifying these subvarieties.

Tannenbaum and Schmidt Typology

The best known typology of decision procedures was proposed by Tannenbaum and Schmidt (1957). Their typology is shown in Figure 8–1. There are three varieties of autocratic procedures. In the first one, the manager simply announces his decision to subordinates. No attempt is made to increase subordinate comprehension or acceptance of the decision. In the second autocratic procedure, the manager makes the decision, but instead of simply announcing it, he tries to "sell" the decision to subordinates. In using this procedure, the manager recognizes the possibility of subordinate resistance and seeks to explain why the decision was necessary and how it will be advantageous to subordinates. The third autocratic procedure also reflects a concern with decision acceptance and comprehension. With this procedure, the manager explains the decision and then invites subordinates to ask questions. The question-and-answer process allows subordinates to clarify their understanding of the decision and its implications. Doubts and fears based on misunderstanding of the decision can be dispelled.

FIGURE 8-1

Tannenbaum and Schmidt Continuum of Decision Participation Procedures

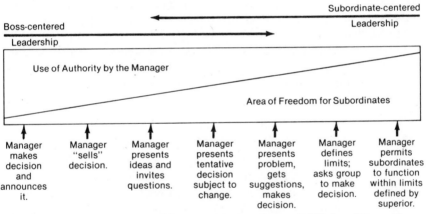

SOURCE: Reprinted by permission of the Harvard Business Review. Exhibit from "How to Choose a Leadership Pattern" by Robert Tannenbaum and Warren H. Schmidt (March–April 1958). Copyright © 1958 by the President and Fellows of Harvard College; all rights reserved.

The next two decision procedures in the Tannenbaum and Schmidt typology are variations of consultation. Unlike the autocratic procedures, subordinates have some influence over the decision. In the first consultation procedure, the manager takes the initiative in identifying and diagnosing the problem, generating alternatives, and identifying the most promising one. This tentative choice is presented to subordinates for their reaction. The decision is subject to change if the manager finds that subordinates have serious objections or criticisms. However, the final decision is still reserved for the manager himself. With the second consultation procedure, slightly more subordinate influence is allowed. The manager presents the problem to subordinates and invites them to diagnose it and suggest solutions. Subordinates may also participate in evaluating the solutions. From the list of alternatives that has been generated, the manager then makes a final choice.

The last two decision procedures in the Tannenbaum and Schmidt typology are variations of joint decision making between a manager and subordinates. In the first variety of group decision, the manager defines the problem and establishes boundaries for the solution. Within these limits, the group generates solutions, evaluates them, and makes a final choice. The manager takes part in the decision process of the group, but is only a discussion coordinator with no more influence over the final choice than any other group member. The maximum degree of subordinate influence occurs with the second variety of group decision. With this decision procedure, the leader allows the group to identify and diagnose problems as well as to generate solutions and make a final choice. The manager may or may not participate in the discussion process, but if he does, his role is once again only that of a discussion coordinator. As with delegation to an individual subordinate, the manager usually specifies certain limits or constraints within which the group is allowed to make decisions. Tannenbaum and Schmidt point out that this procedure is an extreme form of group participation that is only occasionally found in formal organizations.

Appearance of Participation versus Reality

Typologies of decision procedures are helpful, but Strauss (1977) reminds us that it is important to distinguish between overt decision procedures and actual influence patterns. Sometimes what appears to be participation is really only a pretense. For example, a manager may meet with subordinates to make a group decision, but makes it clear that he seeks endorsement of his own choices rather than advice from subordinates. Even when a manager solicits subordinate suggestions and opinions, if he ignores them in making his decision, then no real consultation has occurred. In the same way, a manager may appear to delegate decisions to subordinates, but only after creating conditions where subordinates are afraid to show initiative or to deviate from the choices preferred by the boss. Thus, it takes more than the use of a participative procedure to achieve a real degree of subordinate influence in decision making. The extent to which a leader is genuinely receptive to subordinate ideas and shows respect and appreciation for subordinate contributions is more important than the specific form of participation used (Strauss, 1977).

Strauss also reminds us that participation can occur during informal contacts as well as through formal meetings or formal delegation. For example, a manager may discuss problems with subordinates and get their advice during coffee breaks, during lunch, or at a party. Another variety of informal subordinate participation is "de facto delegation," which occurs when a subordinate or group corrects a problem or changes a procedure without prior authorization, and the boss later accepts the action. Sometimes the cumulative process of repeated small changes by persons at a low level in the authority hierarchy allows them to have a substantial long-term impact on organizational procedures and policies.

Autocratic versus Participative Managers

A typology of decision procedures is helpful for describing how a manager handles a particular decision at a particular time, but such typologies are not appropriate for classifying managers in terms of their overall decision behavior. All managers use a variety of decision procedures depending on the type of decision and other aspects of the situation (Heller & Yukl, 1969; Vroom & Yetton, 1973). Some managers use participative procedures more often than other managers, and thus can be labeled as relatively more participative. However, it is misleading to classify a manager in terms of a simple "autocratic" versus "participative" dichotomy, as many writers have done. Although it is often useful to make a general classification of a manager in terms of how much participation is allowed, it is a matter of degree, not an all-or-none distinction. Furthermore, the pattern of a manager's decision behavior in relation to different kinds of decisions is more important than the overall amount of participation he uses. One manager may have the same composite score as another, yet use a very different pattern of decision procedures. For example, one manager may use consultation most of the time, with only occasional use of autocratic decisions or joint decisions. Another manager may use all three of these decision procedures equally often. Both managers would be regarded as moderately participative, but there are important differences in their behavior patterns that should not be overlooked.

POTENTIAL BENEFITS AND DISADVANTAGES OF PARTICIPATION

Participative management is often recommended as an approach for improving the satisfaction and motivation of subordinates. It is consistent with American ideals of equality, democracy, and individual dignity (Strauss, 1977). A number of reasons have been suggested to explain why participation can improve satisfaction and performance of a leader's subordinates:

1. Participation leads to greater understanding and acceptance of a decision by subordinates when there is likely to be resistance to change based on fears and anxieties about the implications of the decision. Through participation, the subordinates are able to gain a better understanding of the decision. There is also an opportunity for catharsis. Finally, participation allows subordinates to exercise some influence to protect their interests if threatened (Coch & French, 1948; Maier, 1963; Strauss, 1963).

2. Participation leads to greater acceptance of a decision and commitment to implement it effectively when such commitment is not otherwise likely to occur. The process of helping to shape a decision creates subordinate identification with the decision. Subordinates who have considerable influence over a decision tend to perceive it as "their decision" and want it to be successfully implemented (Anthony, 1978; Coch & French, 1948; Strauss, 1963).

3. Participation leads to greater understanding of the objectives involved in a particular decision and of the action plans developed to achieve the objectives. This understanding makes it easier for subordinates to implement the decision, and it enables them to modify the action plans as needed to deal with unanticipated developments (Bass, 1970).

4. Participation provides subordinates with a more accurate perception of the reward contingencies in the organization. If as a result, there is an increase in the expectancy that a high degree of effort will lead to the attainment of positive outcomes (e.g., pay increase, recognition) and the avoidance of negative outcomes (layoff, rejection by coworkers), then subordinate task motivation will be greater (Mitchell, 1973).

5. Participation is consistent with the needs of a mature subordinate for autonomy, achievement, self-identity, and psychological growth, and for such persons a high degree of participation makes the job more interesting and satisfying. Autocratic leadership tends to frustrate these needs and causes resentment, apathy, and withdrawal (Argyris, 1964, 1973; McGregor, 1960).

6. When a group decision is made with a process members perceive as legitimate, the group will apply social pressure on members to increase decision acceptance, or at least compliance with the decision by any members who would otherwise resist implementing it (Likert, 1961; Strauss, 1977).

7. Group decision making provides members with an opportunity to cooperate in solving common problems, and unless there are incompatible goals to disrupt cooperation, mutual understanding will be increased, team identity will be strengthened, and coordination will be facilitated (Anthony, 1978).

8. Some participative procedures establish a bargaining relationship between a manager and subordinates in which differences can be resolved by mutual concessions and exchange of favors. If subordinates have different objectives than the manager, consultation and especially joint decision making provides an opportunity to resolve the conflict and gain subordinate acceptance of the resulting decision (Anthony, 1978; Strauss, 1977).

9. Participation can result in better decisions when subordinates have relevant information or analytical skills not possessed by the leader and are willing to cooperate with him in making a good decision. Participation utilizes the expertise and talents of the entire group rather than merely those of the leader (Anthony, 1978; Maier, 1963; Vroom & Yetton, 1973).

The list of potential advantages of participation is impressive, but other writers (Anthony, 1978; Locke & Schweiger, 1979; Lowin, 1968; Strauss, 1963, 1977) have pointed out potential negative consequences of participation and conditions under which participation will not be effective. Possible disadvantages and limitations of participation are as follows:

1. Participative procedures usually require more time than autocratic decisions. Therefore, participation results in a great deal of wasted time, and it is not appropriate in an emergency where an immediate decision is needed.

2. Participation in some decisions raises subordinate expectations about influencing other decisions. Thus, a leader may find himself in a conflict with subordinates who are trying to extend their participation to a wider range of decisions than the leader is willing to allow.

3. Extensive use of participation may cause a manager to be perceived as lacking in expertise, initiative, and self-confidence. Superiors, peers, and even subordinates may perceive the manager as a weak leader.

4. Extreme forms of participation such as group decisions and

delegation may result in lower-quality decisions if subordinates lack relevant expertise, are apathetic about participating, or have goals and values incompatible with those of the leader.

5. Group decision making diffuses responsibility and makes it difficult to assign responsibility for success and blame for failure. As a consequence, group decisions may result in selection of risky alternatives when these are undesirable for the organization (Clark, 1971; Vinokur, 1971). In addition, with group decisions it is more difficult to reward effective decision making and to select persons for promotion on the basis of their individual problem-solving ability.

6. Participative decision procedures, and especially group procedures, require a great deal of skill on the part of the leader to be used effectively. If these procedures are used by leaders who lack the required skills, the outcomes may be worse than if the leader simply made autocratic decisions.

It is obvious that there is still some controversy about the merits of participation. Many advocates of participative management believe it is applicable to most if not all organizations and is consistent with human nature as well as organizational profit objectives. Other theorists are more pessimistic and critical about participation and view it as a set of procedures with limited potential and applicability. This controversy is reflected in the research literature on participation, to which we will now turn.

RESEARCH ON EFFECTS OF PARTICIPATION

As we saw in Chapter 5, there has been a great deal of research on the consequences of different patterns of leadership behavior. One kind of leader behavior that has been studied extensively is decision participation. As was the case with research on Consideration and Initiating Structure, much of the research on participation consists of correlational field studies in which causality cannot be determined. There have also been quite a few laboratory experiments, but most of these were so unrealistic that the results cannot be readily generalized to leaders in actual organizations. The best studies are again the field experiments, although even these suffer from a variety of limitations. Two of the field experiments will be described to provide examples of this method of investigating the effects of participation on subordinate satisfaction and performance. Then the cumulative findings from all kinds of research on participation will be summarized.

Coch and French Study

One of the earliest studies on the effects of participation was a field experiment by Coch and French (1948) in a garment factory. The study was conducted to see if participation would reduce resistance to change in work procedures among sewing machine operators. Two varieties of participation were compared to each other and to a no-participation condition.

In two "total participation" groups, managers met with the workers and explained the need for a change in work procedures. Then every member of the group was allowed to participate in the design and planning of the new work procedures. In one "representative participation" group, the workers met and selected a few representatives to participate in planning the changes in work procedures. These representatives eventually reported back to their group on what had been decided, and they trained the other group members in the use of the new procedures. In a fourth (control) group, work procedures were decided autocratically by management and simply announced, as had been done in the past.

The effects of participation on worker productivity are shown in Figure 8–2. As can be seen in the graph, the work groups were approximately equal in productivity before transfer to the new work procedure. After the change, the no-participation group showed an immediate decline in productivity, which was the usual reaction to changes in work procedure made in an autocratic manner. The total participation groups had a brief drop in productivity while the new work procedures were being learned, but they returned to their initial level of output within a few days and achieved a 14 percent gain in productivity during the next four weeks. The representative participation group also had an immediate drop in productivity after the work procedure was changed, but they returned to their original level of productivity after two weeks and even exceeded that level slightly in the following weeks. Thus, when compared to no participation, both varieties of participation resulted in better performance.

Additional evidence for the effectiveness of participation was found in a follow-up experiment two and a half months later. The members of the no-participation group, who had been dispersed to different work groups after the first experiment, were reunited and given a job with a new work procedure. The total participation procedure was used to introduce the change, and the results are shown in Figure 8–3, together with productivity data for the same group during the first experiment. It is clear that participation had a beneficial effect on productivity.

FIGURE 8-2
Effects of Employee Participation in a Job Change Decision on Productivity After the Change

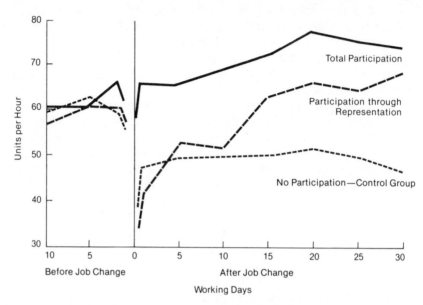

SOURCE: L. Coch and J. R. P. French, Jr., "Overcoming Resistance to Change." *Human Relations*, 1948, 1, 512–532. Published by Plenum Publishing Corporation.

The Coch and French study found some additional effects of participation besides increased productivity. Workers in the no-participation group were not convinced that the changes in work procedure were necessary, and they viewed the new piece rate set by management as arbitrary and unreasonable. Seventeen percent of the employees in this group quit their jobs within the first 40 days after the change, and grievances were filed about the new piece rate. The workers expressed hostility toward the supervisor, refused to cooperate with the supervisor, and deliberately restricted production. On the other hand, in the participation groups, employees worked well with their supervisor and there was no turnover. Employees spoke of the new job as "our job," and the new piece rates were referred to as "our rates." Apparently, participation resulted in identification with the decision and increased motivation to implement it, whereas the autocratic procedure created resistance to change, dissatisfaction, hostility, withdrawal, and reduced motivation.

Bragg and Andrews Study

Another experimental study of participative decision making was conducted by Bragg and Andrews (1973) in a hospital. The foreman of

FIGURE 8–3

Comparison of the Effect of No Participation with Total Participation for the Same Work Group

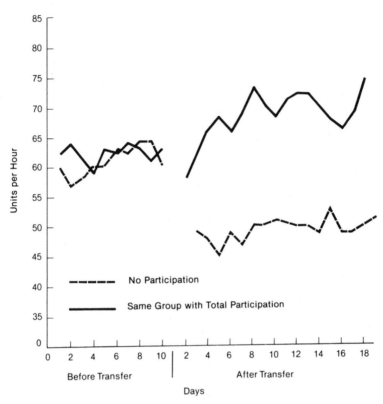

SOURCE: L. Coch and J. R. P. French, Jr., "Overcoming Resistance to Change." *Human Relations,* 1948, 1, 512–532. Published by Plenum Publishing Corporation.

the laundry department of the hospital typically made decisions in an autocratic manner, but he was persuaded by the chief administrator to try a participative approach. The 32 workers in the laundry department were told that group decision meetings would be held to make their job more interesting, not to increase productivity, which was already high. The workers and union were told that the participation program would be discontinued if they found it unsatisfactory. Over the next eighteen months, meetings were held whenever the workers wanted to discuss specific proposals. More than twenty-eight meetings were held to discuss employee proposals about hours of work, working conditions, work procedures, minor equipment modifications, and safety matters. In addition to these problem-solving and decision-making meetings, the foreman consulted regularly with individuals and small groups of workers to discuss problems and new ideas.

The effects of participation were evaluated in terms of changes in employee attitudes, attendance, and productivity. Attitudes were measured at two-month intervals by a questionnaire. The data indicated that, after some initial doubts about the participation program, the attitudes of the workers became increasingly more favorable over the course of fourteen months of measurement.

Productivity for the first eighteen months under participation was compared to productivity in the same department during the preceding year, and to productivity in similar laundry departments in two other hospitals. In the department with the participation program, productivity increased 42 percent over the prior year, whereas in the two comparison groups, productivity declined slightly over the previous year.

Absenteeism for the laundry department was compared to absenteeism during a similar period prior to introduction of the participation program. Even though attendance in the laundry department was initially quite good, it became even better after the participation program was introduced. In contrast, absenteeism during the same time period for the other nonmedical staff in the hospital became worse instead of better.

These results were statistically significant and indicated that the participation program was highly successful. After the program had been in effect for three years, neither the workers nor the supervisor had any desire to return to the old autocratic style of management. The success of the program led to the introduction of participation in the medical records section of the hospital, where it resulted in elimination of grievances and a sharp reduction in turnover. However, an attempt to introduce a participation program in the nursing group was much less successful, due primarily to lack of support by the head nurse and resistance by administrative medical personnel.

Other Research on Participation

Studies on the effects of participation do not always find it to be as successful as the two experiments just described. Results for major field experiments on participation are summarized in Table 8–2. As the table shows, participation has been studied with a variety of different kinds of decisions and samples. Compared to low-participation managers, high-participation managers had better performance in six studies, worse performance in four studies, and there was no clear difference in seven studies. With respect to subordinate absenteeism and turnover, participative managers had better records in four studies, a worse record in one study, and there was no difference in one study.

Subordinate satisfaction with the boss, or with the way decisions are made, was found to be more favorable under high rather than low participation in seven out of eleven studies. Taken together, the results indicate that participation is successful in some situations but not others, and is more likely to improve satisfaction than performance.

A similar pattern of mixed results has been found in correlational field studies and laboratory experiments (see review by Locke & Schweiger, 1979). In these studies, satisfaction was often higher under participatory leadership, but performance was not affected in any consistent manner. Thus, the combined evidence from a large number of studies has failed to resolve the controversy over the consequences of participation. The contradictory results indicate, once again, the importance of the situation. It is unfortunate that so few participation studies have systematically examined the influence of situational variables. Most studies have either ignored the situation entirely, or have identified limiting or facilitating conditions for participation only on a post hoc basis to explain discrepant results or lack of success. Some aspects of the situation found to moderate the effects of participation on subordinate satisfaction and performance include: the importance of the decisions made with a participative procedure (French, et al., 1960), the perceived legitimacy of participation (French, et al., 1960, 1966), the needs and traits of subordinates affecting their desire to participate (French, et al., 1966; Runyon, 1973; Tannenbaum & Allport, 1956; Vroom, 1959), the nature of the task or decision problem (Delbecq, 1965; Lorsch & Morse, 1974; Mott, 1972), the degree of encouragement and support provided by higher management to supervisors using participative procedures (Bragg & Andrews, 1973; Latham & Yukl, 1975), and the leader's own confidence in participation and perception of subordinates' potential contributions (Bragg & Andrews, 1973; Ritchie & Miles, 1970).

CONDITIONS FOR EFFECTIVE USE OF PARTICIPATION

Leadership research and theory suggest that there are certain prerequisites for effective participation. Some of the most important conditions appear to be the following (Anthony, 1978; Tannenbaum & Schmidt, 1958; Strauss, 1977):

1. The leader has authority to make important decisions. There is little opportunity for a leader to use participative procedures if the leader lacks the authority to make decisions on matters that are important to his work unit. As noted earlier, many lower-level managers do not have the authority to decide work procedures, assignments,

TABLE 8–2

Review of Major Field Experiments on Effects of Participation

Researchers and Date of Study	Subordinate Sample	Type of Decision	Measurement Time Span	Satisfaction	Comparison of High and Low Participation Conditions			
					Attendance	Turnover	Ratings	Productivity
Bragg & Andrews (1973)	Hospital laundry workers	Work schedule, procedures, equipment chng.	18 months	Positive effect	Positive effect			Positive effect
Coch & French (1948)	Sewing machine operators	Work procedures	1 month	Positive effect		Positive effect		Positive effect
Dossett, Latham & Mitchell (1978)	Clerical workers	Behavioral goals	4 months				No difference	
Fleishman (1965)	Sewing machine operators	Work procedures	6 months					No difference (both improved)
French (1950)	Sewing machine operators	Work pace & goals	2 months					Positive effect
French, Israel & As (1960)	Footwear product. workers	Assignments & training needs	10 weeks	No difference				No difference
French, Kay & Meyer (1966)	Engineering & mfg. managers	Performance goals	12 weeks	Positive effect			No difference	
Ivancevich (1976)	Sales representatives	Performance goals	11 months	Negative effect				No difference (both improved)

Study	Subjects	Variable	Duration	Negative effect	No difference		No difference	Negative effect (both improved)
Ivancevich (1977)	Production technicians	Performance goals	12 months					Negative effect (both improved)
Latham, Mitchell & Dossett (1978)	Engineers & scientists	Behavioral goals	6 months				No difference	
Latham & Yukl (1975)	Logging crews	Performance goals	8 weeks					Positive in 1 out of 2 samples
Latham & Yukl (1976)	Clerical workers	Performance goals	10 weeks	No difference				No difference (both improved)
Lawler & Hackman (1969)	Janitorial workers	Design of attendance incentive	16 weeks		Positive effect			
Lawrence & Smith (1955)	Office & product. workers	Performance goals	5 weeks			Positive effect		Positive effect
Morse & Reimer (1956)	Clerical workers	Task decisions	1 year	Positive effect				Negative effect (both improved)
Powell & Schlacter (1971)	Road construction crews	Work scheduling	6 months	Positive effect	Negative effect			Negative effect
Seeborg (1978)	Assembly workers (simulation)	Job redesign	1 day	Positive effect				Negative effect
Veen (1972)	Hockey trainees (10–14-yr.-old boys)	Training content	6 weeks	Positive effect				Positive effect (skill test)

compensation, work schedules, and other important issues. Participation is feasible only for problems that fall within the leader's jurisdiction and can be solved by actions the leader is authorized to take. For problems that must be solved in a manner predetermined by organization rules or policy, participation is not appropriate.

2. The decision is made in the absence of strong time pressure. Participation is seldom feasible when there is an emergency or crisis requiring an immediate response by the leader. In a crisis situation of this type, the quality of a prompt autocratic decision will usually be superior to a participative decision that is delayed. Even when there is no crisis, the amount of feasible participation is limited by the time demands on the leader and on subordinates. For example, in an equipment operating crew, it may not be possible for crew members to leave their posts in order to attend a meeting.

3. Subordinates have relevant knowledge. Participation is more likely to be effective if subordinates have information and knowledge relevant to the decision. Without such knowledge, subordinates cannot make much of a contribution to the improvement of a decision. Subordinates are more likely to have relevant knowledge not possessed by the leader when a decision involves an unstructured task or a complex problem.

4. Subordinates are willing to participate. Participative techniques are unlikely to be successful unless subordinates are willing to cooperate with the leader in making decisions. There are many reasons why subordinates may not be willing to participate, including dislike of the leader, aversion to meetings, belief that the leader will ignore subordinate suggestions, unwillingness to assume any responsibility for the decision, and dependence on an authority figure to provide direction. Subordinates may be willing to participate in some kinds of decisions (e.g., important, relevant ones), but not in others. Preferences regarding participation vary from individual to individual, depending on needs, values, and personality traits (Anthony, 1978; Bass & Barrett, 1972). Preferences for participation are also influenced by cultural background, and participation is regarded more favorably in some cultures than in others (Bass, 1968; Haire, Ghiselli & Porter, 1966).

5. The leader has confidence in participative techniques. Participative techniques are less likely to be used by a leader who doubts their relevance and effectiveness. A leader who has no confidence in the knowledge and creativity of subordinates is unlikely to ask them to help him make decisions (Miles, 1975). Regardless of the actual capacity of subordinates to contribute to decisions, if the leader does not recognize their competence, he will see little value in participation. Some leaders have a negative stereotype of subordinates and perceive them as lazy, dishonest, stupid, irresponsible, selfish, and dependent (McGregor, 1960). Participative techniques are most effective when used by a leader who shows enthusiasm and conveys a feeling of confidence and trust in subordinates (Zand, 1972).

6. *The leader is skilled in use of participative techniques.* It is not enough simply to believe in participation and hold meetings to consult with subordinates or make group decisions. A leader must also have the skills necessary to use the participative techniques effectively (Maier, 1963). Without the appropriate skills, the potential benefits of consultation, joint decision making, and delegation are unlikely to be achieved. Group techniques require the greatest degree of skill because so many things can go wrong in a problem-solving or decision-making meeting (see Chapter 9).

Limitations of Participation Research

A major limitation of research on participation has been the conception of participation as a general management style rather than as a set of specific decision procedures that differ from each other as well as from autocratic procedures. In nearly all participation studies, the objective has been to see if participation is successful in improving subordinate performance or satisfaction. When a positive relationship is found, the usual tendency has been to interpret this finding to mean "the more participation, the better." This conclusion is not justified by the research methodology used in these studies. Most of the correlational studies define participation as the overall amount of influence allowed subordinates in decision making, without any concern for the particular mix of decision procedures used by each leader. As noted earlier in this chapter, any composite participation score is an oversimplification that masks important differences in actual leader behavior.

The experimental studies also show little concern for comparing different participative procedures. In most experiments, leaders in the high-participation condition are instructed to use a participative procedure for making certain kinds of decisions, while other decisions are made as they were before the study. In some studies, participation means consultation, whereas in other studies it means a group decision or delegation. The definition of "low participation" also varies. In some studies it is a form of autocratic decision, and in other studies it is a form of consultation.

Hardly any correlational or experimental studies have examined the effect of the pattern of decision procedures used in relation to the different kinds of decisions a leader must make. Some decisions are best made in an autocratic manner, some are best made by consultation, some are best made jointly, and some are best delegated to individual subordinates. Studies that merely test the effect of increased participation seldom consider whether the participative procedures selected are appropriate for the decisions made. When a particular participative procedure is used in an experiment and found to be unsuccessful, this does not mean that all other participative procedures would be unsuccessful, or that the same procedure would be unsuccessful for other kinds of decisions made by the leader. For example, in a study that finds no difference in effectiveness between autocratic decision making and group decision making, it may be that consultation would have proven superior to either of these decision procedures. Group decision making may have been superior to autocratic decisions, or vice versa, for a different set of decisions than those selected. Most prior research on participation simply doesn't answer the most relevant question about it, namely, "When is each decision procedure appropriate?" The Vroom and Yetton (1973) normative model of leadership was formulated to suggest an answer to this question.

THE VROOM AND YETTON MODEL OF DECISION PARTICIPATION

The importance of using decision procedures that are appropriate for the situation has been recognized for some time. In an article published in 1958, Tannenbaum and Schmidt noted that a leader's choice of decision procedures reflects forces in the leader, forces in the subordinates, and forces in the situation. Maier (1963) pointed out the need for leaders to consider both the quality requirements of a decision and the likelihood of subordinate acceptance before choosing a decision procedure. Vroom and Yetton (1973) build upon these earlier approaches, but go further in specifying which decision procedures will be most effective in each of several specific decision situations.

Decision Acceptance and Quality

The Vroom and Yetton model is based on an analysis of how a leader's decision behavior affects decision quality and subordinate acceptance of the decision. These are intervening variables that jointly affect group performance. "Decision acceptance" is the degree of subordinate commitment to implement a decision effectively. In some cases, subordinates will be highly motivated to implement a decision, regardless of whether they have any influence in making it. This is likely to be true when the leader has substantial personal and position power. However, there are many situations where subordinates will not accept an autocratic decision. For example, subordinates may resent not being consulted, they may not understand the reasons for the leader's decision, or they may see the decision as detrimental to their interests. A decision consistent with subordinate preferences is more likely to be made if the leader allows subordinates to participate in the decision making. Moreover, as we saw earlier, if subordinates have considerable influence in making a decision, they will tend to perceive it to be "their decision" and will be more motivated to implement it successfully.

"Decision quality" refers to the objective aspects of a decision that affect group performance, aside from any effects mediated by subordinate acceptance of the decision. A high-quality decision is one where the best available alternative is chosen. For example, an efficient work procedure is selected instead of less efficient alternatives. Decision quality is important when there is a great deal of variability among alternatives, and the decision has important consequences for group performance. When all of the available alternatives are approximately equal in desirability, or when the decision involves a trivial matter, then decision quality is not important. Examples of task decisions that usually have important consequences for group performance include the determination of performance goals and priorities, the assignment of tasks to subordinates who differ in ability, the determination of work procedures, the formulation of strategic plans, and the determination of ways to solve technical problems in the work. When decision quality is important and subordinates have relevant information that the leader does not possess, then a decision procedure that provides for subordinate input into the decision will lead to better decisions.

Decision Procedures

Vroom and Yetton identify five decision procedures that can be used to make decisions involving some or all of the leader's immediate subordinates. These procedures include two varieties of autocratic decision (AI and AII), two varieties of consultation (CI and CII), and joint decision making by leader and subordinates (GII). Each of these decision procedures is defined as follows (Vroom & Yetton, 1973; p. 13):

AI. You solve the problem or make the decision yourself, using information available to you at the time.

AII. You obtain the necessary information from your subordinates, then decide the solution to the problem yourself. You may or may not tell your subordinates what the problem is in getting the information from them. The role played by your subordinates in making the decision is clearly one of providing necessary information to you, rather than generating or evaluating alternative solutions.

CI. You share the problem with the relevant subordinates individually, getting their ideas and suggestions without bringing them together as a group. Then you make the decision, which may or may not reflect your subordinates' influence.

CII. You share the problem with your subordinates as a group, obtaining their collective ideas and suggestions. Then you make the decision, which may or may not reflect your subordinates' influence.

GII. You share the problem with your subordinates as a group. Together you generate and evaluate alternatives and attempt to reach agreement (consensus) on a solution. Your role is much like that of chairman. You do not try to influence the group to adopt "your" solution, and you are willing to accept and implement any solution which has the support of the entire group.

Rules for Determining Optimal Decision Procedures

According to the Vroom and Yetton model, the effectiveness of a decision procedure depends upon a number of aspects of the situation. These include the importance of decision quality and acceptance, the amount of relevant information possessed by the leader and by subordinates, the likelihood that subordinates will accept an autocratic decision, the likelihood that subordinates will cooperate in trying to make a good decision if allowed to participate, and the amount of disagreement among subordinates with respect to their preferred alternatives. The model provides a set of rules for determining what decision procedures should be avoided by the leader in a given situation because decision quality or acceptance would be risked. These rules are shown in Table 8–3.

Vroom and Yetton have developed some decision process flow charts to simplify the application of the rules. One of these charts is shown in Figure 8-4. The rules are presented pictorially in the form of a decision tree. To use the chart, you start at the left side and ask yourself question A. If the answer is no, you then ask yourself question D,

TABLE 8-3
Rules Underlying the Vroom and Yetton Model

RULES TO PROTECT THE QUALITY OF THE DECISION

1. *The Leader Information Rule*
   If the quality of the decision is important and the leader does not possess enough information or expertise to solve the problem by himself, then AI is eliminated from the feasible set.

2. *The Goal Congruence Rule*
   If the quality of the decision is important and subordinates are not likely to pursue the organization goals in their efforts to solve this problem, then GII is eliminated from the feasible set.

3. *The Unstructured Problem Rule*
   In decisions in which the quality of the decision is important, if the leader lacks the necessary information or expertise to solve the problem by himself, and if the problem is unstructured, the method of solving the problem should provide for interaction among subordinates likely to possess relevant information. Accordingly, AI, AII, and CI are eliminated from the feasible set.

RULES TO PROTECT THE ACCEPTANCE OF THE DECISION

4. *The Acceptance Rule*
   If the acceptance of the decision by subordinates is critical to effective implementation and if it is not certain that an autocratic decision will be accepted, AI and AII are eliminated from the feasible set.

5. *The Conflict Rule*
   If the acceptance of the decision is critical, an autocratic decision is not certain to be accepted and disagreement among subordinates in methods of attaining the organizational goal is likely, the methods used in solving the problem should enable those in disagreement to resolve their differences with full knowledge of the problem. Accordingly, under these conditions, AI, AII, and CI, which permit no interaction among subordinates and therefore provide no opportunity for those in conflict to resolve their differences, are eliminated from the feasible set. Their use runs the risk of leaving some of the subordinates with less than the needed commitment to the final decision.

6. *The Fairness Rule*
   If the quality of the decision is unimportant but acceptance of the decision is critical and not certain to result from an autocratic decision, it is important that the decision process used generate the needed acceptance. The decision process used should permit the subordinates to interact with one another and negotiate over the fair method of resolving any differences with full responsibility on them for determining what is fair and equitable. Accordingly, under these circumstances, AI, AII, CI and CII are eliminated from the feasible set.

7. *The Acceptance Priority Rule*
   If acceptance is critical, not certain to result from an autocratic decision, and if subordinates are motivated to pursue the organizational goals represented in the problem, then methods that provide

TABLE 8-3 (continued)

equal partnership in the decision-making process can provide greater acceptance without risking decision quality. Accordingly, AI, AII, CI and CII are eliminated from the feasible set.

SOURCE: V. H. Vroom and A. G. Jago, "On the Validity of the Vroom-Yetton Model." *Journal of Applied Psychology*, 1978, 63, 151–62. Copyright © 1978 by the American Psychological Association. Reprinted by permission.

but if the answer to A was yes, you then ask yourself question B. In other words, you proceed through the decision tree in accordance with your answers until a terminal point is reached. The terminal point indicates which decision procedures are feasible for the decision situation described by your answers to the questions.

For some types of decision situations, the model prescribes more than one feasible decision procedure. In this case, the choice among procedures should be based on other considerations such as time pressure, development of subordinates, and the leader's preferences. Vroom and Yetton have proposed that for decisions involving several subordinates, the amount of time needed to make the decision can be minimized by using the least participative procedure in the feasible set. This additional guideline is based on the finding that less time is usually needed to make an autocratic decision than to make a decision by consultation, and consultation is usually faster than a group decision. Figure 8–5 shows how the model is used in a specific case to select an appropriate decision procedure.

Empirical Evidence for the Model

The Vroom and Yetton model appears to be a promising development in leadership theory. It should be noted, however, that the rules and prescriptions of the model are based on the results of prior research. As yet, there has not been much new research to test the model in its entirety. In one validation study by Vroom and Jago (1978), results were generally supportive of the model. In this study, managers were asked to describe one of their past decisions that was successful, and one that was unsuccessful. By analyzing the conditions under which the decisions were made, the problem type for each decision was identified. The decision procedure used by a manager was compared to the procedure(s) recommended by the model. For decisions judged to be successful, 68 percent were made in accordance with the model, whereas only 22 percent of unsuccessful decisions

FIGURE 8-4

Vroom and Yetton Decision Process Flowchart

A. Does the problem possess a quality requirement?
B. Do I have sufficient information to make a high-quality decision?
C. Is the problem structured?
D. Is acceptance of the decision by subordinates important for effective implementation?
E. If I were to make the decision by myself, am I reasonably certain that it would be accepted by my subordinates?
F. Do subordinates share the organizational goals to be attained in solving this problem?
G. Is conflict among subordinates likely in preferred solutions?

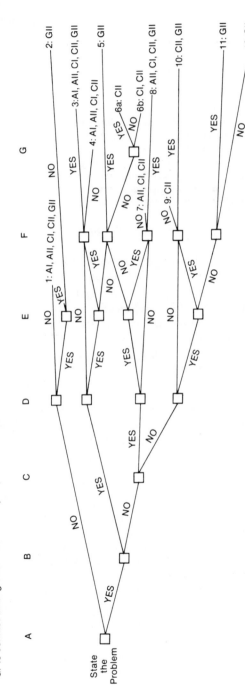

SOURCE: Reprinted, by permission of the publisher, from "Can Leaders Learn to Lead?" V. H. Vroom, *Organizational Dynamics*, Winter 1976, © 1976 by AMACOM, a division of American Management Associations, p. 19. All rights reserved.

DECISION SITUATION

You are a department head with ten subordinates. The company has authorized you to adopt a flexitime schedule with some employees reporting to work earlier than others and leaving earlier. At present, everyone reports to work at the same time. The different arrangements of work schedules possible for your department would not affect the capacity of your subordinates to get the work done. However, you are aware that your subordinates have strong preferences in this matter, and some competition is likely for the "best" times. How would you decide what work schedule to assign to each subordinate?

ANALYSIS BASED ON FIGURE 8-4

Question A (Quality requirement?): NO

Question D (Subordinate acceptance important?):YES

Question E (Is acceptance likely with autocratic decision?):NO

Feasible set of decision procedures: GII

Minimum man-hour solution: GII

Rule violations:

1. AI and AII violate the acceptance rule, the conflict rule, and the fairness rule.
2. CI violates the conflict rule and the fairness rule.
3. CII violates the fairness rule.

were in accordance with the model. Considering the available evidence, it is unlikely that additional research will disconfirm the basic logic of the model, but some refinements or modifications may be necessary.

DELEGATION

As noted earlier, with delegation, the leader has less influence over the decision than he does with any other procedure, and this influence comes primarily from the limitations and guidelines established for the subordinate when the decision is turned over to him. In effect, the leader establishes certain objectives, then allows the subordinate to determine how best to achieve these objectives within specified constraints. The limitations may be communicated in a number of ways, including rules, regulations, standards, policy statements, and direct instructions.

For example, a sales representative may be allowed to negotiate sales within a specified range of prices, quantities, and delivery dates, but cannot exceed these limits without prior approval from the sales manager. The manager could increase delegation further by expanding the limits or by giving the sales representative additional authority, such as the authority to negotiate adjustments for damaged goods and late deliveries.

Reasons for Delegation

Delegation is usually discussed separately from other participative techniques, because it differs from them in important ways. Delegation may be used to improve decision quality and acceptance, but it also serves other purposes not common to consultation and joint decision making. One major purpose is to achieve a more effective division of labor. Decisions may be delegated because the manager responsible for them is overloaded and unable to give the decisions adequate attention. Delegation is also appropriate if a subordinate's job requires quick responses to a changing situation, and the lines of communication do not permit the leader to monitor the situation closely and make rapid adjustments. Since the subordinate is closer to the point of action and has more information than the manager, the subordinate should be able to make better decisions in less time.

Delegation can also be an effective method of management development. When a subordinate is being trained for eventual promotion to the manager's job or one similar to it, the subordinate can be delegated more responsibility for the activities with which he needs to become familiar. Delegation is a form of job enrichment as well as a method of management development. Giving a subordinate more responsibility and authority is a way of making his job more interesting, challenging, and meaningful. Delegation is sometimes necessary to make the job interesting enough to attract and retain competent employees, especially when advancement opportunities in the organization are limited. Giving junior executives more responsibility and authority, with a commensurate increase in salary, reduces the likelihood they will be lured away to other companies in times of stiff competition for managerial talent.

Subordinate Reactions to Delegation

Many subordinates welcome delegation and find it satisfying. However, not all subordinates react favorably to delegation (Solem, 1958). Some persons find it easier to take orders than to make decisions themselves. Persons who lack self-confidence, who fear failure, and who have a low need for achievement and independence are not likely to respond favorably to delegation. Subordinates may also resist delegation of greater responsibility and authority if they are already overburdened with work and lack the information, time, and resources to carry out additional responsibilities effectively (Newman, 1956).

Failure to Delegate

The amount of delegation appropriate for a leader varies greatly, depending on the kind of leader and the situation. In situations where a great deal of delegation is appropriate, failure to delegate can be the cause of serious problems for a manager or administrator. There are a number of reasons why some managers are reluctant to delegate (Terry, 1972).

One reason is lack of confidence in subordinates. "If you want it done right, do it yourself" is an old expression that is still popular. Some leaders avoid delegation because they believe better decisions will be made autocratically or with consultation. In some cases, unwillingness to delegate reflects a fear of being blamed for subordinate mistakes. Delegation is never absolute, because a manager continues to be responsible for the work activities of subordinates. In order to avoid the risk of serious mistakes, a manager may delegate only to one or two trusted subordinates, or not at all. This lack of confidence may become a self-fulfilling prophecy. Subordinates may become apathetic and resentful if their development is stifled by excessive control and direction (Argyris, 1964).

A second reason for lack of adequate delegation is the desire of some managers to maintain absolute control over all aspects of their department's operations. A manager may enjoy the exercise of power and the feeling of being indispensable when subordinates are dependent on him to make all decisions about work procedures, assignments, schedules, task goals, standards, allocation of resources, and so forth.

A third and perhaps more justifiable reason for lack of delegation is that it can cause coordination problems and preclude use of standardization (Strauss & Sayles, 1972). If subordinates have interdependent tasks, they should not make separate decisions about common problems. Here it is appropriate to use a decision procedure that is consistent with the need for coordination. Either a centralized decision by the leader (with or without consultation), or a group decision would be better than delegation for this kind of decision. Even when subordinates are not interdependent in terms of workflow, the leader may find that it is more economical to impose standardization with centralized decisions rather than allowing each subordinate to develop separate procedures or use different equipment and supplies.

Guidelines for Delegating

A number of management writers have proposed guidelines for carrying out delegation effectively (Maier & Thurber, 1969; Newman, 1956; Terry, 1972; Trewatha & Newport, 1978). Important points include the following:

1. Determine how much authority is necessary. After assigning responsiblity for specific activities to a subordinate, a manager should determine how much authority is needed by the subordinate to carry out these responsibilities.

2. Insure subordinate comprehension. When delegating, a manager should make sure that the subordinate clearly understands his new responsibilities and role requirements. Ample time should be allowed to meet with the subordinate to explain new duties, define the scope of responsibility and limits of discretion, and clarify goals and objectives.

3. Obtain subordinate acceptance of responsibilities. The manager should make sure the subordinate explicitly agrees to accept his new responsibility and authority. The manager may find it useful to combine the delegation process with joint decision making on performance goals and career goals for the subordinate, as in many management-by-objectives programs.

4. Monitor subordinate progress. The manager should arrange for regular meetings and reports to monitor subordinate performance in the new role. These checks should be fairly frequent at first, but as the subordinate demonstrates competence and develops confidence, their frequency can be reduced.

5. Provide assistance and psychological support. The manager should provide any necessary assistance to the subordinate, including resources, technical information, coaching, advice, and psychological support (e.g., praise, expression of confidence, encouragement). Need for assistance can be determined from reports, meetings, and observations. During the early learning period, it is important to be supportive rather than critical when a subordinate encounters difficulties or makes mistakes. The manager should be sensitive to the possible problems a subordinate may encounter in handling the new role. A subordinate who needs assistance or support may be unwilling to request it for fear of appearing weak or incompetent.

6. *Discourage excessive dependence.* Some subordinates will try to reduce their doubts and anxieties about their new role by continually asking the manager to review their decisions, or even to make the final choice for them. A manager should avoid development of an overly dependent relationship. When providing assistance and advice, the manager should resist the temptation to reassert domination over the delegated activity. If necessary, a subordinate should be encouraged to act on his own.

Summary

Decision making is one of the most important managerial activities. In making decisions, leaders often consult with other persons, including peers, subordinates, and superiors. Subordinate participation in a leader's decision making can take many forms. There is disagreement about the most suitable typology of decision procedures, but the following four procedures are commonly recognized: autocratic decision, consultation, joint decision, and delegation. The pattern of decision procedures used in relation to different kinds of decisions is more important than the overall amount of subordinate influence as a determinant of leadership effectiveness.

A number of explanations have been proposed for increased subordinate commitment to a decision after participation in making it, but it is not known yet which explanations are most accurate. Controversy remains also about the merits of participation and its applicability to different situations. Research on the effects of participation on subordinate satisfaction and performance has yielded mixed results. Participation often increases subordinate satisfaction, but it does not affect performance in any consistent manner. Participation is most feasible and effective when the leader has authority to make important decisions, there is little pressure for a quick decision, subordinates have relevant knowledge, subordinates are willing to participate and will cooperate in problem solving, the leader has confidence in participative techniques, and the leader has relevant human relations skills.

Vroom and Yetton (1973) formulated a participation model specifying what decision procedures are appropriate in a particular situation. The model rules out certain procedures where their use would jeopardize decision quality or decision acceptance by subordinates. The model is very promising, but more research is needed to validate it in its entirety.

Delegation differs in several ways from other forms of participation. It is a useful procedure for reducing overload on a leader, enriching a subordinate's job, developing subordinate skills, and influencing subordinate commitment. Delegation may or may not increase decision quality and lead to these other benefits, depending on the situation. Despite the potential benefits from delegation, some managers and administrators fail to delegate, due to a lack of confidence in subordinates, desire to retain control, or situational requirements regarding coordination and standardization. A number of guidelines for increasing the effectiveness of delegation were reviewed.

REVIEW AND DISCUSSION QUESTIONS

1. Briefly describe the seven decision procedures identified by Tannenbaum and Schmidt. How does their taxonomy compare to the one proposed by Vroom and Yetton?

2. What are the dangers in trying to label a manager in terms of an overall participation score, as opposed to describing the manager's pattern of decision procedures in relation to different types of decisions he makes?

3. Under what conditions is it advisable for a manager to consult with his boss and with other managers in the organization before making a decision?

4. What are the potential benefits of subordinate participation in making a leader's decisions?

5. What are the possible negative consequences of subordinate participation?

6. Under what conditions is use of participation most likely to be effective?

7. What does the research on participation show? What are the limitations of this research?

8. Briefly explain the essential features of the Vroom–Yetton normative model of decision participation, including the basic logic of the model, the assumptions, the component variables, and the key propositions.

9. How does delegation differ from other participative decision procedures?

10. What advice would you give a leader about effective use of delegation?

11. Define and explain each of the following terms: participation, autocratic decision, consultation, joint decision making, delegation, de facto delegation, decision quality and acceptance, goal congruence.

9

Leadership in Decision-Making Groups

In the preceding chapter, we discussed the conditions under which it is appropriate for a leader to meet with subordinates to make a group decision. Such meetings occur frequently in organizations, especially at higher levels of management. Group decisions are also made by "committees" or "teams" composed of persons who are not in the same organizational subunit and who do not have the same supervisor. Committees and teams may be appropriate when it is necessary to achieve decentralized coordination among different functional subunits in an organization, when power should not be concentrated in a single individual, or when difficult and unpopular decisions need to be made. In general, the reason for establishing committees and holding group meetings is to solve problems and make decisions that cannot be handled as well by a single individual.

The term "conference leader" refers to the person who leads the group in a meeting held to solve problems or make decisions. What leaders should do to make their meetings effective has been the subject of extensive research by behavioral scientists during the last two decades. Consultants and practitioners have also contributed to our accumulation of useful knowledge about effective conference leadership. In this chapter the subject is examined in detail, and guidelines for improving problem solving and decision making by groups will be proposed.

DETERMINANTS OF EFFECTIVE GROUP DECISIONS

When the relevant information necessary to solve a problem is distributed among several persons, a group decision is potentially superior to a decision made by a single individual. However, there are many things that can prevent a group from effectively utilizing its information and achieving its full potential. Whether a group decision is superior to an individual decision depends on the internal group processes that occur during each stage of problem solving and decision making. The extent to which members contribute information and ideas, the clarity of communication, the accuracy of predictions and judgments, the extent to which the discussion proceeds through a logical and orderly sequence, and the manner in which disagreement is resolved will all affect the quality of the group decision. These group processes are influenced by the size and composition of the group, member cohesiveness, status differentials, member knowledge and personality, the immediate environment, and the leader's skill and behavior (Filley, 1970). Let us look more closely at the way each of these determining factors can facilitate or impede group decisions.

Size and Composition of the Group

The size of a decision group can affect group processes in several ways (Shull, et al., 1970). Communication becomes more difficult as the number of members increases, and less time is available for each person to speak. In large groups, it is common for a few talkative and aggressive members to dominate the discussion. The rest of the members are less willing to initiate contributions and tend to feel threatened and dissatisfied. As groups get larger, cliques and coalitions are likely to develop, creating greater potential for conflict. Meetings require more time, and a consensus agreement becomes more difficult to achieve. Clearly, there are some potential disadvantages of meetings with large groups.

On the other hand, some benefits result from increasing group size, at least up to a point. A larger group usually has the advantage of more collective knowledge and a greater variety of perspectives on a problem. Thus, it is a tradeoff between costs and benefits as group size increases, and the trick is to determine what size is optimal in a given situation.

If the leader is able to determine who will attend a particular meeting, he should invite people who have relevant knowledge and people whose participation is necessary to insure effective implementation of the decision. As the size of a group increases beyond eight members, however, the potential contribution of any additional persons should be carefully weighed against the added difficulty of running an effective meeting. Persons who are not needed but who might expect to attend should be tactfully excluded, if possible. If a large group is absolutely necessary, the leader should plan to use subgroups and subcommittees whenever they are feasible (Bradford, 1976).

Group Cohesiveness and Groupthink

Cohesiveness is the degree of mutual affection among members and their attraction to the group. Cohesiveness is a characteristic of the group, but it is dependent on individual characteristics of the members. A group is much more likely to be highly cohesive if its members have similar values, attitudes, and cultural backgrounds.

A high degree of group cohesiveness can be a mixed blessing. A cohesive group is more likely to agree on a decision, but members tend to agree too quickly without a complete, objective evaluation of the alternatives. Members of a cohesive group are less willing to risk social rejection for questioning a majority viewpoint or presenting a dissenting opinion. Consequently, the critical evaluation of ideas is inhibited during decision making, and creativity is reduced during problem solving.

Highly cohesive groups sometimes foster a phenomenon called "groupthink" (Janis, 1972). Groupthink involves certain kinds of illusions and stereotypes that interfere with effective decision making. Members develop an illusion of invulnerability, which is supported by an unfavorable stereotype of outsiders. Critics are ridiculed, and opponents or competitors are underestimated. As a result, the group overestimates the probability that it can attain its objectives with a risky course of action. In the group discussions, any expression of doubts about a preferred but risky alternative is inhibited by "self-censorship" as well as by social pressure from other members.

The group strives to maintain the illusion of internal harmony by avoiding open expression of disagreement. Factual information that doesn't support the preferred alternative is prevented from being seriously considered in the meeting ("mindguarding"), or it is discounted through a process of rationalization. If ethical issues are involved in the decision, the group's illusion of moral superiority makes it easy for them to justify a course of action that would normally be considered unethical by the members.

Groupthink can result in disastrous decisions. Janis (1972) describes some striking examples of horrible groupthink decisions. One of these decisions was the invasion of Cuba at the Bay of Pigs. This decision was made in 1961 by the Kennedy Administration. "The group that deliberated on the Bay of Pigs decision included men of considerable talent. Like the President, all of the main advisors were shrewd thinkers, capable of objective rational analysis, and accustomed to speaking their minds. But collectively they failed to detect the serious flaws in the invasion plans" (p. 19). Not only did the group seriously overestimate the likelihood of overthrowing Castro with only a small brigade of fourteen hundred Cuban exiles, they also ignored the risks involved if the invasion failed. "None of them guessed that the abortive invasion would encourage a military rapprochement between Castro and the Soviet leaders, culminating in a deal to set up installations only ninety miles from the United States shores equipped with nuclear bombs and missiles and manned by more than five thousand Soviet troops, transforming Cuba within eighteen months into a powerful military base of the Soviet Union" (p. 15). If the group had seriously considered such a possibility, they would certainly have rejected the CIA invasion plan as much too risky.

The adverse effects of groupthink can be avoided if the leader is aware of the potential problem and takes steps to increase critical evaluation of alternatives during group decisions. A number of procedures to do this are described later in this chapter.

Status Differentials

When the status differentials in a group are large and obvious, they tend to inhibit information exchange and accurate evaluation of ideas. Low-status members are usually reluctant to criticize or disagree with high-status persons. Moreover, the ideas and opinions of high-status persons have more influence and tend to be evaluated more favorably, even when the basis of their status is irrelevant to the decision problem (Berger, Cohen & Zelditch, 1972; Harvey, 1953). In a group where each member has relevant knowledge and nobody has a monopoly on ideas, it is desirable to minimize the influence of status differences on group decisions.

Member Characteristics

Each member of a group brings to a meeting certain needs, attitudes, values, knowledge, and experience. Some of these characteristics of the members have obvious implications for group processes. We have already seen that the information and knowledge of members is a major determinant of decision quality. Another important determinant is the goal orientation of group members. If the members have personal objectives that are inconsistent with the leader's task objectives, a group decision is unlikely to be successful, because the two parties will be working at cross-purposes. Members may openly promote their point of view in a debate with the leader, but it is more likely that they will become apathetic and uninvolved in the meeting, letting the leader dominate the group decision but later resisting or sabotaging the decision.

The personality traits of group members can also affect group processes and influence the quality of decisions. Certain members may have incompatible personality traits, leading to friction and distrust. Research has shown that groups with compatible members are more productive, especially when agreement is necessary under conditions of time pressure (Liddell & Slocum, 1976; Shutz, 1955). One important aspect of personality is the extent to which members are aggressive and competitive, particularly when they are evaluated on their individual contributions. For example, group members competing for a promotion may try to dominate the discussion in order to appear more knowledgeable and persuasive than other members.

Maturity and emotional stability are also important traits. Groups with a high proportion of immature and neurotic members tend to have more disruptive self-oriented behavior such as attention seeking (e.g., making provocative comments, clowning, bragging, showing off) and domination (e.g., interrupting other members, "shouting them down," threatening to withdraw support to get one's own way). This kind of behavior reduces group effectiveness (Bradford, 1976; Fouriezos, et al., 1950). A leader can ignore such behavior, he can try to suppress it, or he can point out its dysfunctional effects and try to help the person change this behavior pattern.

The Immediate Physical Environment

Meetings occur in a physical environment that helps shape the psychological climate and that indirectly influences group processes (Bradford, 1977; Golde, 1972). One of the most obvious physical factors is the seating arrangement. Some arrangements create psychological separation between the leader and other members, resulting in a climate of stiff formality. Examples are when the leader stands at a lectern, sits behind a desk, or sits at the head of a long rectangular table. A long rectangular table may emphasize status differentials for other members besides the leader if sitting close to the head of the table is based on status (Bradford, 1977; Jay, 1976). This kind of seating arrangement also inhibits conversation among the members if they cannot see each other without leaning inward or moving their chairs outward (Golde, 1972).

A circular arrangement of chairs or a round table is generally considered conducive to open communication and informality. Another good arrangement is to put three rectangular tables in the shape of a

U, with up to nine person seated around the outside of the U. This seating arrangement is appropriate when the leader is using a flip chart, which can be placed at the open end of the U for easy visibility by all members of the group.

A second important aspect of the physical environment is the presence or absence of distractions, such as noise from outside, ringing telephones, and interruptions by the leader's secretary or boss. The leader should try to schedule meetings in a quiet location and plan ways to prevent any interruptions except for emergencies. Visitors, television crews, and reporters should be avoided if their presence is not absolutely necessary.

Quality of Leadership

Assuming that the persons present at the meeting have the knowledge necessary to solve the problems at hand, then the success of the meeting will probably depend more on the quality of conference leadership than on any other single factor. The leadership role can be shared, to some extent, but studies have found that members of decision-making groups usually prefer to have a "take charge" leader who performs many of the essential leadership functions himself. Such leaders tend to have more satisfied and productive groups (Berkowitz, 1953; Schlesinger, Jackson & Butman, 1960). On the other hand, if the leader tries to dominate the discussion with his own ideas ("content control") rather than merely insuring that it proceeds in a systematic manner ("process control"), then the group will be dissatisfied and unproductive. Like any other dominant personality or high-status member, the leader can discourage the contribution of ideas and inhibit critical evaluation of proposals by the group.

Clearly, the job of the conference leader is a difficult one. The group will be ineffective if the leader is either too passive or too domineering. A considerable amount of skill is needed to achieve a delicate balance between these two extremes. The behaviors and procedures used by conference leaders to achieve this balance are discussed in the remaining sections of the chapter.

LEADERSHIP FUNCTIONS IN DECISION GROUPS

As was pointed out in Chapter 5, the most basic way of classifying leadership behavior is to divide it into two broadly defined categories: task-oriented behavior and relationship-oriented behavior. A similar distinction between facilitating problem solving and maintaining interpersonal relations ("group maintenance") can also be applied to leadership behavior in the context of decision-making meetings. Of course, the specific aspects of leadership behavior in each category differ somewhat from those discussed in Chapter 5.

Task-Oriented Behavior

Task-oriented leadership behavior in a group meeting facilitates the systematic communication, evaluation, and analysis of information and ideas, and aids problem solving and decision making. Several writers have proposed typologies of task-oriented behavior (Bales, 1953; Benne & Sheats, 1948; Bradford, 1976; Lord, 1977; Schein, 1969). The following list of categories is a simplified composite based on these earlier typologies.

1. INITIATING–STRUCTURING: to present a problem to the group, to propose an objective and get the group's approval, to introduce a procedure for the group to use in solving a problem or making a decision, to develop an agenda listing topics to be discussed and issues to be decided, to suggest that the group is ready to proceed to a different activity, to direct the discussion back to the task after it has wandered off track, to recess or end the meeting. Some examples of initiating-structuring comments are as follows:

It looks like we are ready to start suggesting solutions.

Why don't we decide first whether to accept the new contract and discuss the other items at the next meeting?

Let's break up into four smaller groups and have each group develop solutions.

2. STIMULATING COMMUNICATION: to seek specific information from group members, to ask members for their opinions, to encourage members to contribute their ideas, to provide specific information yourself. Some examples of comments intended to stimulate communication are as follows:

What are the latest sales figures for product X?

Does anyone know more about this new development?

My survey shows that production costs increased by 20 percent in the last year.

3. CLARIFYING COMMUNICATION: to reduce confusion or clear up a misunderstanding by asking a member to elaborate what he or she has said, by restating in a different way what someone has said, by asking a group member how he interpreted another member's comment, by interpreting ideas and defining terms, or by integrating separate ideas to show how they are related. Some specific examples of comments to clarify communication are as follows:

> *Are you suggesting that we change the amount spent on different advertising media rather than increase the overall budget?*
>
> *Some of us seem to be using the same term in two different ways.*
>
> *I'm not sure that I understand what you mean. Can you give us some specific examples?*

Clarifying is especially important in groups whose members are not proficient in listening skills. Many people try to identify quickly the theme or essence of what is being said, after which the remainder of the message is tuned out as the person formulates a reply or thinks about something else. This kind of listening pattern is often ineffective. It can result in hasty and erroneous initial impressions, and these impressions will tend to persist because the person ignores later information that would otherwise clear up the misunderstanding.

4. SUMMARIZING: to review what has been said or accomplished so far, to review ideas and facts offered during a lengthy period of discussion, to list or post ideas as they are suggested and ask the group to review them. Some specific examples of summarizing comments are as follows:

> *So far we have heard three different ideas of ways to reduce costs. They are . . .*
>
> *We have considered the pros and cons of the first three proposals, but the fourth proposal has not been discussed yet.*
>
> *In the meeting today we agreed that it is desirable to go ahead with the new project. We decided that Bob and John should meet tomorrow to draft the revised proposal, and Linda said she would work on the specifications. We also decided . . .*

Summarizing has several important benefits, including (a) checking and aiding understanding after a complex discussion, (b) avoiding loss of ideas, (c) organizing contributions, (d) assessing progress to maintain interest, (e) keeping a discussion on course, and (f) demonstrating "non-evaluative listening" by the person making the summary (Maier, 1963). Summarizing is especially important at the end of a meeting to insure that members leave with an understanding of what has been decided and what each person is supposed to do next.

5. CONSENSUS TESTING: to check on the amount of agreement among group members with respect to objectives, interpretation of information, evaluation of different alternatives, and readiness to reach a decision. Some specific examples of comments intended to test for consensus include the following:

Are we in agreement that layoffs are the best way to cut labor costs?

Perhaps someone has doubts about the market survey for the new product. Let's check and see if we agree about the meaning of the figures.

There seems to be a feeling that we need to get a lot more information before this issue can be resolved. Are we in agreement with Bill's suggestion to postpone the decision until the next meeting?

The five types of behavior do not exhaust all of the possibilities, but they seem to be the most essential aspects of task-oriented leadership in meetings. Bradford (1976) reminds us that it is not sufficient for a leader simply to engage in these behaviors; a sense of proper timing is also essential. Any specific task-oriented behavior can be useless or even detrimental if it is premature or overdone. For example, summarizing too soon may discourage contribution of additional ideas on a subject. A discussion may be excessively prolonged if the leader keeps on stimulating communication instead of testing for a consensus. It is also important for the leader to have considerable skill in the use of each kind of task-oriented behavior. For example, an unskilled leader who tries to clarify a member's statement may succeed only in creating more confusion. A leader who is unskilled in summarizing may make a summary that leaves out key points and fails to organize contributions in a meaningful way.

Group-Maintenance Functions

Task-oriented leadership behavior in a meeting is essential for group effectiveness, but group-maintenance behavior is also important. Group maintenance includes leadership behavior that increases cohesiveness, improves interpersonal relations, aids resolution of conflict, and satisfies the personal needs of members for acceptance, respect, and involvement. Just as machines need periodic maintenance to keep them running smoothly, so also do human relationships in a group. As with machines, preventative maintenance should be carried out frequently rather than waiting to do corrective maintenance after a serious breakdown. Group maintenance should be an ongoing activity designed to build teamwork and prevent the development of chronic apathy, withdrawal, interpersonal conflict, and power-status struggles. If these problems are allowed to develop, they will disrupt the task-oriented activity in a group and reduce group effectiveness. The following list of group-maintenance behaviors is a simplified, composite typology based on the typologies proposed by earlier writers (Bales, 1953; Benne & Sheats, 1948; Bradford, 1976; Schein, 1969).

1. GATEKEEPING: to regulate and facilitate the participation of group members, to suggest ways of increasing participation, to encourage contributions by quiet members and prevent dominant members from monopolizing the discussion. Some specific examples of gatekeeping comments are as follows:

> *That is an interesting point, Fred. I'd like to hear more about what you have in mind.*

> *We haven't heard anything yet from the production people. It might be helpful to get their reaction to this proposal.*

> *George, why don't you hold off giving us all those technical details until later, so that we can find out what other kind of general approaches the group wants to consider.*

2. HARMONIZING: to smooth over conflict between members or mediate it by suggesting compromises, to reduce tension with humor, to ask members to reconcile their differences in a constructive manner, to discourage personal attacks, insults, and threats. Some specific examples of harmonizing comments are as follows:

> *Let's try to keep personalities out of this discussion.*

> *Let's not allow this difference to be blown out of proportion. We seem to be in agreement on all of the other points.*

> *Is there some way we can combine the best features of both proposals rather than having to make a choice between them?*

3. SUPPORTING: to be friendly and supportive to group members, to be responsive to their needs and feelings, to come to the aid of a member or help the person save face, to show appreciation for the contributions of members. Some specific examples of supporting comments are as follows:

I think your idea is a very creative one, Carol, despite Tom's doubts about its feasibility. Why don't we all try to think of some ways to overcome the limitation that Tom has pointed out?

I would like to express the appreciation of the group for Nancy's special efforts in preparing this report.

You seem very upset about this aspect of the proposal, Joe. I can see how you might have some doubts about it.

4. STANDARD SETTING: to suggest norms and standards of behavior (e.g., objectivity, fairness), to encourage the group to establish norms, to remind the group of norms that it established previously, to point out implicit group norms and check how members really feel about them. Some specific examples of standard-setting comments are the following:

Didn't we agree before not to blame individual members for this problem?

I think we should all agree to be completely candid about our feelings, rather than holding back or making up phony reasons for objecting to a proposal.

I have noticed that the group seems to feel personnel problems should not be discussed in these meetings. Is this a subject that should be avoided all the time?

5. PROCESS ANALYZING: to examine group processes in order to identify process problems and dysfunctional member behavior, to point out process problems to the group, to ask members for their perception of the group meetings (e.g., effectiveness of communication, degree of trust, amount of cooperation, effectiveness of procedures, etc.). Some specific examples of process analyzing are the following:

Let's spend the last fifteen minutes discussing how well the meeting has gone and see if we're satisfied with the new procedure for evaluating alternative proposals.

The group has avoided dealing with the tough issues in this meeting. Why is this happening?

I get the impression that people are not really leveling with each other on this subject. Has communication been as open as it should be?

Some group-maintenance behavior occurs in any meeting, but this aspect of conference leadership is often neglected by leaders unaware of its importance. Standard setting and process analyzing are the aspects of behavior that are least likely to occur, perhaps because they require an explicit recognition of maintenance needs. As in the case of task-oriented behaviors, the group-maintenance behaviors require skill and a sense of proper timing to be performed effectively. Table 9–1 summarizes the objectives of each kind of task-oriented and group-maintenance behavior discussed in this chapter.

TABLE 9–1

Major Types of Leadership Behavior in Decision Groups

Task-Oriented Behavior	Specific Objective
1. Initiating–Structuring	Guide and Sequence Discussion
2. Stimulating Communication	Increase Information Exchange
3. Clarifying Communication	Increase Comprehension
4. Summarizing	Check Understanding and Monitor Progress
5. Consensus Testing	Check on Agreement

Group-Maintenance Behavior	Specific Objective
1. Gatekeeping	Increase and Equalize Participation
2. Harmonizing	Reduce Tension and Hostility
3. Supporting	Prevent Withdrawal
4. Standard Setting	Regulate Behavior
5. Process Analyzing	Discover and Resolve Process Problems

ROLE OF THE CONFERENCE LEADER

Behavioral scientists generally agree that task-oriented behavior and group-maintenance behavior are both essential for the effectiveness of decision groups. However, there is some disagreement about who should perform these functions and about their relative priority. One part of the controversy began when some behavioral scientists proposed that the two functions are basically incompatible and should be performed by separate task and maintenance leaders in each group (e.g., Slater, 1955). Other behavioral scientists took the position that it is best for the designated leader in a group to perform both roles if he or she is capable of doing so (Borgatta, Couch & Bales, 1954). This early controversy has been largely superseded by a debate over whether leaders should perform both kinds of functions alone or encourage group members to share in the responsibility for performing them.

Bradford (1976) suggests that there are two opposing viewpoints regarding the proper role of a decision group leader. He refers to these viewpoints as the "traditional approach" and the "group-centered" approach. A summary comparison of the two approaches is shown in Table 9–2, and each approach is described in more detail in the following sections.

TABLE 9–2
Comparison of Traditional and Group-Centered Leadership

Basis for Comparison	Traditional	Group-Centered
1. Responsibility for Group Effectiveness	Leader Responsible	Responsibility Shared by Group
2. Control over Final Choice	Control Held by Leader	Control Vested in Group
3. Importance of Position Power as Source of Leader Influence	Emphasized and Guarded Carefully	Deemphasized
4. Leader Perceives Group	As Set of Individuals	As Interacting, Collective Entity
5. Task-Oriented Functions	Performed by Leader Only	Shared by Group
6. Group-Maintenance Functions	Not Performed Systematically	Emphasized and Shared by Group
7. Socioemotional Processes and Interactions	Mostly Ignored by Leader	Observed Closely by Leader
8. Expression of Member Needs and Feelings	Discouraged by Leader; Emphasis on Objective Analysis	Encouraged by Leader and Dealt with in Meetings

Based on Bradford, 1976

Traditional Leadership

The traditional view is that leaders should have "the initiative and power to direct, drive, instruct, and control those who follow" (Bradford, 1976; p. 8). This definition of the leader's role points to the following prescriptions:

1. The leader should focus on the task and ignore personal feelings and relationships whenever possible.
2. The leader should seek opinions and try to get agreement but never relinquish the right to make final choices.
3. The leader should stay in control of the group discussion at all times, and should politely but firmly stop disruptive acts and irrelevant discussion.

4. The leader should discourage members from expressing their feelings and should strive to maintain a rational, logical discussion without any emotional outbursts.

5. The leader should guard against threats to his power position in the group and should fight if necessary to maintain his authority.

According to Bradford, this kind of group leadership produces some favorable results, but at an unacceptable price. Meetings are orderly and decisions get made, but members become apathetic and resentful, which leads to a loss of potential contributions and a reduction in quality of decisions. Acceptance of decisions by group members may also be reduced, if members feel manipulated and unable to influence the decisions significantly.

Group-Centered Leadership

Bradford (1976) contends that much better results can be attained by using group-centered leadership in meetings. The group-centered conception of leadership is an outcome of extensive experience with T-groups and process consultation by behavioral scientists associated with the NTL Institute of Applied Behavioral Science, beginning in 1947. According to this view of leadership, the group as a whole must share the responsibility for its effectiveness. Group-maintenance functions are considered to be as important as task-oriented functions, because feelings and interactions profoundly affect the problem-solving and decision-making processes in a group. Performance of both kinds of functions should be shared with the members, because no one person can be sensitive to all of the process problems and needs of the group. Sharing the responsibility for leadership functions will make members more satisfied with the group, according to Bradford. The following prescriptions for leaders are indicated by group-centered leadership:

1. The leader should listen attentively and observe nonverbal cues so as to be aware of member needs, feelings, interactions, and conflict: in doing so, the leader should view the group as a collective entity or social system rather than as merely a collection of individuals.

2. The role of the leader should be to serve as a consultant, advisor, teacher, and facilitator, rather than as a director or manager of the group.

3. The leader should model appropriate leadership behaviors and encourage members to learn to perform these behaviors themselves by imitating him.

4. The leader should establish a climate of approval for expression of feelings as well as ideas.

5. The leader should encourage the group to deal with any maintenance needs and process problems within the context of the regular group meetings. However, the leader should not try to move too quickly in encouraging group self-evaluation.

6. The leader should relinquish control to the group and allow the group to make the final choice in all appropriate kinds of decisions.

Evaluation of the Group-Centered Approach

Bradford (1976) recognizes some difficulties in implementing group-centered leadership. He notes that this kind of leadership requires considerable skill on the part of both the leader and group members, and that this skill is learned gradually. Leaders who are used to the traditional approach may be afraid to risk sharing control with group members or dealing openly with emotional behavior. There may be concern by such leaders that the new approach will make them appear weak or incompetent. Resistance to the new approach may also come from group members who are afraid of dealing openly with emotions or who prefer to avoid assuming more responsibility for leadership functions in the group. The traditional approach is often reinforced by ritual and tradition, which represent additional obstacles to the introduction of group-centered leadership. In some kinds of organizations, decision groups are legally required by their charter or bylaws to follow cumbersome procedural methods such as Robert's Rules of Order.

Despite these many obstacles, Bradford is optimistic about the prospects for successful implementation of group-centered leadership. In his book, he provides examples that show how the new approach has been used effectively in a variety of different kinds of groups. Nevertheless, there remain some questions about the applicability of group-centered leadership. Like other humanistic ideas for improving employee satisfaction (e.g., job enrichment, industrial democracy, participative management), the approach is based on rather optimistic assumptions about human nature. It is doubtful that all groups have members with sufficient maturity and emotional stability to respond favorably to group-centered leadership It is also doubtful that some groups can achieve the high degree of interpersonal skill and sensitivity needed by members to make the approach successful. Many committees are only temporary and do not meet over a long enough time to develop the necessary trust and skills. Other committees are composed of persons who represent competing constituent groups, and these persons may be unwilling to support committee activities that are incompatible with the interests of their constituent group. Still other committees have no real authority or power, and are staffed by unwilling members who are required to fulfill committee duties. In such committees, members usually prefer to meet as seldom as possible and to assume as little responsibility as possible for committee activities.

Group-centered leadership sounds very appealing, and it has been found to be effective in some groups, but further research is needed to determine the limits of its usefulness. This research is likely to indicate the need for a contingency theory of conference leadership. Such a theory would prescribe more sharing of leadership functions in some situations than in others. The contingency approach may also indicate a need to modify the relative priority of task-oriented and group-maintenance functions in different kinds of groups and in different stages of development within the same group.

LEADER FACILITATION OF GROUP PROBLEM SOLVING

Up to now we have discussed conference leadership in terms of general types of behavior that a leader or other group members can use (e.g., clarifying, supporting, etc.). There are also some standardized procedures that can be used by a leader to improve group effectiveness. Some procedures (e.g., agendas) are appropriate for both problem solving and decision making, but certain procedures are relevant only for one or the other of these group processes. Ways to improve problem solving will be discussed first, and ways to improve decision making will be discussed later in the last portion of the chapter.

Preparation of an Agenda

In preparation for a meeting, it is usually advisable to plan an agenda and circulate it two or three days before the meeting (Jay, 1976). If the agenda is circulated too far in advance, it may be forgotten or lost, and if circulated too late, some group members may not have a chance to study it. The agenda can be of help in planning what items to include in the meeting and how much time to devote to each item. The time allocated to each item and the purpose of the item (e.g., "for information," "for discussion," "for decision") can be indicated on the agenda next to the item (Jay, 1976). When there is an important problem to solve or decision to make, it is best to devote an entire meeting to it, rather than try to cram too many items into a single meeting. If there are reports and proposals to be studied by members in preparation for the meeting, they should be circulated in advance with the agenda. Of course, if the information is highly sensitive or confidential, it will sometimes be advisable to present this information at the meeting rather than circulating written reports.

Presentation of the Problem

The first step in a problem-solving meeting is to present the problem to the group. The manner in which the problem is presented can either hinder or facilitate group problem solving (Maier, 1963). A presentation that is vague and ambiguous creates confusion, misunderstanding, and possibly even anxiety. A presentation that implies the group is to blame for the problem stimulates defensiveness. A presentation that implies a favored solution by the leader tends to discourage consideration of other solutions and may engender resentment by group members. Maier (1963, p. 76) offers several recommendations about the way a problem should be presented to the group:

1. Use Situational Terms.   The problem should be stated in situational terms rather than in behavioral terms. Describing the problem in situational terms avoids the implication that certain persons are behaving improperly and is less likely to threaten group members and make them defensive. The leader sounds like he is asking for help in solving a mutual problem rather than making an accusation. Examples of behavioral problem statements and corresponding situational problem statements are as follows:

How can we get people to stop their excessive use of the duplicating machines? (Behavioral)

How can we reduce duplicating expenses? (Situational)

How can we get employees to do more work? (Behavioral)

How can we increase productivity in our department? (Situational)

2. Avoid Suggesting Causes.   The problem statement should not suggest the reasons for the problem or possible solutions to it. This kind of statement would limit the consideration of different problem diagnoses by the group. Instead, the problem statement should be worded in a way that encourages exploration of a variety of causes and a variety of possible solutions. An example of a restrictive problem statement is as follows:

How can we introduce incentives to increase employee productivity?

This problem statement implies that the cause of low productivity is poor motivation, and it also implies that the appropriate solution is use of incentives. A less restrictive problem statement would be the following:

How can we increase employee productivity?

This statement leaves it up to the group to discover the cause of low productivity and generate solutions.

   3. *Invoke mutual interests.*   The problem statement should incorporate mutual interests of group members. Problem solving will be more effective if the members are interested in the problem and perceive that its solution will benefit them as well as the organization. Consider the following examples:

How can we hold down production costs?

How can we protect our jobs by keeping our production costs from rising above those of competitors?

The second problem statement will be more effective with group members who are not initially concerned about holding down production costs, because it indicates how this objective is relevant to their interests.

   4. *Specify only one objective.*   The problem statement should specify only one major objective. Other objectives should be regarded as secondary, and any benefits and costs relevant to these objectives should be treated as positive or negative byproducts of achieving the primary objective. This guideline is intended to facilitate diagnosis of the problem and simplify the evaluation of solutions. Consider the following example:

How can we reduce errors and delays in deliveries to customers?

Two objectives are stated, but it is not clear which one is paramount. It is also unclear whether there is one complex problem or two unrelated ones. It is easier to make an initial problem diagnosis for each objective to see if errors and delays have different and completely unrelated causes, with a need for different kinds of solutions. If a common cause is later found for the two problems, then they can be solved together.

5. Be brief. In most cases, it should be possible to present the problem in no more than five minutes. Conference leaders usually spend too much time introducing the problem before inviting discussion. Long introductions give the impression that the leader is trying to sell his own point of view. Another disadvantage of long introductions is that they usually create confusion and misunderstanding. Too much information at one time "overloads" people, and they are unable to digest all of it. The leader should briefly introduce the problem, then pause, and wait for the group to respond. If the problem statement is not clear, someone will ask questions indicating a lack of understanding. At that point, the leader can make a more detailed description of the problem or call upon an expert member to do so. Sometimes the group will test the leader by asking him what he thinks is the reason for the problem or a likely solution. If this occurs, the leader should point out that the purpose of the meeting is to obtain the group's ideas, not to promote his own.

6. Share essential information. When the problem is presented, essential facts should be reviewed briefly including an indication of how long the problem has been evident, the nature of the problem symptoms, and what if anything has been done about the problem up to that time. The amount of information that should be presented depends on the nature of the problem and on how well informed the group members are already. The leader should be careful to present facts with as little interpretation as possible. For example, if the problem is how to increase sales, it is better simply to review sales figures for each district than to make judgments such as "sales are terrible in the central district." If there are definite constraints on solutions available to the group, such as spending limits or legal restrictions, these should also be mentioned briefly when the problem is presented.

Problem Diagnosis and Solution Generation

After the problem is presented to the group, the next step is to determine the cause of the problem. There are basically two different kinds of problems: "control-deviation problems" and "goal-attainment problems." In a control-deviation problem, the objective is to restore conditions to a previously satisfactory state. For example, some equipment that was operating properly suddenly starts having defective output. The cause of a control-deviation problem is determined by a logical analysis of data on the exact nature of the deviation from normal, satisfactory conditions and the exact timing of the deviations (e.g., when did they start, how often do they occur, how long do they last?). The main reason for holding a meeting to solve a control-deviation problem is that the leader does not have all of the information needed to determine the nature and cause of the problem by himself. In making the problem diagnosis, the leader should have the group follow a systematic procedure to describe the deviation and identify single or multiple changes that occurred prior to the onset of the deviations (Kepner & Tregoe, 1965).

In a goal-attainment problem, a new or higher goal has been established, and the problem is how to attain the goal. The problem is caused by obstacles that prevent the goal from being attained in some easy, obvious manner. The main reason for the meeting is that the leader does not have all of the relevant information about the nature of the problem, and he wants to utilize the collective knowledge of the group to diagnose the problem as well as to generate more creative solutions than he could develop by himself.

As a first step in problem diagnosis for a goal-attainment problem, Maier (1963) recommends the leader should stimulate group members to express different conceptions of the problem. Since a complex problem has many elements to be considered, alternative problem diagnoses help to identify different parts of the problem and suggest different ways of solving it. The leader can initiate a procedure to facilitate idea generation (e.g., brainstorming, nominal group technique), but he should be careful not to express his own ideas about the nature of the problem. In order to avoid dominating and inhibiting the group's thinking, the leader should refrain from offering his own ideas, except, if absolutely necessary, after all other members have presented their ideas. This guideline can be waived, however, if the leader uses a procedure for anonymous idea generation.

Several common errors occur in problem diagnosis, regardless of whether the diagnosis is made by an individual or a group. These common errors include: (1) confusing facts with opinions or assumptions, (2) confusing symptoms with causes, (3) looking for scapegoats to blame, (4) proposing solutions before the problem is clearly understood, (5) defining the problem in a way that implies there is only one solution, (6) defining the problem in a way that implies a choice must be made between two particular solutions, and (7) defining the problem in such a way that it could not possibly be solved without exceeding the discretion and authority of the leader and group. The leader can help the group avoid making these types of errors.

Comparison of alternative problem statements is easier if members are encouraged to provide supporting facts and explain the logic behind their inferences and hypotheses. In making this comparison, it may be possible for the group to agree which problem statement is the most accurate and useful one. However, it is not absolutely necessary for the group to agree on a single problem statement. In some cases, where there is disagreement about the nature of the problem, it is advisable to adjourn the meeting to collect additional information needed to understand the problem. In other cases, where additional information is unnecessary or unavailable, the group can select one problem statement that appears especially promising and consider possible solutions in an effort to make further progress. Sometimes in the course of exploring solutions the understanding of the problem will change (Gordon, 1961).

Some common mistakes made by groups when generating solutions to a problem include the following: (1) discussing what should have been done in the past instead of what can be done in the present, (2) discussing solutions that exceed the discretion and authority of the group, (3) focusing on solutions that have been used in the past without any attempt to create novel solutions, and (4) evaluating solutions as they are generated instead of waiting until after everyone has had an opportunity to suggest solutions. Once again, the leader can help the group avoid making these common mistakes. As in problem diagnosis, the leader should be careful to avoid dominating the discussion of solutions with his own ideas and preferences.

PROCEDURES FOR INCREASING IDEA GENERATION

Creative idea generation is a vital element of problem solving for goal-attainment problems. It is important both for development of alternative problem definitions and for development of potential solutions to the problem. As noted earlier in this chapter, the contribution of ideas by group members can be inhibited in many ways. Much of the problem stems either from domination of the discussion by certain individuals or from members' fears that their ideas will be evaluated unfavorably. Research on problem solving in groups has found that idea generation is less inhibited when it is separated from idea evaluation (Maier & Hoffman, 1960; Maier & Maier, 1957; Maier & Solem, 1952). Based on this and other research, some new procedures have been developed to facilitate idea generation in groups. The procedures are applicable both to problem diagnosis and solution generation.

Brainstorming

Brainstorming is a procedure wherein members are encouraged to suggest any idea about the problem that comes to mind. The ideas are written on a blackboard or flip chart, and no positive or negative evaluation of ideas is permitted, including scowls, groans, sighs, or gestures. Contribution of ideas is supposed to be completely spontaneous, and members are encouraged to build on each other's ideas.

Brainstorming was the first of the new procedures devised to reduce inhibition and facilitate idea generation. It was hoped that inhibition would be reduced by deferring evaluation of ideas, domination would be reduced by making contributions brief and spontaneous, and creativity would be increased by mutual facilitation of ideas and a climate of acceptance for strange and novel ideas. Brainstorming was only partially successful. It is likely to improve idea generation in comparison with a regular interacting group, but some inhibition continues to occur when ideas are initially suggested out loud in a face-to-face meeting.

Nominal Group Technique

The nominal group technique for idea generation was undoubtedly inspired by research that found more and better ideas were generated by a set of persons working separately ("nominal group") than by the same persons (or the same number of persons) working together in an interacting group, even when brainstorming was used (Dunnette, Campbell & Jaastad, 1963; Van de Ven & Delbecq, 1971). The nominal group technique attempts to capitalize on the advantages of both nominal and interacting groups, while avoiding their limitations.

The conditions for a nominal group are simulated by having members first write their ideas on a slip of paper without discussing them. A period of from five to fifteen minutes is usually required to write ideas, and the leader insures that there is no talking during this time. The next step in the procedure recommended by Delbecq, Van de Ven and Gustafson (1975) is a round-robin contribution of ideas. Each member in turn is asked to contribute one of his or her ideas. As an idea is suggested, it is written by the leader on a blackboard or flip chart. No evaluation of ideas or discussion of them is permitted during the posting. As the round robin continues, some members may pass if they have no more ideas differing from those already posted. A person may suggest ideas not on his original list, and members are encouraged to build on each other's ideas. After all ideas are posted, the leader goes down the list of ideas and asks if there are any questions, statements of clarification, or statements of agreement or disagreement regarding the relevance of the ideas to the problem. The procedure is applicable for groups of up to nine persons, but it should not be used in larger groups unless carried out within subgroups (ideas can be combined after the subgroups have finished.).

An alternative approach to the one recommended by Delbecq, et al. (1975) is simply to have members write their ideas, then have the leader post all of the ideas at the same time. To save time in posting, the ideas can be written by members on large sheets of paper, using large printed letters to insure easy readability and the sheets can be taped to the wall of the conference room. After the ideas are posted, they are discussed and additional ideas can be added as they occur to members. The advantage of this procedure over the round-robin procedure is that anonymity of contributors is maintained, which may or may not be important, depending on how sensitive the topic is and how worried members may be that other members will judge them unfavorably for suggesting bizarre, silly, or controversial ideas. A disadvantage is that many of the same ideas are likely to occur on each list. Either the leader will have to merge and simplify the lists before posting, or the group will have to spend some time doing this after all of the original sheets are posted.

Synectics Techniques

Synectics techniques utilize fantasy and analogy to facilitate creativity and encourage new ways of looking at a problem (Gordon, 1961). Some of the techniques can be used by an individual problem solver, but they are more appropriate for use in a diverse group of people who can take advantage of mutual stimulation and acceleration of the "kind of semi-conscious mental activity which might take months of incubation for a single person" (Gordon, 1961; p. 11). Groups can stimulate more daring and psychological risk taking in abandonment of familiar ways of looking at things and temporary suspension of tendencies to organize perception in a rational manner. The primary objective of synectics techniques is to stimulate creativity by overcoming internal inhibitions resulting from normal, rational ways of perceiving and thinking. Inhibition of contributions due to group processes is regarded as a secondary barrier to creative idea generation, and procedures comparable to brainstorming and the nominal group technique are used together with special training to minimize this additional source of inhibition.

According to Prince (1969, 1970), the following steps should be followed in a problem-solving meeting. First, the leader makes a brief statement of the problem. One or more members with specialized knowledge about the problem are asked to provide a more detailed explanation and answer any questions. Then all members are asked to write one or more restatements of the problem as they understand it. In making these problem restatements, members are encouraged to use fantasy and think in terms of wishful goals, regardless of how unrealistic these are. For example, in a group working on the problem of how to "enter the pet food market with an advantage over the competition," some of the problem restatements were as follows (Prince, 1969; p. 102):

Why don't we devise a pet food that makes addicts out of pets?

How can we make pet food that perfectly fits the buyer's image of what the pet needs and loves?

Why can't we devise a pet food that the pet will choose every time in a taste test?

The problem restatements are collected and posted on a blackboard or flip chart.

After the group has had an opportunity to study the problem restatements, the leader selects one of them to focus on initially. No attempt is made to get the group to agree on a single definition of the problem. Prince (1970) argues that it is not only impossible but also undesirable to achieve consensus about the nature of a highly complex problem. Members will naturally view it differently, and once these differences are recorded, they can tolerate the differences and go on to find a solution that will be acceptable to everyone.

The next step is called an "excursion." Its purpose is to get group members to put the problem out of mind temporarily, but at the same time to use imagery and knowledge about other subjects as a source of creative solutions. In one type of excursion, the leader asks for images from some field of natural science and selects a promising example for the group to discuss. Another kind of excursion is generation of two-word phrases that capture the essence of a paradox (e.g., aggressive–surrender, familiar–surprise, disciplined–freedom). A third kind of excursion is a "personal analogy" in which members discuss what it would feel like to be a physical object, such as a tree, wall, or cloud.

The leader next asks members to apply their metaphorical images or their two-word phrases to the problem restatement, regardless of how irrelevant they first appear to be. If this "force fit" is successful, it is considered as a possible solution. A number of fantasy excursions may be necessary to develop a viable set of solutions.

The leader of a synectics group plays an important role, although the leadership can be rotated among group members from meeting to meeting if desired. The leader's role is to insure that appropriate procedures are followed, everyone has an opportunity to participate, members are not put on the defensive, enthusiasm is maintained, communication is effective, and incomplete new ideas are protected and nurtured.

One of the most useful supplementary techniques is to ask members to restate another member's idea and find something worthwhile about it before saying anything critical. If a member points out a deficiency or limitation of another's idea, he is also encouraged to suggest a way to correct the deficiency or overcome the limitation. The emphasis is on careful listening and constructive, helpful behavior. This technique is applicable in any decision group, regardless of whether the other synectics procedures are used. The amount of published research on synectics techniques is quite limited, but the available evidence suggests the techniques can be very effective (Bouchard, 1971).

LEADER FACILITATION OF GROUP DECISIONS

After a set of alternative solutions has been generated by a group, or by a leader acting alone, the alternatives must be evaluated and the best one selected. This process is called "decision making," and as we saw in Chapter 8, it can be carried out either by the leader himself or in a meeting with the group. If the group is involved, it may be asked merely to make a recommendation for the leader to consider ("consultation"), or the group may be allowed to make the final choice ("group decision"). When the group is involved in decision making, the leader should be aware of certain process problems that are likely to reduce group effectiveness. These process problems include: (1) hasty decisions, (2) incomplete participation, (3) polarization, and (4) superficial action planning. In this section of the chapter, each of the process problems will be discussed, and some procedures leaders find useful for avoiding or correcting them will be described.

Hasty Decisions

A "hasty decision" is one made without an adequate evaluation of the available alternatives. We saw earlier in the chapter that highly cohesive groups are likely to agree too quickly because nobody is willing to disagree strongly with other members or to criticize a popular alternative. Even when there are uninhibited critics and dissenters in a group, a strong majority coalition may ram through a decision quickly before the critics have an opportunity to explain its weaknesses and gather support. The pressure of time is another reason for hasty decisions. Such decisions commonly occur when a meeting is about to end, and members desire to resolve matters quickly so they can adjourn and avoid another meeting.

When alternatives are not carefully evaluated, the result is likely to be a poor quality decision. Careful consideration of the possible consequences of each alternative course of action is necessary to identify adverse consequences that were not foreseen when the alternative was proposed. Sometimes the actions taken to solve a problem create new problems that are worse than the original one. When a solution is selected without due consideration to the cost of implementing it, the cost may prove to be greater than the benefits.

There are several things the leader can do to prevent hasty decisions and improve the accuracy of the solution evaluation process. One important step is to plan meetings in which enough time is available to explore adequately the implications and consequences of each alternative. If an important decision is being considered and the meeting must end before an adequate solution evaluation is possible, the leader should try to postpone the decision until another meeting. If it is obvious that more information is needed and an immediate decision is not necessary, the leader may want to adjourn the meeting and arrange for the necessary information to be obtained. If a preliminary evaluation of alternatives reveals that one alternative is strongly favored and has no critics, the leader should try to postpone the decision until a later meeting and assign some group members to investigate further possible weaknesses of this alternative (Janis, 1972).

A number of procedures have been devised to facilitate careful consideration of the positive and negative aspects of each alternative. These procedures are generally useful for solution evaluation, and they are especially appropriate when a cohesive group is reluctant to disagree, or an impatient group is pushing for a quick decision. Some of the procedures are complex, highly sophisticated methods of analyzing quantitative data (e.g., mathematical models, linear programming, nonlinear programming, etc.). Only two, less complex approaches will be described below:

1. Two-column method. This procedure is recommended by Maier (1963) when there is no single solution that is clearly superior to all of the others, and each solution has both positive and negative features. The procedure is feasible only if there are few solutions being considered. If more than four solutions are available, the list should first be reduced, otherwise the procedure will be too time-consuming. Each alternative being evaluated is written on a blackboard or flip chart. Under each alternative, the leader makes two columns and labels one "advantages" and the other "disadvantages." Then the leader asks members to work together as a group in exploring the advantages and disadvantages of each alternative. The alternatives can be discussed one at a time, or they can all be discussed together. The important point is to involve every group member in the identification of both the advantages and the disadvantages of each alternative. The procedure is intended to avoid the usual tendency people have to support their preferred alternative and criticize competing ones. As the group members point out advantages and disadvantages, the leader abbreviates each comment and writes it in the appropriate column. After the posting of comments is completed, objections to any items are considered by the group, and those that lack factual support or are irrelevant can be deleted.

2. Cost-benefit analysis. This procedure is appropriate when the consequences of each alternative are fairly certain, and it is possible to make reasonably accurate estimates of the benefits and costs involved. The analysis consists of identifying benefits and costs in monetary terms, using cost accounting and other quantitative techniques. It is important for the leader to insure that this analysis is as objective as possible. The analysis should be conducted in a systematic manner, and care should be taken to avoid biasing estimates of costs and benefits to support a preferred solution. After the alternatives have all been analyzed, the group selects the best one by using whatever economic criterion seems most appropriate (e.g., maximize net benefit, maximize return on investment, etc.).

Incomplete Participation

Just as group members may be inhibited during problem solving, they may be inhibited about contributing their opinions and knowledge during solution evaluation and choice. Incomplete participation sometimes results in a "false consensus." When some members loudly advocate a particular solution, and other members remain silent or fail to take a position, the silent ones are usually assumed to be in agreement. In fact, silence may indicate dissent rather than agreement. A false consensus will result in a lower quality decision if the inhibited members have important information indicating that the alternative favored by the more vocal members is in fact deficient. This information is likely to be suppressed by members who are afraid to oppose openly the vocal minority, especially if the leader or other high-status persons support the dominant position. A false consensus will also lead to a low level of decision acceptance by members of the "silent majority".

The leader can do much to facilitate complete participation by engaging in appropriate gatekeeping behavior. Each member should be encouraged to contribute to the evaluation of solutions, and members should be discouraged from using social-pressure tactics (e.g., threats, derogatory comments) to intimidate persons who disagree with them. The leader should be careful to continue discussion long enough to provide minority factions with ample opportunity to influence the decision.

The procedure used to make the final choice of the best alternative has important implications for the acceptance of the decision by group members. Two kinds of procedures can be used to insure that members have an equal influence over the final choice.

1. Voting. With this technique, each group member is asked to indicate his or her single preferred choice from among the alternatives being considered. Voting can be done by a show of hands, by going around the group to hear each member's preference, or with a secret written ballot. The secret ballot is appropriate if there is indication that members will be inhibited about expressing their real preference publicly. A voting procedure is easy to use when there are only a few alternatives, but it is not very effective when there are many alternatives. As the number of alternatives increases, it is more and more likely that the votes will be widely distributed among alternatives, without a clear majority or even a strong plurality for any one of them. Rather than go through successive ballots when there are many alternatives, it is better initially to reduce the list by some other procedure besides regular voting. Maier (1963) suggests having each member write his or her three most preferred alternatives on a slip of paper, after which the leader posts the tally for each alternative. In studying decision groups, Maier finds that invariably three or four solutions stand out by getting well over half of the votes, and each group member is likely to have at least one of his preferred choices among them. The list of alternatives can be reduced to these three or four most popular ones, and it is then feasible to make the final choice with a regular voting procedure.

When voting is used with a short list of alternatives, the leader should encourage the group to try to reach a consensus rather than deciding on the basis of a simple majority. A consensus occurs when all members of the group agree that a particular alternative is acceptable to them. This alternative is not necessarily the first choice of every member, but any members who do not regard it as their first choice are willing to accept it and support the group decision (Schein, 1969). A consensus decision usually generates more commitment than a majority decision, but more time is typically needed to make the decision. A group member must feel that he has had ample opportunity to present his point of view before he will be willing to go along with a nonpreferred alternative. A group consensus is not easy to achieve. When the group has a large majority in support of one alternative, but there are still a few dissenters, the leader should carefully weigh the possible benefits of winning them over against the cost of spending additional discussion time. If adequate time has already been devoted to discussion of alternatives, it is usually not worthwhile to prolong the discussion merely to persuade one or two stubborn members. In this situation, the leader should take the initiative and diplomatically declare that a group decision has been reached.

2. *Ranking and ratings.* These procedures are an application of the "nominal group technique" to decision making. The consequences of each alternative solution are discussed by the group, but group members do not openly indicate their perferences among alternatives. Then preference judgments are made privately. When rankings are to be used, Delbecq, et al. (1975) suggest the following procedural steps:

a. The leader posts the alternatives and assigns each a code number.
b. Each member selects his five preferred alternatives and writes the code number of each alternative on a different 3 x 5 card.
c. Each member ranks the alternatives by ordering the cards from most to least preferable, then writes on each card the rank assigned to that alternative (5 is first choice, 1 is fifth choice).
d. The rank scores are tallied by the leader on the blackboard or flip chart.
e. If the group is generally in agreement, the alternative with the highest tally of rank scores is selected as the final choice.
f. If there is substantial disagreement, the group discusses the results and explores reasons why members have different preferences. During the discussion, some members may change their preferences, leading to general agreement.
g. If necessary, a final ballot can be used to determine which alternative has the most support.

A similar procedure is followed if ratings are used instead of rankings. Rather than ranking their five preferred alternatives, the members rate them on a scale of from 0 (least desirable) to 10 (most desirable). Otherwise, the same sequence of steps is followed (Delbecq, et al., 1975).

Polarization

Polarization occurs when group members form two opposing factions, each strongly committed to its own preferred alternative. When this happens, each faction tends to ignore the good features of the opposing position. Discussion is focused on differences between positions while similarities are ignored. As each faction concentrates on attacking the weaknesses of the opposing position, emotional debate replaces objective analysis. Each faction selects different facts or makes a different interpretation of facts to support its own position. Loud arguments are likely to ensue as people struggle to be heard or try to interrupt opposing speakers to refute their arguments. Since members are not listening carefully to opposing speakers, they seldom understand what is being said (Blake, Shepard & Mouton, 1964).

Polarization may lead to a number of undesirable outcomes. One possible outcome is a prolonged stalemate in which the group is unable to reach a decision. Another outcome is a forced decision in which the politically stronger faction imposes its choice on the weaker faction. If this happens, it is unlikely that members of the weaker faction will be committed to implement the decision effectively, and they may try to subvert it or sabotage it. Another possible outcome is that the two factions will agree on a compromise decision. Such compromises are usually only marginally acceptable to either faction, and member commitment to the decision is likely to be weak (Schein, 1969).

Polarization can often be prevented by an alert leader who is sensitive to its early signs. The leader can try to reduce tension and hostility by use of "harmonizing" behavior, such as discouraging derogatory comments, pointing out areas of agreement, and interjecting some humor into the discussion. Misunderstandings due to poor listening can be minimized by restating comments ("clarifying communication") or asking a group member to restate the comment made by someone in the opposing faction. The leader can point out to the group that they appear to be drifting toward polarization and ask them to discuss ways to avoid it ("process analyzing" behavior). When there are rival alternatives and the group is having difficulty reaching agreement, the following specific procedures can be used to prevent polarization or resolve a stalemate:

1. *Posting advantages.* If the group has not already used the two-column method to evaluate alternatives, a variation of this procedure can be helpful for preventing polarization (Maier, 1963). Instead of posting both the advantages and the disadvantages for two competing alternatives, only the advantages are posted. This procedure delays

criticism and requires each member to consider the positive aspects of both alternatives. When negative aspects of each alternative are later considered, they can be restated as positive aspects of the other alternative. The procedure tends to depersonalize the discussion, minimize tension and hostility, and develop an understanding and appreciation of both alternatives. However, the success of the procedure depends greatly on the skill of the leader in using it. The leader plays an important role in getting members to participate actively in development of a supporting case for each alternative, and in preventing intrusion of critical judgments during posting of positive aspects.

2. Solution integration.   The group is encouraged to develop an integrative solution that encompasses the rival solutions, or at least their principal features. One way to begin this procedure is to examine both alternatives closely to identify what features they have in common as well as how they differ. This comparison develops a better understanding and appreciation of the opposing alternative, especially if all group members become actively involved in the discussion. The leader should encourage participation, keep the discussion analytical rather than critical, and post the results of the comparison to provide a visual summary of the similarities and differences.

When members disagree about which alternative is best, it is helpful to determine whether the disagreement is due primarily to different objectives or to a different estimate of consequences. Members may disagree because they do not have the same objectives or priorities, and each faction prefers the alternative most consistent with its own objectives or priorities. Finding a single solution to satisfy different objectives is very difficult, especially if the objectives are essentially incompatible. It is usually necessary to resolve this kind of disagreement by a compromise in which each faction makes some concessions. The process of finding an integrative solution, or at least a good compromise, is facilitated by having members separately rate the importance of each objective being used as a criterion for evaluating the alternatives. The results can be posted by the leader and examined by the group to see how much agreement there is in objectives and priorities. If there is substantial disagreement, a discussion of the reasons for the differences is sometimes helpful in reducing disagreement, or at least in developing a better understanding of why other people feel the way they do.

When members have the same objectives and priorities, but disagree about the likely outcomes of each alternative, the discussion should focus on the reasons for the different estimates. The facts and inferences used in making each estimate about consequences of the alternatives should be reviewed carefully to see if more agreement can be achieved. It is easier to find an integrative solution if the disagreement is over means rather than over objectives. The process of finding an integrative solution requires a return to the use of problem-solving procedures such as those described earlier. In effect, the group is asked to generate either a composite solution using the best features of the rival solutions or a completely new solution that both factions can agree is superior to the initial ones.

   3. Experimentation.   When a group is sharply divided in support of competing alternatives, it is sometimes feasible to conduct a limited test of one or both of them to evaluate their likely consequences. Whether such a test is feasible will depend on time pressures, the cost of experimentation, and the possibility of conducting a limited, reversible trial for either alternative. Experimentation is highly desirable when it is likely to provide accurate information about consequences, and different estimates of the consequences are the primary source of the disagreement over which alternative is better. The most direct procedure is to conduct a limited test of both alternatives simultaneously, then compare the results. It is also possible to use a sequential strategy in which only one alternative is tested initially. If the consequences are satisfactory to both factions, the other alternative does not need to be tested.

   4. Leader decision.   Another way for the leader to resolve a stalemate is to make the final choice himself after carefully considering the ideas and preferences of group members. In effect, the leader reverts to use of "consultation" rather than "group decision making." Some leaders make it clear to group members in advance that this will be done if the group cannot reach agreement in a specified time period. A leader decision is sometimes necessary when a decision needs to be reached quickly, experimentation is not feasible, and other methods of resolving the deadlock are unsuccessful.

Superficial Action Planning

   The final step in decision making is planning how the decision will be implemented. Detailed action steps should be specified, and procedures for monitoring progress should be established. Some good decisions are unsuccessful simply because nobody bothers to see that action plans are made.
   One important part of action planning is what Kepner and Tregoe (1973) call "potential problem analysis." It is the process of anticipat-

ing what may go wrong with the chosen alternative, planning how to prevent undesirable but avoidable events, and planning how to minimize any damage caused by unavoidable events. In their book, Kepner and Tregoe recommend detailed procedures for carrying out a potential problem analysis.

Another important part of action planning is the assignment of responsibility for different tasks involved in implementing the decision. If the group members are going to implement the decision, it is necessary to determine who will be responsible for which tasks. The leader may want to allow group members to select tasks, or he may prefer to make the task assignments himself. If the decision is to be implemented by persons not involved in making it, they may not understand why the decision was made, and the decision may not be implemented in an enthusiastic manner. The best way to avoid this potential problem is to invite some of the persons responsible for implementing the decision to participate in making it. If it is not feasible to involve some of these persons directly, they should at least be informed in detail about the reasons for the decision (Schein, 1969).

Summary

For some kinds of problems, a group decision is potentially superior to a decision made by a single individual such as the leader. However, many things can prevent a group from realizing its potential. Aspects of a group that affect its problem-solving capacity include group size, group cohesiveness, status differentials, member characteristics, and the physical environment. If group members have the knowledge necessary to solve their problem and are motivated to do so, then the success of the group will depend more on the quality of leadership than on any other single factor. The leadership role is a difficult one, because the decision process will be adversely affected if the leader is either too passive or too domineering.

Task-oriented leadership functions in the context of decision groups include: initiating activities, stimulating communication, clarifying communication, summarizing, and consensus testing. Group-maintenance functions include: gatekeeping, harmonizing, providing support, standard setting, and process analyzing. All of the leadership functions require skill and a sense of proper timing to be performed effectively.

Both kinds of leadership behavior appear essential for the success of a decision group, but there is some disagreement about the extent to which these functions should be shared with subordinates. Proponents of what is called "traditional leadership" emphasize the need to direct and control group activities. Proponents of "group-centered leadership" contend that better results are obtained when group-maintenance functions are given equal priority with task-oriented functions, and group members share in carrying out both kinds of leadership. Group-centered leadership sounds appealing, but it requires considerable skill and maturity on the part of both the leader and the group members. Additional research is needed to resolve the controversy and determine if either style of leadership is universally superior, or if the optimal style of conference leadership varies depending on the situation.

Research and the practical experience of group trainers suggests a number of ways to improve group problem solving. Recommended steps include planning for the meeting, circulating an agenda, presentation of the problem in an unbiased way, considering alternative conceptions of the problem, and deferring solution generation until after the problem diagnosis is completed. A number of procedures have been developed to increase idea generation, and these include brainstorming, the nominal group technique, and synectics techniques.

Typical kinds of obstacles encountered by groups during the evaluation and choice of alternatives include: hasty decisions, incomplete participation, polarization, and superficial action planning. There are several techniques a skilled leader can use to deal with these obstacles and improve group decision processes.

REVIEW AND DISCUSSION QUESTIONS

1. How are group decisions affected by the size and composition of the group?

2. What is groupthink, and under what conditions is it most likely to occur?

3. What are the major types of task-oriented leadership behavior in decision groups and the objectives of each behavior?

4. What are the major types of group-maintenance leadership behavior in decision groups and the objectives of each behavior?

5. What is group-centered leadership, and how does it differ from the so-called traditional view of group leaders?

6. What are Maier's recommended steps for presenting a problem to a group?

7. What common errors occur in problem diagnosis by groups?

8. Briefly compare brainstorming, nominal group procedure, and synectics procedures for idea generation.

9. How can a leader help the group avoid hasty decisions?

10. How can a leader deal with polarization in a decision group?

11. Define and explain each of the following terms: groupthink, gatekeeping, process analyzing, agenda, brainstorming, nominal group technique, synectics techniques, polarization, two-column method, cost-benefit analysis, false consensus, solution integration, action planning.

10

Overview and Integration

The field of leadership is presently in a state of ferment and confusion. Some writers (Miner, 1975) question whether leadership is even a useful concept, while other writers argue strongly for its utility (Hunt & Larson, 1975). Some writers doubt that leaders have any substantial influence on the performance of their organization (Pfeffer, 1978), whereas other writers believe an organization's leaders are a major determinant of its success or failure (Katz & Kahn, 1978). Current theories of leadership processes are beset with conceptual weaknesses and lacking strong empirical support. Many hundreds of studies have been conducted on leader traits, power, and behavior as predictors of leadership effectiveness, but for each type of predictor the results have been contradictory and inconclusive. More recent research on situational moderator variables has not lived up to its promise.

The confused state of the field has been lamented by several writers. As early as 1959, in reaction to the lack of success in the trait and behavior approaches, Bennis (1959, p. 259) made the following observation:

> Of all the hazy and confounding areas in social psychology, leadership theory undoubtedly contends for the top nomination. And, ironically, probably more has been written and less known about leadership than about any other topic in the behavioral sciences.

In 1974, after making an extensive review of more than 3,000 leadership studies, Stogdill (1974, p. vii) concluded:

> Four decades of research on leadership have produced a bewildering mass of findings. . . . The endless accumulation of empirical data has not produced an integrated understanding of leadership.

Even more pessimistic was the evaluation made by Salancik, Calder, Rowland, Leblebici, and Conway (1975, p. 81):

> There is perhaps no area of study in organizational behavior which has more blind alleys and less critical knowledge than the area of leadership.

Practitioners and researchers alike have groped for years with such questions as: What is leadership? How does it work? How does one become an effective leader? Yet after many years of investigation, it appears we have no ready useful answers.

INTEGRATING FRAMEWORK AND REVIEW OF MAJOR APPROACHES

In the preceding nine chapters of this book, the major theories and lines of leadership research were examined. In contrast to the cynicism of most other reviewers, there is reason to conclude that substantial progress has been made in developing an understanding of leadership processes and identifying the determinants of leadership effectiveness. The disparity of approaches, the proliferation of terms, the tendency of researchers to concentrate on a narrow aspect of leadership, and the absence of an integrating conceptual framework have created an exaggerated impression of chaos and contradiction. The sheer volume of publications on the subject of leadership is so great that it is "difficult to see the forest for the trees." However, when the sets of variables from different approaches are viewed as parts of a larger network of interacting variables, they appear to be interrelated in a meaningful way. Figure 10–1 provides an integrating framework that encompasses each of the important variable sets discussed in this book, including leader traits, power, behavior, situational variables, intervening variables, and end-result variables.

This conceptual framework builds on recent attempts to catalog the variables essential for understanding leadership effectiveness (Bass & Valenzi, 1974; Barrow, 1977; Halal, 1974; Karmel & Egan, 1976; Melcher, 1977; Stogdill, 1974).

The conceptual framework indicates that leadership effectiveness is determined by a complex interaction among the major sets of variables and can best be understood by considering all types of variables simultaneously. Unfortunately, few researchers and theoreticians have taken a broad perspective of leadership that recognizes the importance of each type of variable. The dominant tendency has been to ignore other types of variables besides those of immediate interest. Consequently, we have little specific knowledge about the precise manner in which the different kinds of variables interact. Until research is carried out to investigate these complex relationships, it will not be possible to develop the sketchy conceptual framework into a full-fledged leadership theory. In the meantime, the best way to see how the different kinds of variables fit together is to find points of convergence in results from different research approaches. Some of the

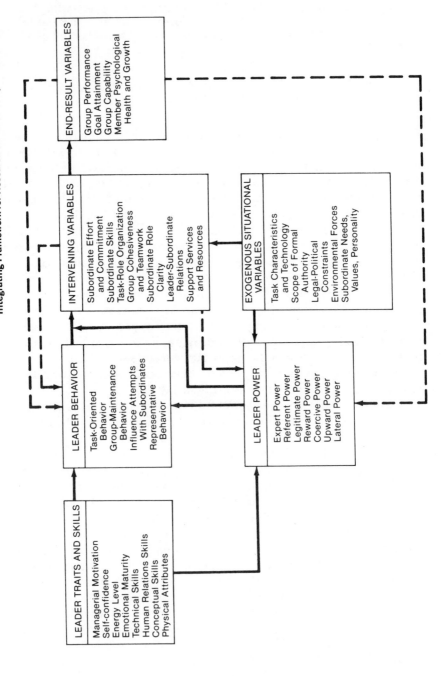

FIGURE 10–1

Integrating Framework for Research on Leadership Effectiveness

LEADER TRAITS AND SKILLS

Managerial Motivation
Self-confidence
Energy Level
Emotional Maturity
Technical Skills
Human Relations Skills
Conceptual Skills
Physical Attributes

LEADER BEHAVIOR

Task-Oriented
Behavior
Group-Maintenance
Behavior
Influence Attempts
With Subordinates
Representative
Behavior

LEADER POWER

Expert Power
Referent Power
Legitimate Power
Reward Power
Coercive Power
Upward Power
Lateral Power

INTERVENING VARIABLES

Subordinate Effort
and Commitment
Subordinate Skills
Task-Role Organization
Group Cohesiveness
and Teamwork
Subordinate Role
Clarity
Leader-Subordinate
Relations
Support Services
and Resources

EXOGENOUS SITUATIONAL
VARIABLES

Task Characteristics
and Technology
Scope of Formal
Authority
Legal-Political
Constraints
Environmental Forces
Subordinate Needs,
Values, Personality

END-RESULT VARIABLES

Group Performance
Goal Attainment
Group Capability
Member Psychological
Health and Growth

more obvious points of convergence will be discussed after a brief review of results found to date in each major research approach.

Power-Influence Approach

The study of reciprocal influence processes between the leader and each follower has been an important line of research for gaining knowledge about emergent leadership and accumulation of power by leaders. Research on the consequences of using different kinds of power and different forms of influence has provided insight into the causes of leadership effectiveness. The amount of research on influence processes is meager, and much remains to be learned. Nevertheless, the results appear to support some important conclusions. One conclusion is that leaders are better off if they have at least a moderate amount of position power, especially the authority to make necessary changes and dispense tangible rewards and benefits. A second finding is that the manner in which power is used largely determines whether it results in enthusiastic commitment, passive compliance, or resistance by followers. Effective leaders usually develop personal power to supplement their position power, and influence is exerted in a subtle, easy fashion that minimizes status differentials and avoids threats to the self-esteem of subordinates. The most effective forms of personal power appear to be the leader's expertise based on demonstrated competence, the leader's attractiveness based on his personal qualities (e.g., character, appearance, charismatic appeal) and loyalty to the leader developed during a history of satisfactory exchange relationships wherein the leader provided benefits to subordinates and treated them in a fair and considerate manner. The leader's capacity to provide tangible benefits and satisfying work roles to subordinates depends on the leader's upward influence in a hierarchical organization. Upward influence can be viewed either as a source of additional position power or as a way of bypassing the constraints of formal authority to get things accomplished.

Trait Approach

The primary focus of the trait approach has been on the implications of various leader attributes for leadership effectiveness, although a limited number of studies have examined the relationship between traits and behavior. The most promising trait predictors of leadership effectiveness are managerial motivation and managerial skills. Effective managers and administrators in large, hierarchical organizations tend to have a strong need for power, a fairly strong need for achievement, and a somewhat weaker need for affiliation. Effective leaders tend to have high self-esteem, energy, maturity, stress tolerance and a favorable attitude toward authority figures. They are inclined to be pragmatic and results oriented, rather than introspective, philosophical or idealistic. Technical skills, conceptual skills and human relations skills are necessary for most leadership roles, but the relative importance of these skills varies from situation to situation. In addition, the optimal mix of specific kinds of conceptual and human relations skills, and the nature of the technical knowledge required by a leader vary from one kind of organization to another.

Behavior Approach

The behavior approach has been concerned with discovering what activities leaders carry out, and with identifying those activities that account for differences between effective and ineffective leaders. Difficulties in the conceptualization and measurement of leadership behavior have impeded progress, and the literature is full of contradictory findings. There is little agreement about what categories of leadership behavior are meaningful, except at the most abstract level of conceptualization. Most writers acknowledge that task-oriented behavior, group-maintenance behavior, and external-representational behavior are generally relevant aspects of leadership behavior, but there is as yet no widely accepted typology of specific behaviors.

It would appear that effective leaders carry out whatever task-related behaviors are essential in their given situation, and these may include such things as planning, organizing, coordinating, setting goals, clarifying subordinate roles, providing skill training, disseminating information, solving technical problems and facilitating work by obtaining necessary supplies and resources. In group meetings, effective leaders use task behaviors that facilitate communication, problem solving and decision making.

In the realm of group-maintenance activities, effective leaders usually establish and maintain favorable relationships with subordinates by acting in a considerate, supportive manner and treating them fairly. Effective leaders also try to maintain group cohesiveness and cooperation at a level appropriate for the situation by engaging in team building and conflict management behavior. In the context of group meetings to make decisions, maintenance behaviors include gatekeeping, harmonizing, supporting, standard setting and process analyzing.

With respect to external representative behavior, observational studies indicate that it is an essential part of the leadership role. Effective leaders usually establish mutually beneficial relationships with peers, superiors, and persons outside of the immediate organization. Representational behavior includes acting as a spokesperson for the group, negotiating on behalf of the group, lobbying for resources, soliciting support and cooperation from other groups, carrying out public relations activities, maintaining contacts with people who are important sources of information, and forming alliances with influential people to promote and defend the group's vital interests.

Attempts by the leader to influence and motivate subordinates directly can be regarded as a fourth general category of leadership behavior. Although influence attempts are generally neglected in research on leadership behavior, there is evidence from several studies that effective leaders provide praise, recognition and tangible rewards to subordinates with outstanding performance. Effective leaders are also more likely to use decision participation and delegation when appropriate to elicit subordinate involvement and commitment.

Situational Approach

The situational approach has been concerned with identifying aspects of the situation that influence a leader's behavior and determine whether it will be effective. Situational theories of leadership effectiveness typically examine the moderating influence of situational variables on the relationship between leader behavior and its consequences. These situational theories are so complex and imprecisely formulated that complete empirical verification has not yet been feasible. Aspects of the situation found to be important in situational research include: task structure, interdependence of subordinate tasks, technology, external workflow dependencies, environmental uncertainty, leader position power, level of management, span of control, centralization, formalization, and subordinate characteristics such as needs, traits, expectations, and competence.

POINTS OF CONVERGENCE IN DIFFERENT APPROACHES

Studies on leader traits, power, and behavior have generated a number of convergent findings. That is, some of the findings from different research approaches are consistent and mutually supportive. In this section, several interesting points of convergence will be examined.

Importance of Task-Relevant Expertise

One theme recurring in findings from different kinds of leadership research is the importance of leader expertise in matters involving group activities. In the research on Social Exchange Theory, task-relevant knowledge and skill in planning and problem solving were determinants of a leader's continuing status and influence over subordinates. Such expertise is the basis for expert power, and it is essential for use of influence forms such as rational faith and rational persuasion. Expertise is an important source of upward and lateral power as well as downward power in hierarchical organizations.

In the trait approach, task-related knowledge, technical skill, intelligence, analytical ability, judgment and originality were found in early studies to predict leadership success to a limited extent. Later research with broad skill categories found the relative importance of technical and conceptual skills varied across situations, but both were essential for most kinds of leaders.

The behavior approach indicated that effective leaders usually organize and structure group activities. Depending on the situation, leaders engage in varying amounts of planning, coordinating, clarifying roles, setting goals, training subordinates, and solving technical problems. These leadership behaviors require considerable technical knowledge about work processes, rules, procedures, equipment, and so on in order to be carried out effectively. Functions like planning, organizing, and coordinating require substantial conceptual skills in addition to technical skill. Research on leadership behavior in decision groups also indicates the importance of technical and conceptual skills. In order to perform functions like structuring the discussion, clarifying communication, and summarizing, the leader needs to be well versed in the technical aspects of the problems discussed by the group.

A final aspect of leader behavior for which task-relevant expertise is important is external representation. Leaders are occasionally required to serve as an expert spokesperson for their group and as a consultant to higher management and other groups in their organization. In order to perform this function effectively, the leader needs a thorough understanding of his group's activities and the technical aspects of his functional specialization.

Importance of Leader–Subordinate Relations

Another recurrent theme is the advantage of establishing generally harmonious and cooperative relationships with subordinates. The research on power indicated the importance of referent power as a source of influence over subordinates. Effective leaders usually have a relationship of trust and mutual loyalty with subordinates. This relationship may be based on the leader's attractiveness and charisma, but in work-oriented organizations referent power is likely to develop gradually over time as a result of social exchange processes. Leaders gain the support and loyalty of subordinates by demonstrating concern, showing trust, providing benefits in an equitable manner, and avoiding forms of influence that cause resentment.

Similar findings are apparent in the research on leader behavior. The extent to which a leader is considerate and supportive in his treatment of subordinates has been shown to be the most important determinant of subordinate satisfaction with the leader. Leaders who are friendly, open, sympathetic, and helpful are more likely to develop favorable relations with subordinates. Consideration does not necessarily imply that a leader is intimate with subordinates, only that he treats them fairly and demonstrates concern for their needs and feelings. It is possible to do this and still maintain some social distance if the leader chooses to do so. Finally, some other aspects of leadership behavior like providing recognition, providing equitable rewards, allowing subordinate participation in decision making when appropriate, reducing role ambiguity and representing group interests in external contacts also contribute to better leader–subordinate relations. The relative importance of different aspects of leader behavior as a determinant of subordinate satisfaction will depend to some extent on the needs and values of subordinates and the kind of role expectations they have for the leader.

Several traits and skills that predict leadership success appear important for developing effective relationships with subordinates. Relevant human relations skills include tact and diplomacy, social insight, empathy for other people's needs and feelings, listening skills, ability to relate to people, and skill in providing counseling and psychological support. Since charismatic leaders are usually able to develop strong support and loyalty among followers, the traits and skills facilitating charismatic leadership are also likely to be relevant, including speaking and acting ability, self-confidence, and insight into follower values, hopes and fears.

Importance of Decision Participation

The primary concern in the earliest studies of participation was with the implications for subordinate motivation and satisfaction. In cases where subordinate commitment is in doubt, participation usually increases the likelihood of commitment, although it doesn't necessarily improve the quality of the decision. The degree of subordinate commitment to the decision is greater when subordinates have a dominant influence over the decision (as in a group decision) than when the final choice rests with the leader (as in consultation). However, both forms of participation tend to increase the amount of reciprocal influence beyond the level existing for leaders who make most decisions in an autocratic manner.

The behavior research includes studies on leadership behavior in the context of meetings in which subordinates participate in diagnosing problems, generating solutions, evaluating solutions, and making decisions. Effective leaders are more likely to carry out any necessary task-oriented and group-maintenance functions in decision-making groups, although these functions can be shared to a certain extent with subordinates. Leader effectiveness is also enhanced if the leader makes appropriate use of procedures developed to avoid or deal with typical problems encountered in decision groups, such as inhibition, deadlocks, "groupthink," and so forth.

Only a few trait studies have been concerned with decision participation, but these studies suggest that certain leader traits predispose a leader to use a greater amount of participation. A leader who perceives people (including subordinates) as generally creative, responsible, mature, and cooperative is more likely to encourage participation than a leader with a negative stereotype of people consisting of the opposite characteristics. A leader who has an extreme need for achievement or an intense desire for absolute power will be inclined to control every aspect of his group's activities and make all important decisions himself. A leader with little task-relevant expertise will find it necessary to consult more with subordinates than a leader with a great deal of expertise. The extent to which participation will contribute to better decisions depends on the leader's skills in selecting and using an appropriate participative procedure. For example, tact and diplomacy seem essential for effective performance of gatekeeping functions, and other human relations skills appear equally relevant. The task-oriented functions of conference leadership appear to require considerable conceptual skill. For example, analytical ability and logical reasoning seem essential for recognizing how the multitude of facts and ideas contributed by group members are interrelated.

Importance of Upward and Lateral Influence

Research on upward and downward leader power indicate the two are related. Without sufficient upward influence to obtain necessary resources, protect group interests, and gain approval for proposed changes, a leader is unlikely to develop an effective exchange relationship with subordinates. A leader will lose status and influence in his own group if he lacks the "clout" to represent them effectively in competition among groups for scarce organizational resources. Leaders gain upward influence if they possess critical knowledge and expertise, perform some vital function for the organization, and cannot easily be replaced. Upward influence also depends on the capacity of the leader's group to perform essential activities effectively. Influence over superiors and peers is developed through a political process, and may be enhanced by forming alliances and coalitions with other parties inside or outside of the organization.

Research on managerial activities shows that managers spend considerable time in interactions with peers and superiors. Many of these interactions involve the leader's representative role wherein the leader is promoting and defending the interests of his group and obtaining necessary information, resources, cooperation, and support. In some of the earliest research on leadership behavior, Likert (see Chapter 5) emphasized the importance of the "linking pin" function, which involves the leader's facilitation of vertical communication, the integration of group activities with the objectives and policies of higher management, and the coordination of subordinate activities with the activities of other groups.

Some of the traits and skills found to be predictive of managerial success in the trait studies are relevant to the effective performance of representative functions. Aspects of managerial motivation like desire to exercise influence, a positive attitude toward authority figures, and a desire to compete with peers seem to be important determinants of a manager's efforts to influence superiors and compete with other groups for limited resources. Technical expertise and human relations skills like persuasive ability, tact and diplomacy, and social insight appear to be important factors determining the success of a manager in upward influence attempts and political gamesmanship.

Importance of Managerial Motivation

The trait research revealed that the motivational pattern of managers in large organizations was an important determinant of managerial success. Managerial motivation appears relevant in several respects. First, a person is unlikely to seek a leadership position unless he has a strong need for power and a strong desire for advancement to a prominent position. Second, a person is unlikely to enjoy being in an administrative position unless he has a high degree of managerial motivation and other relevant traits like self-esteem, stress tolerance, and emotional stability. The hectic pace of managerial work, the stress created by conflicting pressures, the heavy burden of responsibility for the fate of others, and the need to take risks in making critical decisions under uncertainty are typical aspects of an administrative job that many people find intolerable. Such people are likely either to seek a nonadministrative position or to use coping mechanisms that reduce leadership effectiveness (e.g., daydreaming, fixation on trivial duties, avoidance of hard decisions, excessive dependence on superiors).

Managerial motivation is also related to functional leadership behavior and the manner in which a leader exerts influence over subordinates. A leader is more likely to develop subordinate loyalty and dedication to the organization if he has a high need for power tempered by emotional maturity and inhibition. Such a leader is less likely to exercise power in a manipulative, impulsive manner, or to rely on forms of influence that result in passive compliance or resistance rather than commitment to task goals. This type of leader is less autocratic and more willing to use decision participation and delegation when appropriate.

In comparison to leaders with a dominant need for affiliation, the leader with a dominant power need and a relatively high need for achievement is more willing to make necessary but unpopular decisions to dispense rewards contingent on performance, and to administer rules equally without showing favoritism. This kind of leader experiences achievement through leading his group to successful attainment of difficult objectives, rather than through individual performance of some task. His high degree of ambition, initiative, persistence, and energy is more likely to be channeled into necessary leadership behavior such as planning, organizing, coordinating, setting goals, coaching subordinates, initiating improvement programs, and emphasizing performance. These behaviors, in turn, require a substantial degree of technical expertise and conceptual skill to be carried out proficiently.

IMPLICATIONS FOR IMPROVING LEADERSHIP

The knowledge gained from extensive research on leadership effectiveness has important implications for practitioners. This knowledge can be utilized to improve managerial leadership. There are three general approaches for improving leadership: (1) selection, (2) training, and (3) situational engineering. Organizational development interventions may be regarded either as a fourth approach or as a variation of training.

Selection

Use of personnel selection to improve leadership is closely associated with the trait approach and utilizes the findings from trait studies. When there is a vacant leadership position, the necessity of selecting a person to fill the position provides an opportunity to have an impact on the quality of leadership in the organization. The recommended procedure for selecting a qualified person is, first, to analyze the nature of the position to determine what traits and skills are most relevant. Next, candidates for the position are assessed by tests, interviews, and situational exercises to measure the relevant traits and skills. Information about effectiveness of candidates in any prior leadership positions is also useful. Finally, the candidate with the most suitable combination of traits, skills, and prior experience is selected. Assessment centers like those described in Chapter 4 have been quite effective for identifying persons with high potential as a manager or administrator (Huck, 1973). Assessment centers are increasing in popularity and are now used in hundreds of organizations in the United States and in other countries.

Training

Training is the most widely used method for improving leadership. Most large companies have management development programs of one kind of another, and many organizations send their managers to attend outside seminars and workshops. Of the three categories of managerial skills, technical knowledge is most easily increased by training. Special training methods have been developed to facilitate the learning of technical information. These methods include programmed textbooks, teaching machines, computer-aided instruction, equipment simulators, and videotaped demonstrations. Conceptual skills are harder to acquire through short-term training, but specialized training methods have also been developed for this kind of training. Cases and business games are widely used as supplementary methods for learning skills in problem analysis, forecasting, planning, and decision making. Creativity can be enhanced by various forms of specialized training, including instruction in the use of the idea generation techniques discussed in Chapter 9. Descriptions of the training methods mentioned above can be found in most textbooks on training and personnel administration (Goldstein, 1974; Wexley & Yukl, 1977).

Until recently, the effectiveness of human relations training was questioned. The earlier studies evaluating this kind of training failed to find evidence of significant long-term improvement in behavior or performance. However, with the introduction of more effective train-

TABLE 10–1

Selected Leadership Training Experiments with Managers and Independent Criteria of Behavior or Performance

Investigators	Sample Description	N	Design	Type of Training	Criterion	Results
Aronoff & Litwin (1971)	Managers	11 11	T-M C-M	Achievement motive workshop (5 days)	Salary increase & advancement	Trained group was more successful
Boyd & Ellis (1962)	Managers in public utility	42 12 10	T1-M T2-M C-M	T-groups vs. lecture–discussion vs. no training control grp.	Behavior changes observed by peers, boss, subords.	T-groups had more behavior change
Bunker (1965)	Managers and other professionals	229 112	T-M C-M	T-groups	Descriptions by coworkers	Trained group had more behavior change
Burnaska (1976)	GE middle managers	62 62	M-T-M M-C-M	Behavior modeling	1. Observer ratings of interpersonal skill in role play 2. Subordinate ratings	1. Trained group improved, control group did not 2. Few significant changes
Byham, et al. (1976)	Accounting supervisors	8 8	M-T-M M-C-M	Behavior modeling (3 3-hr. sessions)	Ratings of interpersonal skill from subord. interviews	Trained group improved more
Fleishman (1953)	Industrial foremen	90 32	M-T-M M-C-M	Lecture–discussion & role playing (2 wks.)	SBD (subordinates)	No significant, lasting effects
Goldstein & Sorcher (1974)	Industrial foremen in GE	100 100	M-T-M M-C-M	Behavior modeling (10 2-hr. sessions)	Subordinate productivity	Trained group improved
Goodacre (1963)	Tire company managers	400 400	M-T-M M-C-M	Feedback & instruction (6 1½-hr. sessions)	Subordinate report on leader behavior in appraisal interview	Trained group improved more

T = training
M = measurement of criteria
C = control group without training

TABLE 10–1

Selected Leadership Training Experiments with Managers and Independent Criteria of Behavior or Performance

Investigators	Sample Description	N	Design	Type of Training	Criterion	Results
Hand & Slocum (1970, 1972)	Managers in steel plant	21 21	M-T-M M-C-M	Lecture & group exercises (41 hrs.)	1. SBQ (subords.) 2. Ratings by boss	Higher consideration & ratings in trained group
Handyside (1956)	Production supervisors	40 ?	M-T-M M-C-M	Human relations skill training?	1. Productivity 2. Subord. attitudes	Trained group had higher productivity
Jennings (1954)	First-line supervisors	20 20	M-T1-M M-T2-M	Forced leadership method vs. conference method (16 sessions)	Performance ratings	Forced leadership method had improved ratings
Latham & Saari (1979)	Foremen in paper company	20 20	M-T-M M-C-M-T-M	Behavior modeling	1. Knowledge test 2. Ratings by boss 3. Ratings of skill in role play	Training led to impoved skill and higher ratings
Lawshe, et al. (1959)	Supervisors (Study 5)	14 15	M-T-M M-C-M	Role playing	Ratings of skill in test with filmed case	Trained group increased in social sensitivity
Maier (1953)	First-line & middle managers	176 144	T-M C-M	Role playing & lecture (8 hrs.)	Ratings of skill in role-play test	Trained group was better
Mayo & Dubois (1963)	Military officers	211 211	M-T-M M-C-M	Leadership classes (5-wk. school)	Ratings by superiors	Trained group improved more

T = training
M = measurement of criteria
C = control group without training

TABLE 10-1

Selected Leadership Training Experiments with Managers and Independent Criteria of Behavior or Performance

Investigators	Sample Description	N	Design	Type of Training	Criterion	Results
Miles (1965)	High school principals	34 29 148	M-T-M* M-C-M C-M*	T-groups	1. LBDQ (subords.) *2. Perceived behavior change	1. No change 2. Trained group had more behavior change
Miner (1965)	R & D managers	52 49	M-T-M* M-C-M*	Managerial motivation workship	1. Projective test of motivation 2. Advancement over 5-yr. period 3. Rehiring recommendation	Trained managers had stronger managerial motivation and advanced more to higher positions
Moon & Hariton (1958)	Engineering managers at GE	50 ?	T-M C-M	Lecture–discussion & role plays (30 hrs.)	Subordinate ratings of leader behavior	Trained group had improved behavior
Moses & Richie (1976)	Telephone company supervisors	90 93	T-M C-M	Behavior modeling	Ratings of interpersonal skill in role-play test	Trained group was better
Schwartz, et al. (1968)	57 managers in insurance company		M-T-M* C-M*-T-M	Lecture–discussion, role plays (6 days)	1. LBDQ-XII (subords.) *2. Self-reported critical incidents	Trained group better in motivating & developing their subordinates
Smith (1976)	IBM managers (Study 1)	18 13	M-T-M M-C-M	Behavior modeling	Subordinate ratings of boss & of group	Trained group improved more

T = training
M = measurement of criteria
C = control group without training

TABLE 10–1

Selected Leadership Training Experiments with Managers and Independent Criteria of Behavior or Performance

Investigators	Sample Description	N	Design	Type of Training	Criterion	Results
Smith (1976) (continued)	(Study 2)	36 12 12	M-T1-M M-T2-M M-T3-M	Behavior modeling & team building (2 days) vs. behavior modeling vs. lecture–discussion	1. Ratings of communication skills 2. Sales (% of quota)	1. Both modeling groups improved 2. Combined treatment group improved
Stroud (1959)	Supervisors in telephone company	11 11	T-M C-M	Human relations skill training?	1. LBDQ (superiors) 2. Self-reported incidents	Trained group was more considerate
Underwood (1965)		15 15	T-M C-M	T-groups	Descriptions by coworkers	Trained group had more behavior change, but not all of it desirable
Valiquet (1968)	Managers	39	T-M	T-groups	Descriptions by coworkers	Trained group had more behavior change
Wexley & Nemeroff (1975)	Supervisors in large hospital	9 9 9	M-T1-M M-T2-M M-T3-M	Role plays, goal setting, & feedback (2 half-day workshops)	1. LBDQ (subords.) 2. Subordinate absenteeism	1. Feedback & goal setting increased Consideration 2. Decreased absenteeism

T = training
M = measurement of criteria
C = control group without training

ing methods and the accumulation of knowledge about leadership effectiveness, there has been increasing success in human relations training. It is unfortunate that very few management development programs include rigorous procedures for evaluating training effectiveness. A well designed study includes an untrained control group as well as an experimental group of persons receiving training, and some external criterion of behavior change or performance improvement is used. Most of the relatively small number of studies meeting these requirements are summarized in Table 10–1. The studies all evaluate the effects of training in leadership skills or managerial motivation. It is evident from the results that this kind of training can be quite effective for improving managerial skills, altering leadership behavior, and strengthening managerial motivation.

Situational Engineering

The third approach for improving leadership in organizations is situational engineering. Instead of trying to select or train leaders to fit the existing situation, the situation is changed to be more compatible with the leader. Examples of this approach include a change in the organization of work and reporting relationships, an increase or decrease in a manager's authority, and an increase or decrease in a manager's span of control. Changes like these are usually made by the top management of an organization. Fiedler goes a step further by suggesting that lower-level managers can be trained to change some aspects of their own situation. Fiedler, Chemers and Mahar (1976) have developed a programmed textbook to teach leaders how to analyze their situation and change it if necessary in accordance with the prescriptions of Fiedler's Contingency Model of Leadership (see Chapter 6). In several studies evaluating the effects of Fiedler's Leader Match training, improvements in group performance were found (Csoka & Bons, 1978; Fiedler and Mahar 1979a, 1979b; Leister, Borden & Fiedler, 1977). A major limitation of these studies is failure to determine how much situational engineering actually occurred and whether any changes were consistent with Fiedler's model. Other than this research, there has been little effort to evaluate situational engineering, but the approach appears promising.

Organizational Development and Leadership Improvement

Organizational development (OD) programs are designed to improve interpersonal processes in organizations with a variety of interventions by specially trained change agents. Many of these interventions include, as one of their objectives, the improvement of leadership processes. For example, in survey feedback interventions, information about the attitudes and perceptions of subordinates is collected by means of interviews and/or questionnaires. This information is fed back to the manager and is used to identify problems in communication, decision making, and interpersonal relations. The feedback by itself may act as a catalyst for changes in the attitude and behavior of managers, but other forms of intervention are usually included to facilitate the change process. Goal setting, training sessions (e.g., sensitivity training, behavior modeling), team building meetings, process consultation, situational engineering, and career counseling are types of interventions likely to contribute to the effectiveness of a broadly conceived OD program. The reader is referred to books on organizational development for more information about specific techniques and their effectiveness (French & Bell, 1973; Huse, 1975). Recent studies by Bass (1976), Hegarty (1974), and Nemeroff and Cosentino (1979) demonstrate how a goal-setting and/or feedback intervention can be used to improve the leadership effectiveness of managers.

DIRECTIONS FOR FUTURE RESEARCH

In this book we have reviewed what is known about managerial leadership. Now it is worthwhile to consider where the field should go from here. Trying to provide guidelines for future research is a little like giving detailed directions to someone without knowing his or her destination. It is easier to anticipate what research methods will be useful than to forecast the most productive line of inquiry, but both will be attempted.

Knowledge Gaps

One source of ideas for future research is examination of the gaps in our present knowledge about the sets of variables in Figure 10-1. The first place to start is with the variable sets themselves. Despite increasing attention to situational variables in the last decade, only a limited variety of situational variables has been examined in most of the research. The range of end-result variables used in leadership research has also been quite limited. Most studies have used subordinate satisfaction, ratings of leader effectiveness by superiors, or objective measures of group performance. As pointed out in Chapter 1, other end-result variables are also relevant.

Intervening variables have received very little attention in the leadership research, despite attempts by some writers to make a case for their necessity in understanding leadership effectiveness (Likert, 1961; Yukl, 1971). The intervening variables are especially useful as indicators of leader effectiveness in situations where there are no accurate measures of end-result variables. In the rare instances where intervening variables were included in leadership research, the variety of these variables has been quite limited. There is need for more research to examine the effect of leaders on observable subordinate behavior, on subordinate perception and interpretation of events, on group cohesiveness and teamwork, on group problem-solving processes, and on subordinate commitment, compliance, and resistance in reaction to influence attempts by the leader. Finally, the feedback effects of intervening variables on leader perception and behavior has received inadequate attention due to the predominant emphasis on forward-acting, unidirectional causation.

With respect to leader power, traits, and behavior, most of the research effort has been devoted to the latter two variable sets. Despite the centrality of influence processes in the definition of leadership, relatively little attention has been paid to the manner in which leaders influence subordinates. Much remains to be learned about the dynamics of reciprocal influence processes and the consequences of having and using different forms of power.

Even within the trait and behavior approaches, many questions remain unanswered. Managerial motivation appears important for leaders in large, bureaucratic organizations, but it is unclear whether the same motivational pattern is optimal for other kinds of leadership situations (e.g., legislative leaders, leaders of social movements, leaders of collegial associations). With respect to managerial skills, conceptualization and measurement are still primitive, and very little research has been conducted.

The many hundreds of studies on leadership behavior have provided only limited insight into what leaders do and why they are or are not effective. Much more needs to be learned about the frequency, timing, and content of managerial activities and how these activities are affected by role expectations, the nature of the task, and other aspects of the situation. Improvements are needed in the conceptualization and measurement of leadership behavior, although some recent research on behavior taxonomies is a step in the right direction (e.g., Mintzberg, 1973; Yukl & Nemeroff, 1979). Most research on leadership behavior has focused on the leader's behavior toward subordinates, even though an important part of the leadership role is interaction with peers, superiors, and outsiders. Much more research is needed to discover how leaders gain power and exert influence in the competitive arena of organizational politics.

The most obvious gap revealed by the literature review in this book is due to the predominant pattern of narrowly focused studies limited to a single class of predictor variables. Despite the many apparent points of convergence between the trait research, the power research, and the behavior research, few studies include more than one set of variables in the same investigation, and even these studies fall short of the broad perspective required of truly integrative research. To advance the integration of approaches, some studies are needed with a perspective broad enough to encompass leader traits, behavior, influence processes, intervening variables, situational variables, and end-result variables. It is not necessary in a single study to investigate every possible variable in each variable set, but researchers should be aware of variables likely to be relevant to the research question being explored. If some of these variables cannot be measured quantitatively, the researcher should at least make an effort to assess qualitatively how they fit into the leadership process.

Recommended Research Topics

A number of writers have surveyed the state of the field in recent years and made suggestions about specific topics deserving more research. Some of these suggestions are summarized below in the form of questions:

1. How do leader personality, values, and behavior interact with follower personality, values, and behavior? (Stogdill, 1974)
2. How do some persons emerge as leaders and maintain their position when challenged by others? (Stogdill, 1974)
3. To what extent are self-reinforcing cycles involved in reciprocal influence processes, and how does the leader adjust to the situation as well as trying to change it? (Campbell, 1977; Katz & Kahn, 1978; Melcher, 1976)
4. What kinds of reactive behavior occur in the daily routine of leaders, as opposed to the careful, deliberate analysis and rational choice usually assumed to occur? (McCall, 1977)
5. How do leaders influence the organizational environment by using, modifying, ignoring, or circumventing structural mechanisms? (McCall, 1977)
6. How are leadership processes related to organizational variables beyond the immediate group situation, such as technology, environmental uncertainty, organizational climate, formalization, and centralization of authority? (Osborn & Hunt, 1975; McCall, 1977; Melcher, 1975)

7. To what extent do leaders typically vary their behavior across different subordinates and over time as the situation changes? (Dansereau & Dumas, 1977; Evans, 1977)

8. How does charismatic leadership differ from other types of leadership processes, and when does it enhance organizational effectiveness as opposed to being dysfunctional? (Berlew, 1974; House, 1977; McCall & Lombardo, 1978; Sashkin, 1977)

9. How do leadership processes differ when there are multiple leaders (e.g., formal assistant manager, dual managers with joint authority, executive team, informal lieutenant, or key advisor) as opposed to a single leader who deals directly with each subordinate? (McCall & Lombardo, 1978)

10. How do effective leaders obtain and process information and communicate relevant feedback to subordinates? (McCall, 1977)

11. How do leaders plan and make decisions effectively in the midst of their chaotic, fragmented activities? (McCall, Morrison & Hannan, 1978)

12. How do leaders accumulate power through political activities, and how is the use of power related to its enhancement or depletion?

This list is not exhaustive by any means, but it provides a good sense of the concerns writers have about what needs to be studied next in order to gain a better understanding about leadership.

Methodological Issues

Several writers have recently concluded that the lack of faster progress in leadership research is largely attributable to the prevailing methodology. One of the strongest criticisms is overreliance on questionnaires as a source of information about leadership processes. The large majority of leadership studies in the last two decades used questionnaires that measure respondent perception of a leader's behavior rather than the actual behavior. A number of recent studies show responses on these questionnaires are biased by the respondent's stereotypes about people, by knowledge about group performance, and by the wording of the questions themselves (see Chapter 5). Most critics of questionnaires have recommended using observational methods along with questionnaires, or in place of them (Campbell, 1977; Graen & Cashman, 1975; McCall & Lombardo, 1978; Sims, 1979). In general, use of multiple methods of measurement is advisable to avoid the limitations of any single method.

A related criticism concerns "reductionism" (McCall & Lombardo, 1978). We need more descriptive, in-depth observational studies in which researchers seek to comprehend the total system of relationships and processes, rather than trying to break it down into tiny components. McCall and Lombardo (1978, p. 11) propose that researchers "need to get out there and see what is going on, . . . to feel the subtle eddies of events just as the members of the system do." Leadership researchers should make more use of the methods of anthropologists who immerse themselves in a culture over a period of weeks or months in order to learn about its intricate processes.

A third theme running through recent critiques of leadership research is the inadequacy of short-term studies for gathering information about events that unfold over a much longer period of time and involve reciprocal causality (Greene, 1977; Katz & Kahn, 1978; Melcher, 1977). Regardless of whether correlational analysis or experimental manipulation is used, two-way causality cannot be determined without longitudinal research that involves repeated measurement of variables over time. Sophisticated methods for analyzing data from this kind of research are being refined (Eastman, 1976; Emmett, 1976; Heise, 1975; Melcher, 1976; Billings & Wroten, 1978), but the difficulties have not been entirely resolved. At present, the best way to proceed is probably to use a variety of research designs and a variety of analytical methods. Experimental field studies are badly needed, and there is also a place for carefully designed experiments in a laboratory setting. In the latter type of experiments, it is imperative to use a simulation capturing the essential qualities of the leadership situation to which researchers want to generalize their results.

Conclusions

The purpose of this book was to present a review of the leadership literature and take stock of what progress has been made in learning about leadership processes. It is apparent that we know more about leadership effectiveness than is commonly realized. However, the development of the field has been much slower than would be expected from the large number of studies conducted and the great amount of effort expended. With such a vital subject as this, it is imperative that we begin to do better. By improving the quality of leadership research, there are good prospects for extending our knowledge and making rapid progress in the coming years.

REVIEW AND DISCUSSION QUESTIONS

1. Some writers have asserted that we know hardly anything about leadership. Evaluate this assertion.

2. What methodological weaknesses have prevented better progress in leadership research?

3. What are some points of convergence among the trait, behavior, and power-influence approaches to leadership, according to the chapter?

4. Can you think of some additional points of convergence among different lines of research described in this book?

5. What are some major gaps in our knowledge about leadership?

6. Briefly describe three major approaches for improving leadership. Which approach do you think is most promising, and why?

7. What do you think should be the focus of future research on leadership (what subjects should be explored and what research approaches should be used)?

References

Aldag, R.J., and Brief, A.P. *Task design and employee motivation.* Glenview, Illinois: Scott, Foresman, 1979.

Allport, G.W., Vernon, P.E., and Lindzey, G. *A study of values* (Third Edition). Boston: Houghton Mifflin, 1960.

Andersson, B., and Nilsson, S. "Studies in the reliability and validity of the critical incident technique." *Journal of Applied Psychology,* 1964, 48, 398–413.

Anthony, W.P. *Participative management.* Reading, Massachusetts: Addison-Wesley, 1978.

Argyris, C. *Integrating the individual and the organization.* New York: Wiley, 1964.

Argyris, C. "Personality and organization theory revisited." *Administrative Science Quarterly,* 1973, 18, 141–167.

Aronoff, J., and Litwin, G.H. "Achievement motivation training and executive advancement." *Journal of Applied Behavioral Science,* 1971, 7(2), 215–229.

Arvey, R.D., and Ivancevich, J.M. "Punishment in organizations: A review, propositions, and research suggestions." *Academy of Management Review,* 1980, 5, 123–132.

Ashour, A.S. "The contingency model of leadership effectiveness: An evaluation." *Organizational Behavior and Human Performance,* 1973, 9, 339–355.

Ashour, A.S., and England, G. "Subordinates' assigned level of discretion as a function of leader's personality and situational variables." *Journal of Applied Psychology,* 1972, 56, 120–123.

Bachman, J.G. "Faculty satisfaction and the dean's influence: An organizational study of twelve liberal arts colleges." *Journal of Applied Psychology,* 1968, 52, 55–61.

Bachman, J.G., Smith, C.G., and Slesinger, J.A. "Control, performance, and satisfaction: An analysis of structural and individual effects." *Journal of Personality and Social Psychology,* 1966, 4, 127–136.

Bales, R.F. "A set of categories for the analysis of small group interaction." *American Sociological Review,* 1950, 15, 257–263.

Bankhart, C.P., and Lanzetta, J. "Performance and motivation as variables affecting the administration of rewards and punishments." *Representational Research in Social Psychology,* 1970, 1, 1–10.

Barnard, C.I. "A definition of authority." In R.K. Merton, A.P. Gray, B. Hockey, and H.C. Selven (Eds.), *Reader in bureaucracy.* New York : Free Press, 1952.

Barrow, J.C. "Worker performance and task complexity as causal determinants of leader behavior style and flexibility." *Journal of Applied Psychology,* 1976, 61, 433–440.

Barrow, J.C. "The variables of leadership: A review and conceptual framework." *Academy of Management Review,* 1977, 2, 231–251.

Bass, B.M. "A preliminary report on manifest preferences in six cultures for participative management." Technical Report 21, Management Research Center, University of Rochester, 1968.

Bass, B.M. "When planning for others." *Journal of Applied Behavioral Science,* 1970, 6, 151–171.

Bass, B.M. "A systems survey research feedback for management and organizational development." *Journal of Applied Behavioral Science,* 1976, 12, 215–229.

Bass, B.M., and Barrett, G.V. *Man, work, and organizations.* Boston: Allyn & Bacon, 1972.

Bass, B.M., and Valenzi, E.R. "Contingent aspects of effective management styles." In J.G. Hunt and L.L. Larson (Eds.), *Contingent approaches to leadership.* Carbondale: Southern Illinois University Press, 1974.

Bauer, R. "The study of policy formation: An introduction." In R. Bauer and K. Gergen (Eds.), *The study of policy formation.* New York: Free Press, 1968.

Behling, D., and Starke, F.A. "The postulates of expectancy theory." *Academy of Management Journal,* 1973, 16, 373–388.

Benne, K.D., and Sheats, P. "Functional roles of group members." *Journal of Social Issues,* 1948, 2, 42–47.

Bennis, W.G. "Leadership theory and administrative behavior: The problem of authority." *Administrative Science Quarterly*, 1959, 4, 259–260.

Bentz, V.J. "The Sears experience in the investigation, description, and prediction of executive behavior." In F.R. Wickert and D.E. McFarland (Eds.), *Measuring executive effectiveness*. New York: Appleton-Century-Crofts, 1967.

Berger, J., Cohen, B.P., and Zelditch, M. "Status characteristics and social interaction." *American Sociological Review*, 1972, 37, 241–255.

Berkowitz, L. "Sharing leadership in small decision-making groups." *Journal of Abnormal and Social Psychology*, 1953, 48, 231–238.

Berlew, D.E. "Leadership and organizational excitement." In D.A. Kolb, I.M. Rubin, and J.M. McIntyre (Eds.), *Organizational psychology: A book of readings*. Englewood Cliffs, New Jersey: Prentice-Hall, 1974.

Billings, R.S., and Wroten, S.P. "Use of path analysis in industrial–organizational psychology: Criticisms and suggestions." *Journal of Applied Psychology*, 1978, 63, 677–688.

Blake, R.R., and Mouton, J.S. *The managerial grid*. Houston: Gulf Publishing Co., 1964.

Blake, R.R., Shepard, H.A., and Mouton, J.S. *Managing intergroup conflict in industry*. Houston: Gulf Publishing Co., 1964.

Blankenship, L.V., and Miles, R.E. "Organizational structure and managerial decision behavior." *Administrative Science Quarterly*, 1968, 13, 106–120.

Blau, P.M. "Patterns of interaction among a group of officials in a government agency." *Human Relations*, 1954, 7, 337–388.

Blau, P.M. *Bureaucracy in modern society*. New York: Random House, 1956.

Blau, P.M. *Exchange and power in social life*. New York: Wiley, 1974.

Borgotta, E.G., Couch, A.S., and Bales, R.F. "Some findings relevant to the Great Man Theory of leadership." *American Sociological Review*, 1954, 19, 755–759.

Borman, W.C.   *First line supervisor validation study*. Minneapolis: Personnel Decisions, 1973.

Borman, W.C., Dunnette, M.D., and Johnson, P.D.   *Development and evaluation of a behavior-based naval officer performance assessment package*. Minneapolis: Personnel Decisions, 1974.

Bouchard, T.J.   "Whatever happened to brainstorming?" *Journal of Creative Behavior*, 1971, 5, 182–189.

Bowers, D.G.   "Hierarchy, function, and the generalizability of leadership practices." In J.G. Hunt and L.L. Larson (Eds.), *Leadership frontiers*. Kent, Ohio: Kent State University Press, 1975.

Bowers, D.G., and Seashore, S.E.   "Predicting organizational effectiveness with a four-factor theory of leadership." *Administrative Science Quarterly*, 1966, 11, 238–263.

Boyd, J.B., and Ellis, J.D.   *Findings of research into senior management seminars*. Toronto: Hydro-electric Power Commission of Ontario, 1962.

Bradford, L.P.   *Making meetings work*. La Jolla, California: University Associates, 1976.

Bragg, J., and Andrews, I.R.   "Participative decision making: An experimental study in a hospital." *Journal of Applied Behavioral Sciences*, 1973, 9, 727–735.

Brass, D.J., and Oldham, G.R.   "Validating an In-Basket test using an alternative set of leadership scoring dimensions." *Journal of Applied Psychology*, 1976, 61, 652–657.

Bray, D.W., Campbell, R.J., and Grant, D.L.   *Formative years in business: A long term AT&T study of managerial lives*. New York: Wiley, 1974.

Brewer, E., and Tomlinson, J.W.C. "The manager's working day." *Journal of Industrial Ergonomics*, 1964, 12, 191–197.

Brooks, E. "What successful executives do." *Personnel*, 1955, 32, 210–225.

Bunker, D.R. "Individual applications of laboratory training." *Journal of Applied Behavioral Science*, 1965, 1, 131–147.

Burke, W.W. "Leadership behavior as a function of the leader, the follower, and the situation." *Journal of Personality*, 1965, 33, 60–81.

Burnaska, R.F. "The effects of behavior modeling training on managers' behaviors and employee's perceptions." *Personnel Psychology*, 1976, 29, 329–335.

Burns, J.M. *Leadership.* New York: Harper & Row, 1978.

Burns, T. "The directions of activity and communication in a departmental executive group: A quantitative study in a British engineering factory with a self-recording technique." *Human Relations*, 1954, 7, 73–97.

Burns, T. "Management in action." *Operational Research Quarterly*, 1957, 8, 45–60.

Byham, W.C., Adams, D., and Kiggins, A. "Transfer of modeling training to the job." *Personnel Psychology*, 1976, 29, 345–349.

Campbell, J.P. "The cutting edge of leadership: An overview." In J.G. Hunt and L.L. Larson (Eds.), *Leadership: The cutting edge.* Carbondale: Southern Illinois University Press, 1977, p. 221–246.

Campbell, J.P., Dunnette, M.D., Arvey, R.D., and Hellervik, L.W. "The development and evaluation of behaviorally based rating scales." *Journal of Applied Psychology*, 1973, 57, 15–22.

Campbell, J.P., Dunnette, M.D., Lawler, E.E., and Weick, K.E., Jr. *Managerial behavior, performance, and effectiveness.* New York: McGraw-Hill, 1970.

Carlson, S. *Executive behavior.* Stockholm: Strombergs, 1951.

Cartwright, D. "Leadership, influence, and control." In J.G. March (Ed.), *Handbook of organizations.* Chicago: Rand McNally, 1965.

Cashman, J., Dansereau, F., Jr., Graen, G., and Haga, W.J. "Organizational understructure and leadership: A longitudinal investigation of the managerial role-making process." *Organizational Behavior and Human Performance*, 1976 15, 278–296.

Chemers, M.M., and Skrzypek, G.J. "An experimental test of the contingency model of leadership effectiveness." *Journal of Personality and Social Psychology*, 1972, 24, 172–177.

Clark, R.D. "Group induced shift toward risk." *Psychological Bulletin*, 1971, 76, 251–270.

Coch, L., and French, J.R.P., Jr. "Overcoming resistance to change." *Human Relations*, 1948, 1, 512–532.

Cohen, M.D., and March, J.G.   *Leadership and ambiguity.* New York: McGraw-Hill, 1974.

Collins, O.F., Moore, D.G., and Unwalla, D.B.   *The enterprising man.* East Lansing: Bureau of Business and Economic Research, Michigan State University, 1964.

Comrey, A.L., Pfiffner, J.M., and High, W.S.   *Factors influencing organizational effectiveness: A final report.* Los Angeles: University of Southern California, Technical Report, 1954.

Crowe, B.J., Bochner, S., and Clark, A.W.   "The effects of subordinates' behavior on managerial style." *Human Relations,* 1972, 25, 215–237.

Csoka, L.S., and Bons, P.M.   "Manipulating the situation to fit the lender's style: Two validation studies of Leader Match." *Journal of Applied Psychology,* 1978, 63, 295–300.

Cummin, P.C.   "TAT correlates of executive performance." *Journal of Applied Psychology,* 1967, 51, 78–81.

Curtis, B., Smith, R.E., and Smoll, F.L.   "Scrutinizing the skipper: A study of leadership behavior in the dugout." *Journal of Applied Psychology,* 1979, 64, 391–400.

Dahl, R.A.   "The concept of power." *Behavioral Science,* 1957, 2, 201–218.

Dahl, T., and Lewis, D.R.   "Random sampling device used in time management study." *Evaluation,* 1975, 2(2), 20–22.

Dale, E.   "Management must be made accountable." *Harvard Business Review,* 1960, 38, (March–April). 49–59.

Dale, E., and Urwick, L.F.   *Staff in organization.* New York: McGraw-Hill, 1960.

Dalton, M.   "Conflicts between staff and line managerial officers." *American Sociological Review,* 1950, 15, 342–351.

Dansereau, F., Jr., and Dumas, M.   "Pratfalls and pitfalls in drawing inferences about leader behavior." In J.G. Hunt and L.L. Larson (Eds.), *Leadership: The cutting edge.* Carbondale: Southern Illinois University Press, 1977.

Dansereau, F., Jr., Graen, G., and Haga, W.J.   "A vertical dyad linkage approach to leadership within formal organizations: A longitudinal investigation of the role making process." *Organizational Behavior and Human Performance,* 1975, 13, 46–78.

Davis, K. "Attitudes toward the legitimacy of management efforts to influence employees." *Academy of Management Journal*, 1968, 11, 153–162.

Dawson, J.E., Messe, L.A., and Phillips, J.L. "Effect of instructor-leader behavior on student performance." *Journal of Applied Psychology*, 1972, 56, 369–376.

Day, R.C. "Some effects of combining close, punitive, and supportive styles of supervision." *Sociometry*, 1971, 34, 303–327.

Day, R.C., and Hamblin, R.L. "Some effects of close and punitive styles of supervision." *American Journal of Sociology*, 1964, 69, 499–510.

Delbecq, A.L. "Managerial leadership styles in problem solving conferences." *Academy of Management Journal*, 1965, 8, 32–44.

Delbecq, A.L., Van de Ven, A.H., and Gustafson, D.H. *Group techniques for program planning: A guide to nominal and delphi processes*. Glenview, Illinois: Scott, Foresman, 1975.

Donley, R.E., and Winter, D.G. "Measuring the motives of public officials at a distance: An exploratory study of American presidents." *Behavioral Science*, 1970, 15, 227–236.

Dossett, D.L., Latham, G.P., and Mitchell, T.R. "The effects of assigned versus participatively set goals, KOR, and individual differences in employee behavior when goal difficulty is held constant." *Journal of Applied Psychology*, 1979, 64, 291–298.

Dubin, R., and Spray, S.L. "Executive behavior and interaction." *Industrial Relations*, 1964, 3, 99–108.

Dubrin, A.J. *Human relations: A job oriented approach*. Reston, Virginia: Reston Publishing Co., 1978.

Dunne, E.J., Jr., Stahl, M.J., and Melhart, L.J., Jr. "Influence sources of project and functional managers in matrix organizations." *Academy of Management Journal*, 1978, 21, 135–139.

Dunnette, M.D. "Multiple assessment procedures in identifying and developing managerial talent." In P. McReynolds (Ed.), *Advances in psychological assessment* (Vol. 2). Palo Alto, California: Science and Behavior Books, 1971.

Dunnette, M.D., Campbell, J., and Jaastad, K. "The effect of group participation on brainstorming effectiveness for two industrial samples." *Journal of Applied Psychology*, 1963, 47, 30–37.

Dutton, J.M., and Walton, R.E. "Interdepartmental conflict and co-operation: Two contrasting studies." *Human Organization,* 1965, 25(3), 207–220.

Dyer, W.G. *Team building: Issues and alternatives.* Reading, Massa-chusetts: Addison-Wesley, 1977.

Eastman, J. "Methods of describing and analyzing dynamic rela-tionships." In L.K. Bragaw and E.K. Winslow (Eds.), *Eastern Acad-emy of Management Proceedings,* 1976.

Eden, D., and Leviatan, U. "Implicit leadership theory as a determi-nant of the factor structure underlying supervisory behavior scales." *Journal of Applied Psychology,* 1975, 60, 736–741.

Emmett, D. "Methods for describing and analyzing dynamic lead-ership." In L.K. Bragaw and E.K. Winslow (Eds.), *Eastern Academy of Management Proceedings,* 1976.

England, G.W. "Personal value systems of American managers." *Academy of Management Journal,* 1967, 10, 53–68.

Etzioni, A. *A comparative analysis of complex organizations.* New York: Free Press, 1961.

Evan, W.M., and Zelditch, M. "A laboratory experiment on bureau-cratic authority." *American Sociological Review,* 1961, 26, 883–893.

Evans, M.G. "The effects of supervisory behavior on the path-goal relationship." *Organizational Behavior and Human Performance,* 1970, 5, 277–298.

Evans, M.G. "Extensions of a path-goal theory of motivation." *Jour-nal of Applied Psychology,* 1974, 59, 172–178.

Evans, M.G. "On the advancement of leadership theory." In J.G. Hunt and L.L. Larson (Eds.), *Leadership: The cutting edge.* Carbon-dale: Southern Illinois University Press, 1977.

Ewing, D.W. *The managerial mind.* New York: Free Press, 1964.

Farris, G.F., and Lim, F.G., Jr. "Effects of performance on leadership, cohesiveness, satisfaction, and subsequent performance." *Journal of Applied Psychology,* 1969, 53, 490–497.

Feldman, H. *Problems in labor relations.* New York: Macmillan, 1937.

Fiedler, F.E. "A contingency model of leadership effectiveness." In L. Berkowitz (Ed.), *Advances in experimental social psychology,* New York: Academic Press, 1964.

Fiedler, F.E.   *A theory of leadership effectiveness.* New York: McGraw-Hill, 1967.

Fiedler, F.E.   "Validation and extension of the contingency model of leadership effectiveness: A review of empirical findings." *Psychological Bulletin,* 1971, 76, 128–148.

Fiedler, F.E.   "Personality, motivational systems, and the behavior of high and low LPC persons." *Human Relations,* 1972, 25, 391–412.

Fiedler, F.E.   "The contingency model: A reply to Ashour." *Organizational Behavior and Human Performance,* 1973, 9, 356–368.

Fiedler, F.E.   "What triggers the person–situation interaction in leadership?" In D. Magnusson and N.S. Endler (Eds.), *Personality at the crossroads: Current issues in interactional psychology.* Hillsdale, N.J.: Lawrence Erlbaum & Associates, Inc., 1977. (A)

Fiedler, F.E.   "A rejoinder to Schriesheim and Kerr's premature obituary of the contingency model." In J.G. Hunt and L.L. Larson (Eds.), *Leadership: The cutting edge.* Carbondale: Southern Illinois University Press, 1977. (B)

Fiedler, F.E.   "The contingency model and the dynamics of the leadership process." In L. Berkowitz (Ed.), *Advances in experimental social psychology.* New York: Academic Press, 1978.

Fiedler, F.E., Chemers, M.M., and Mahar, L.   *Improving leadership effectiveness: The leader match concept.* New York: Wiley, 1976.

Fiedler, F.E., and Mahar, L.   A field experiment validating contingency model leadership training. *Journal of Applied Psychology,* 1979, 64, 247–254. (A)

Fiedler, F.E., and Mahar, L.   The effectiveness of contingency model training: A review of the validation of leader match. *Personnel Psychology,* 1979, 32, 45–62. (B)

Filley, A.C.   "Committee management: Guidelines from social science research." *California Management Review,* 1970, 13(1) 13–21.

Filley, A.C., House, R.J., and Kerr, S.   *Managerial process and organizational behavior.* Glenview, Illinois: Scott, Foresman, 1976.

Flanagan, J.C.   "Defining the requirements of an executive's job." *Personnel,* 1951, 28, 28–35.

Fleishman, E.A.   "The description of supervisory behavior." *Personnel Psychology,* 1953, 37, 1–6. (A)

Fleishman, E.A.   "Leadership climate, human relations training, and supervisory behavior." *Personnel Psychology*, 1953, 6, 205–222. (B)

Fleishman, E.A.   "A leader behavior description for industry." In R.M. Stogdill and A.E. Coons (Eds.), *Leader behavior: Its description and measurement*. Columbus: Bureau of Business Research, Ohio State University, 1957.

Fleishman, E.A.   "Attitude versus skill factors in work group productivity." *Personnel Psychology*, 1965, 18, 253–266.

Fleishman, E.A., and Harris, E.F.   "Patterns of leadership behavior related to employee grievances and turnover." *Personnel Psychology*, 1962, 15, 43–56.

Fleishman, E.A., Harris, E.F., and Burtt, H.E.   *Leadership and supervision in industry*. Columbus: Bureau of Educational Research, Ohio State University, 1955.

Fouriezos, N.T., Hutt, M.L., and Guetzkow, H.   "Measurement of self-oriented needs in discussion groups." *Journal of Abnormal and Social Psychology*, 1950, 45, 682–690.

French, J.R.P.   "Field experiments: Changing group productivity." In J.G. Miller (Ed.), *Experiments in social process*. New York: McGraw-Hill, 1950.

French, J.R.P., Israel, J., and As, D.   "An experiment on participation in a Norwegian factory." *Human Relations*, 1960, 13, 3–19.

French, J.R.P., Kay, E., and Meyer, H.H.   "Participation and the appraisal system." *Human Relations*, 1966, 19, 3–20.

French, J.R.P., and Raven, B.   "The bases of social power." In D. Cartwight (Ed.), *Studies in social power*. Ann Arbor, Michigan: Institute for Social Research, 1959.

French, J.R.P., Jr., and Snyder, R.   "Leadership and interpersonal power." In D. Cartwright (Ed.), *Studies in social power*. Ann Arbor, Michigan: Institute for Social Research, 1959.

French, W.L., and Bell, C.H., Jr.   *Organization development*. Englewood Cliffs, New Jersey: Prentice-Hall, 1973.

Gardner, J.W.   The anti-leadership vaccine. *Annual Report of the Carnegie Corporation of New York*, New York, 1965.

Gellerman, S.W.   "Supervision: Substance and style." *Harvard Business Review*, 1976 (March–April), 89–99.

Georgopoulos, B.S., Mahoney, G.M., and Jones, N.W., Jr. "A path-goal approach to productivity." *Journal of Applied Psychology,* 1957, 41, 345–353.

Ghiselli, E.E. *The validity of occupational aptitude tests.* New York: Wiley, 1966.

Gibb, C. A. "Leadership." In G. Lindzey and E. Aronson (eds.), *The handbook of social psychology.* Reading, Massachusetts: Addison-Wesley, 1954.

Gilmore, D.C., Beehr, T.A., and Richter, D.J. "Effects of leader behavior on subordinate performance and satisfaction: A laboratory experiment with student employees." *Journal of Applied Psychology,* 1979, 64, 166–172.

Golde, R.A. "Are your meetings like this one?" *Harvard Business Review,* 1972, (January–February), 68–77.

Goldner, F.H. "The division of labor: Processes and power." In M.N. Zald (Ed.), *Power in organizations.* Nashville, Tennessee: Vanderbilt University Press, 1970.

Goldstein, A.P., and Sorcher, M. *Changing supervisory behavior.* New York: Pergamon, 1974.

Goldstein, I.I. *Training: Program development and evaluation.* Monterey, California: Brooks/Cole, 1974.

Goodacre, D.M. "Stimulating improved man management." *Personnel,* 1963, 16, 133–143.

Goodstadt, B., and Kipnis, D. "Situational influences on the use of power." *Journal of Applied Psychology,* 1970, 54, 201–207.

Gordon, L.V. *The measurement of interpersonal values.* Chicago: Science Research Associates, 1975.

Gordon, L.V. *Survey of interpersonal values: Revised manual.* Chicago: Science Research Associates, 1976.

Gordon, W.J. *Synectics.* New York: Collier Books, 1961.

Graen, G., Alvares, K.M., Orris, J.B., and Martella, J.A. "Contingency model of leadership effectiveness: Antecedent and evidential results." *Psychological Bulletin,* 1970, 74, 285–296.

Graen, G., and Cashman, J.F. "A role making model of leadership in formal organizations: A developmental approach." In J.G. Hunt and L.L. Larson (Eds.), *Leadership frontiers.* Kent, Ohio: Kent State University Press, 1975.

Greene, C.N. "The reciprocal nature of influence between leader and subordinate." *Journal of Applied Psychology*, 1975, 60, 187–193.

Greene, C.N. "Disenchantment with leadership research: Some causes, recommendations, and alternative directions." In J.G. Hunt and L.L. Larson (Eds.), *Leadership: The cutting edge.* Carbondale: Southern Illinois University Press, 1977.

Greene, C.N. "Questions of causation in the Path-Goal theory of leadership." *Academy of Management Journal*, 1979, 22, 22–41. (A)

Greene, C.N. "A longitudinal investigation of modification to a situational model of leadership effectiveness." Paper presented at the Academy of Management Convention, Atlanta, 1979. (B)

Green, S.G., and Mitchell, T.R. "Attributional processes of leaders in leader–member exchanges." *Organizational Behavior and Human Performance*, 1979, 23, 429–458.

Grimes, A.J. "Authority, power, influence, and social control: A theoretical synthesis." *Academy of Management Review*, 1978, 3, 724–735.

Guest, R.H. "Of time and the foreman." *Personnel*, 1956, 32, 478–486.

Guest, R.H. *Organizational change: The effect of successful leadership.* Homewood: Irwin–Dorsey, 1964.

Guion, R.M., and Gottier, R.F. "Validity of personality measures in personnel selection." *Personnel Psychology*, 1965, 18, 135–164.

Hackman, J.R., and Lawler, E.E. "Employee reactions to job characteristics." *Journal of Applied Psychology*, 1971, 55, 259–286.

Hackman, J.R., and Oldham, G.R. "Development of the job diagnostic survey." *Journal of Applied Psychology*, 1975, 60, 159–170.

Hackman, J.R., and Oldham, G.R. "Motivation through the design of work: Test of a theory." *Organizational Behavior and Human Performance*, 1976, 16, 250–279.

Haimann, T., and Hilbert, R.L. *Supervision: Concepts and practices of management.* Cincinnati: South-Western, 1977.

Haire, M., Ghiselli, E.E., and Porter, L.W. *Managerial thinking: An international study.* New York: Wiley, 1966.

Halal, W.E. "Toward a general theory of leadership." *Human Relations*, 1974, 27, 401–416.

Halpin, A.W. "The leadership behavior and combat performance of airplane commanders." *Journal of Abnormal and Social Psychology*, 1954, 49, 19–22.

Halpin, A.W., and Winer, B.J. "A factorial study of the leader behavior descriptions." In R.M. Stogdill and A.E. Coons (Eds.), *Leader Behavior: Its description and measurement*. Columbus: Bureau of Business Research, Ohio State University, 1957.

Hammer, T. "Towards an understanding of the leadership construct: Construct validation of a leadership process model." Unpublished paper, New York School of Industrial and Labor Relations, Cornell University, 1973.

Hamner, W.C., and Hamner, E.P. "Behavior modification on the bottom line." *Organizational Dynamics*, 1976, 4(4), 2–21.

Hamner, W.C., and Organ, D.W. *Organizational behavior: An Applied Approach*. Dallas: Business Publications, 1978.

Hand, H., and Slocum, J. "Human relations training for middle management: A field experiment." *Academy of Management Journal*, 1970, 13, 403–410.

Hand, H., and Slocum, J. "A longitudinal study of the effect of a human relations training program on managerial effectiveness." *Journal of Applied Psychology*, 1972, 56, 412–418.

Handyside, J.D. "The effectiveness of supervisory training: A survey of recent experimental studies." *Personnel Management*, 1956, 38, 96–107.

Harvey, O.J. "An experimental approach to the study of status relationships in informal groups." *American Sociological Review*, 1953, 18, 357–367.

Heckman, R.W., Groner, D.M., Dunnette, M.D., and Johnson, P.D. *Development of psychiatric standards for police selection: A first year's report*. Minneapolis: Personnel Decisions, 1972.

Hegarty, W.H. "Using subordinate ratings to elicit behavioral changes in supervisors." *Journal of Applied Psychology*, 1974, 59, 764–766.

Heise, D.R. *Causal analysis*. New York: Wiley, 1975.

Heizer, J.H. "Manager action." *Personnel Psychology*, 1972, 25, 511–521.

Heller, F. *Managerial decision making: A study of leadership style and power sharing among senior managers.* London: Tavistock, 1971.

Heller, F., and Yukl, G.A. "Participation, managerial decision making, and situational variables." *Organizational Behavior and Human Performance,* 1969, 4, 227–241.

Hellervik, L.W., Dunnette, M.D., and Arvey, R.D. *Development and pretesting of behaviorally defined job performance measures for foremen in Ford Motor Company's transmission and automobile assembly divisions.* Minneapolis: Personnel Decisions, 1971.

Hemphill, J.K. "Relations between the size of the group and the behavior of "superior" leaders." *Journal of Social Psychology,* 1950, 32, 11–22.

Hemphill, J.K. "Job descriptions for executives." *Harvard Business Review,* 1959, 37 (September–October), 55–67.

Hemphill, J.K. *Dimensions of executive positions.* Columbus: Bureau of Business Research, Ohio State University, Research Monograph Number 98, 1960.

Hemphill, J.K., and Coons, A.E. "Development of the leader behavior description questionnaire." In R.M. Stogdill and A.E. Coons (Eds.), *Leader Behavior: Its Description and Measurement.* Columbus: Bureau of Business Research, Ohio State University, 1957.

Herold, D. "Two way influence processes in leader–follower dyads." *Academy of Management Journal,* 1977, 20, 224–237.

Hersey, P., and Blanchard, K.H. *Management of organizational behavior* (Third Edition). Englewood Cliffs, N.J.: Prentice-Hall, 1977.

Hickson, D.J., Hinings, C.R., Lee, C.A., Schneck, R.E., and Pennings, J.M. "A strategic contingencies theory of intra-organizational power." *Administrative Science Quarterly,* 1971, 16, 216-229.

Hill, W.A., and Hughes, D. "Variations in leader behavior as a function of task type." *Organizational Behavior and Human Performance,* 1974, 11, 83–96.

Hinrichs, J.R. "Communications activity of industrial research personnel." *Personnel Psychology,* 1964, 17, 193–204.

Hinrichs, J.R. "Where has all the time gone?" *Personnel,* 1976, 53(4), 44–49.

Hollander, E.P. "Conformity, status, and idiosyncrasy credit." *Psychological Review*, 1958, 65, 117–127.

Hollander, E.P. "Competence and conformity in the acceptance of influence." *Journal of Abnormal and Social Psychology*, 1960, 61, 361–365.

Hollander, E.P. "Some effects of perceived status on responses to innovative behavior." *Journal of Abnormal and Social Psychology*, 1961, 63, 247–250.

Hollander, E.P. "Leadership and social exchange processes." In K. Gergen, M.S. Greenberg, and R.H. Willis (Eds.), *Social exchange: Advances in theory and research.* New York: Winston–Wiley, 1979.

Hollander, E.P., and Julian, J.W. "Studies in leader legitimacy, influence, and innovation." In L. Berkowitz (Ed.), *Advances in experimental social psychology* (Vol. 5). New York: Academic Press, 1970.

Hollander, E.P., and Julian, J.W. "A further look at leader legitimacy, influence and innovation." In L. Berkowitz (Ed.), *Group processes.* New York: Academic Press, 1978.

Homans, G.C. "Social behavior as exchange." *American Journal of Sociology*, 1958, 63, 597–606.

Homans, G.C. "Effort, supervision and productivity." In R. Dubin, G.C. Homans, F.C. Mann, and D.C. Miller (Eds.), *Leadership and productivity.* San Francisco: Chandler, 1965.

Horne, J.H., and Lupton, T. "The work activities of 'middle managers.'" *Journal of Management Studies*, 1965, 1, 14–33.

House, R.J. "A path goal theory of leader effectiveness." *Administrative Science Quarterly*, 1971, 16, 321–339.

House, R.J. "A 1976 theory of charismatic leadership." In J.G. Hunt and L.L. Larson (Eds.), *Leadership: The cutting edge.* Carbondale: Southern Illinois University Press, 1977.

House, R.J., and Dessler, G. "The path goal theory of leadership: Some post hoc and a priori tests." In J. Hunt and L. Larson (Eds.), *Contingency approaches to leadership.* Carbondale: Southern Illinois University Press, 1974.

House, R.J., Filley, A.C., and Gujarati, D.N. "Leadership style, hierarchical influence, and the satisfaction of subordinate role expectations." *Journal of Applied Psychology*, 1971, 55, 422–432.

House, R.J., and Mitchell, T.R. "Path-goal theory of leadership." *Contemporary Business*, 1974, 3 (Fall), 81–98.

House, R.J., Shapiro, H.J., and Wahba, M.A. "Expectancy theory: Reevaluation of empirical evidence." *Decision Sciences*, 1974 (December/Special Issue), 54–77.

Huck, J.R. "Assessment centers: A review of external and internal validities." *Personnel Psychology*, 1973, 26, 191–212.

Hundal, P.S. "A study of entrepreneurial motivation: Comparison of fast and slow progressing small scale industrial entrepreneurs in Punjab, India." *Journal of Applied Psychology*, 1971, 55, 317–323.

Hunt, J.G., and Larson, L.L. "We march to the beat of a different drummer: An overview." In J.G. Hunt and L.L. Larson (Eds.), *Leadership frontiers*. Kent, Ohio: Kent State University Press, 1975.

Hunt, J.G., and Osborn, R.N. "A multiple influence approach to leadership for managers." In J. Stinson and P. Hersey (Eds.), *Leadership for practitioners*. Athens, Ohio: Center for Leadership Studies, 1978.

Huse, E.F. *Organization development and change.* New York: 1975.

Ivancevich, J.M. "An analysis of control, bases of control, and satisfaction in an organizational setting." *Academy of Management Journal*, 1970, 13, 427–436.

Ivancevich, J.M. "Effects of goal setting on performance and job satisfaction." *Journal of Applied Psychology*, 1976, 61, 605–612.

Ivancevich, J.M. "Different goal setting treatments and their effects on performance and job satisfaction." *Academy of Management Journal*, 1977, 20, 406–419.

Ivancevich, J.M., and Donnelly, J.H. "Leader influence and performance." *Personnel Psychology*, 1970, 23, 539–549.

Jakcson, J.M. "The effect of changing the leadership of small work groups." *Human Relations*, 1953, 6, 25–44.

Jacobs, T.O. *Leadership and exchange in formal organizations.* Alexandria, Virginia: Human Resources Research Organization, 1970.

Janda, K.F. "Towards the explication of the concept of leadership in terms of the concept of power." *Human Relations*, 1960, 13, 345–363.

Janis, I.L. *Victims of Groupthink*. Boston: Houghton Mifflin, 1972.

Jasinski, F.J. "Foreman relationships outside the work group." *Personnel*, 1956, 33, 130–136.

Jay, A. "How to run a meeting." *Harvard Business Review*, 1976 (March–April), 43–57.

Jenkins, W.O. "A review of leadership studies with particular reference to military problems." *Psychological Bulletin*, 1947, 44, 54–79.

Jennings, E.E. "The dynamics of forced leadership training." *Journal of Personnel Administration and Industrial Relations*, 1954, 1, 110–118.

Kahn, R.L., and Quinn, R.P. "Role stress: A framework for analysis." In A. McLean (Ed.), *Mental health and work organizations*. Chicago: Rand McNally, 1970.

Kahn, R.L., Wolfe, D.M., Quinn, R.P., and Snoek, J.D. *Organizational stress: Studies in role conflict and ambiguity*. New York: Wiley, 1964.

Karmel, B. "Leadership: A challenge to traditional research methods and assumptions." *Academy of Management Review*, 1978, 3, 475–482.

Karmel, B., and Egan, D.M. "Managerial performance: A new look at underlying dimensionality." *Organizational Behavior and Human Performance*, 1976, 15, 322–334.

Katz, D., and Kahn, R.L. "Some recent findings in human relations research." In E. Swanson, T. Newcomb, and E. Hartley (Eds.), *Readings in social psychology*. New York: Holt, Rinehart, and Winston, 1952.

Katz, D., and Kahn, R.L. *The social psychology of organizations* (Second Edition). New York: Wiley, 1978.

Katz, D., Maccoby, N., Gurin, G., and Floor, L. *Productivity, supervision, and morale among railroad workers*. Ann Arbor: Survey Research Center, University of Michigan, 1951.

Katz, D., Maccoby, N., and Morse, N. *Productivity, supervision, and morale in an office situation*. Ann Arbor, Michigan: Institute for Social Research, 1950.

Katz, R.L. "Skills of an effective administrator." *Harvard Business Review*, 1955 (January–February), 33–42.

Katzell, R.A., Barrett, R.S., Vann, D.H., and Hogan, J.M. Organizational correlates of executive roles. *Journal of Applied Psychology*, 1968, 52, 22–28.

Kay, B.R. "Key factors in effective foreman behavior." *Personnel*, 1959, 36, 25–31.

Kay, E., and Meyer, H.H. "The development of a job activity questionnaire for production foremen." *Personnel Psychology*, 1962, 15, 411–418.

Keller, R.T., and Szilagyi, A.D. "Employee reactions to leader reward behavior." *Academy of Management Journal*, 1976, 19, 619–627.

Kelly, J. "The study of executive behavior by activity sampling." *Human Relations*, 1964, 17, 277–287.

Kepner, C.H., and Tregoe, B.B. *The rational manager: A systematic approach to problem solving and decision making.* New York: McGraw-Hill, 1965.

Kepner, C.H., and Tregoe, B.B. *Executive problem analysis and decision making.* Princeton, New Jersey: Kepner-Tregoe, 1973.

Kerr, S., and Harlan, A. "Predicting the effects of leadership training and experience from the contingency model: Some remaining problems." *Journal of Applied Psychology*, 1973, 57, 114–117.

Kerr, S., and Jermier, J.M. "Substitutes for leadership: Their meaning and measurement." *Organizational Behavior and Human Performance*, 1978, 22, 375–403.

Kerr, S., and Schriesheim, S. "Consideration, initiating structure, and organizational criteria—an update of Korman's 1966 review." *Personnel Psychology*, 1974, 27, 555–568.

Kerr, S., Schriesheim, C.A., Murphy, C.J., and Stodgill, R.M. "Toward a contingency theory of leadership based on the consideration and initiating structure literature." *Organizational Behavior and Human Performance*, 1974, 12, 62–82.

Kipnis, D. "Does power corrupt?" *Journal of Personality and Social Psychology*, 1972, 24, 33–41.

Kipnis, D., and Lane, W.P. "Self confidence and leadership." *Journal of Applied Psychology*, 1962, 46, 291–295.

Kochan, T.A., Schmidt, S.S., and De Cotiis, T.A. "Superior–subordinate relations: Leadership and headship." *Human Relations*, 1975, 28, 279–294.

Korda, M. *Power! How to get it, how to use it.* New York: Ballantine Books, 1975.

Korman, A.K. "Consideration, initiating structure, and organizational criteria—a review." *Personnel Psychology*, 1966, 19, 349–362.

Korman, A.K. "The prediction of managerial performance: A review." *Personnel Psychology*, 1968, 21, 295–322.

Korman, A.K. "On the development of contingency theories of leadership: Some methodological considerations and a possible alternative." *Journal of Applied Psychology*, 1973, 58, 384–387.

Korman, A.K., and Tanofsky, R. "Statistical problems of contingency models in organizational behavior." *Academy of Management Journal* 1975, 18, 393–397.

Kraut, A.I. "Developing managerial skills via modeling techniques: Some positive research findings—A symposium." *Personnel Psychology*, 1976, 29, 325–370.

Kuhn, A. *The study of society: A unified approach.* Homewood, Illinois: Irwin, 1963.

Landsberger, H. "The horizontal dimension in bureaucracy." *Administrative Science Quarterly*, 1961, 6, 299–332.

Latham, G.P., Fay, C.H., and Saari, L.M. "The development of behavioral observation scales for appraising the performance of foremen." *Personnel Psychology*, 1979, 32, 299–311.

Latham, G.P., Mitchell, T.R., and Dossett, D.L. "Importance of participative goal setting and anticipated rewards on goal difficulty and job performance." *Journal of Applied Psychology*, 1978, 63, 163–171.

Latham, G.P., and Saari, L. "The application of social learning theory to training supervisors through behavioral modeling." *Journal of Applied Psychology*, 1979, 64, 239–246.

Latham, G.P., and Wexley, K.N. "Behavioral observation scales for performance appraisal purposes." *Personnel Psychology*, 1977, 30, 255–268.

Latham, G.P., and Yukl, G.A. "A review of research on the application of goal setting in organizations." *Academy of Management Journal*, 1975, 18, 824–845. (A)

Latham, G.P., and Yukl, G.A. "Assigned versus participative goal setting with educated and uneducated woods workers." *Journal of Applied Psychology*, 1975, 60, 299–302. (B)

Latham, G.P., and Yukl, G.A. "Effects of assigned and participative goal setting on performance and job satisfaction." *Journal of Applied Psychology*, 1976, 61, 166–171.

Lawler, E.E., III, and Hackman, J.R. "Impact of employee participation in the development of pay incentive plans: A field experiment." *Journal of Applied Psychology*, 1969, 53, 467–471.

Lawler, E.E., Porter, L.W., and Tennenbaum, A. "Managers' attitudes toward interaction episodes." *Journal of Applied Psychology*, 1968, 52, 432–439.

Lawrence, L.C., and Smith, P.C. "Group decision and employee participation." *Journal of Applied Psychology*, 1955, 39, 334–337.

Lawshe, C.H., Bolda, R.A., and Brune, R.L. "Studies in management training evaluation. II: The effects of exposure to role playing." *Journal of Applied Psychology*, 1959, 43, 287–292.

Lee, J.A. "Leader power for managing change." *Academy of Management Review*, 1977, 2, 73–80.

Leister, A.F., Borden, D., and Fiedler, F.E. "Validation of contingency model leadership training: Leader Match." *Academy of Management Journal*, 1977, 20, 464–470.

Liddell, W.W., and Slocum, J.W., Jr. "The effects of individual role compatibility upon group performance: An extension of Schutz's FIRO theory." *Academy of Management Journal*, 1976, 19, 413–426.

Likert, R. *New patterns of management.* New York: McGraw-Hill, 1961.

Likert, R. *The human organization: Its management and value.* New York: McGraw-Hill, 1967.

Litwin, G.H., and Stringer, P.A. *Motivation and organizational climate.* Boston: Division of Research, Harvard Business School, 1966.

Locke, E.A., and Schweiger, D.M.   "Participation in decision making: One more look." *Research on Organizational Behavior,* 1979, 1, 265–339.

Lord, R.G.   "Functional leadership behavior: Measurement and relation to social power and leadership perceptions." *Administrative Science Quarterly,* 1977, 22, 114–133.

Lord, R.G., Binning, J.F., Rush, M.C., and Thomas, J.C.   "The effect of performance cues and leader behavior on questionnaire ratings of leader behavior." *Organizational Behavior and Human Performance,* 1978, 21, 27–39.

Lorsch, J.W., and Morse, J.J.   *Organizations and their members: A contingency approach.* New York: Harper & Row, 1974.

Lowin, A.   "Participative decision-making: A model, literature critique, and prescriptions for research." *Organizational Behavior and Human Performance,* 1968, 3, 68–106.

Lowin, A., and Craig, J.R.   "The influence of level of performance on managerial style: An experimental object lesson in the ambiguity of correlational data." *Organizational Behavior and Human Performance,* 1968, 3, 440–458.

Lowin, A., Hrapchak, W.J., and Kavanagh, M.J.   "Consideration and initiating structure: An experimental investigation of leadership traits." *Administrative Science Quarterly,* 1969, 14, 238–253.

Lusk, E.J., and Oliver, B.L.   "American managers' personal value systems—revisited." *Academy of Management Journal,* 1974, 17, 549–554.

Mahoney, R.A., Jerdee, T.H., and Carroll, S.J.   "The job(s) of management." *Industrial Relations,* 1965, 4, 97–110.

Maier, N.R.F.   *Problem solving discussions and conferences: Leadership methods and skills.* New York: McGraw-Hill, 1963.

Maier, N.R.F., and Hoffman, L.R.   "Using trained 'developmental' discussion leaders to improve further the quality of group decisions." *Journal of Applied Psychology,* 1960, 44, 247–251.

Maier, N.R.F., and Maier, R.A.   "An experimental test of the effects of 'developmental' vs. 'free' discussions on the quality of group decisions." *Journal of Applied Psychology,* 1957, 41, 320–323.

Maier, N.R.F., and Solem, A.R. "The contribution of a discussion leader to the quality of group thinking: The effective use of minority opinions." *Human Relations*, 1952, 5, 277–288.

Maier, N.R.F., and Thurber, J.A. "Problems in delegation." *Personnel Psychology*, 1969, 22, 131–139.

Mann, F.C. "Toward an understanding of the leadership role in formal organization." In R. Dubin, G.C. Homans, F.C. Mann, and D.C. Miller (Eds.), *Leadership and productivity*. San Francisco: Chandler, 1965.

Mann, F.C., and Dent, J. "The supervisor: Member of two organizational families." *Harvard Business Review*, 1954, 32(6), 103–112.

Mann, F.C., and Hoffman, L.R. *Automation and the worker: A study of social change in power plants*. New York: Holt, 1960.

Mann, R.D. "A review of the relationships between personality and performance in small groups." *Psychological Bulletin*, 1959, 56, 241–270.

Marples, D.L. "Roles in a manufacturing organization." *Journal of Management Studies*, 1968, 11, 183–204.

Martin, N.H. "Differential decisions in the management of an industrial plant." *Journal of Business*, 1956, 29, 249–260.

Mass, H.S. "Personal and group factors in leaders' social perception." *Journal of Abnormal and Social Psychology*, 1950, 45, 54–63.

Mayo, G.D., and Dubois, P.H. "Measurement of gain in leadership training." *Educational and Psychological Measurement*, 1963, 23, 23–31.

McCall, M.W., Jr. "Leaders and leadership: Of substance and shadow." In J. Hackman, E.E. Lawler, Jr., and L.W. Porter (Eds.), *Perspectives on Behavior in Organizations*. New York: McGraw-Hill, 1977.

McCall, M.W., Jr., and Lombardo, M.M. *Leadership: Where else can we go?* Durham, North Carolina: Duke University Press, 1978.

McCall, M.W., Jr., Morrison, A.M., and Hannan, R.L. *Studies of managerial work: Results and methods*. Greensboro, North Carolina: Center for Creative Leadership, Technical Report 9, 1978.

McClelland, D.C. "N-achievement and entrepreneurship: A longitudinal study." *Journal of Personality and Social Psychology*, 1965, 1, 389–392.

McClelland, D. The two faces of power. *Journal of International Affairs*, 1970, 24(1), 29–47.

McClelland, D. *Power: The inner experience.* New York: Irvington, 1975.

McClelland, D., and Burnham, D.H. "Power is the great motivator." *Harvard Business Review*, 1976 (March–April), 100–110.

McClelland, D.C., and Winter, D.G. *Motivating economic achievement.* New York: Free Press, 1969.

McFillen, J.M. "Supervisory power as an influence in supervisor-subordinate relations." *Academy of Management Journal*, 1978, 21, 419–433.

McGregor, D. *The human side of enterprise.* New York: McGraw-Hill, 1960.

McLennan, K. "The manager and his job skills." *Academy of Management Journal*, 1967, 3, 235–245.

McMahon, J.T. "The contingency theory: Logic and method revisited." *Personnel Psychology*, 1972, 25, 697–711.

Mechanic, D. "Sources of power of lower participants in complex organizations." *Administrative Science Quarterly*, 1962, 7, 349–364.

Melcher, A.J. "Leadership models and research approaches." In J.G. Hunt and L.L. Larson (Eds.), *Leadership: The cutting edge.* Carbondale: Southern Illinois University Press, 1977.

Melcher, B. "Relationships of static and dynamic analysis." In L.K. Bragaw and E.K. Winslow (Eds.), *Eastern Academy of Management Proceedings*, 1976.

Miles, M.B. "Changes during and following laboratory training." *Journal of Applied Behavioral Science*, 1965, 1, 215–242.

Miles, R.E. *Theories of management: Implications for organizational behavior and development.* New York: McGraw-Hill, 1975.

Miller, D.C. "Supervisors: Evolution of an organizational role." In R. Dubin, G.C. Homans, F.C. Mann, and D.C. Miller (Eds.), *Leadership and productivity.* San Francisco: Chandler, 1965.

Miner, J.B. *Studies in management education.* Atlanta, Georgia: Organizational Measurement Systems Press, 1965.

Miner, J.B. "The school administrator and organizational character." Eugene, Oregon: Center for the Advanced Study of Educational Administration, University of Oregon, 1967.

Miner, J.B. "The uncertain future of the leadership concept: An overview." In J.G. Hunt and L.L. Larson (Eds.), *Leadership frontiers.* Kent, Ohio: Comparative Administration Research Institute, Kent State University, 1975.

Miner, J.B. *Motivation to manage: A ten-year update on the "Studies in Management Education" research.* Atlanta, Georgia: Organizational Measurement Systems Press, 1977.

Miner, J.B. "Twenty years of research on role motivation theory of managerial effectiveness." *Personnel Psychology,* 1978, 31, 739–760.

Mintzberg, H. "Structured observation as a method to study managerial work." *Journal of Management Studies,* 1970, 7 (February), 87–104.

Mintzberg, H. *The nature of managerial work.* New York: Harper & Row, 1973.

Misshauk, M.J. "Supervisory skills and employee satisfaction." *Personnel Administration,* 1971 (July–August), 29–33.

Misumi, J., and Seki, F. "Effects of achievement motivation on the effectiveness of leadership patterns." *Administrative Science Quarterly,* 1971, 16, 51–60.

Misumi, J., and Shirakashi, S. "An experimental study of the effects of supervisory behavior on productivity and morale in a hierarchical organization." *Human Relations,* 1966, 19, 297–307.

Mitchell, T.R. "Motivation and participation: An integration." *Academy of Management Journal,* 1973, 16, 660–679.

Mitchell, T.R. "Expectancy models of job satisfaction, occupational preference, and effort: A theoretical, methodological, and empirical appraisal." *Psychological Bulletin,* 1974, 81, 1053–1077.

Mitchell, T.R., Larson, J.R., Jr., and Green, S.G. "Leader behavior, situational moderators, and group performance: An attributional analysis." *Organizational Behavior and Human Performance,* 1977, 18, 254–268.

Mitchell, T.R., and Wood, R.E. "Supervisor's responses to subordinate poor performance: A test of an attributional model." *Organizational Behavior and Human Performance,* 1980, 25, 123–138.

Moon, C.G., and Hariton, T. "Evaluating an appraisal and feedback training program." *Personnel,* 1958, 35, 36–41.

Morse, J.J., and Wagner, F.R. "Measuring the process of managerial effectiveness." *Academy of Management Journal,* 1978, 21, 23–35.

Morse, N.C., and Reimer, E. "The experimental change of a major organizational variable." *Journal of Abnormal and Social Psychology,* 1956, 52, 120–129.

Moses, J.L., and Ritchie, R.J. "Supervisory relationships training: A behavioral evaluation of a behavior modeling program." *Personnel Psychology,* 1976, 29, 337–343.

Mott, P.E. *Characteristics of effective organizations.* New York: Harper & Row, 1972.

Mowry, H.W. *Leadership evaluation and development scale casebook.* Los Angeles: Psychological Services, 1964.

Mulder, M., Ritsema van Eck, J.R., and de Jong, R.D. "An organization in crisis and non-crisis situations." *Human Relations,* 1970, 24, 19–41.

Mulder, M., and Stemerding, A. "Threat, attraction to group, and need for strong leadership." *Human Relations,* 1963, 16, 317–334.

Nash, A.V. "Vocational interest of effective managers: A review of the literature." *Personnel Psychology,* 1965, 18, 21–38.

Nash, A.V. "Development and evaluation of a SVIB key for selecting managers." *Journal of Applied Psychology,* 1966, 50, 250–254.

Nealy, S.M., and Fiedler, F.E. "Leadership functions of middle managers." *Psychological Bulletin,* 1968, 5, 313–329.

Nebecker, D.M., and Mitchell, T.R. "Leader behavior: An expectancy theory approach. *Organizational Behavior and Human Performance,* 1974, 11, 355–367.

Nemeroff, W., and Cosentino, J. "Utilizing feedback and goal setting to increase performance appraisal interviewer skills of managers." *Academy of Management Journal,* 1979, 22, 566–576.

Newman, W.H. "Overcoming obstacles to effective delegation." *Management Review,* 1956, (January), 36–41.

Oldham, G.R.   "The motivational strategies used by supervisors: Relationships to effectiveness indicators." *Organizational Behavior and Human Performance*, 1976, 15, 66–86.

O'Neill, H.E., and Kubany, A.J.   "Observation methodology and supervisory behavior." *Personnel Psychology*, 1959, 12, 85–96.

Osborn, R.N.   "Discussant comments." In J.G. Hunt and L.L. Larson (Eds.), *Contingency approaches to leadership*. Carbondale: Southern Illinois University Press, 1974.

Osborn, R.N., and Hunt, J.G.   "An adaptive-reactive theory of leadership: The role of macro variables in leadership research." In J.G. Hunt and L.L. Larson (Eds.), *Leadership frontiers*. Kent, Ohio: Kent State University Press, 1975.

Patchen, M.   "Supervisory methods and group performance norms." *Administrative Science Quarterly*, 1962, 7, 275–294.

Patchen, M.   "The locus and basis of influence on organizational decisions." *Organizational Behavior and Human Performance*, 1974, 11, 195–221.

Paul, W.J., Robertson, K.B., and Herzberg, F.   "Job enrichment pays off." *Harvard Business Review*, 1969 (March–April), 61–78.

Peabody, R.L.   *Organizational authority: Superior–subordinate relationship in three public service organizations*. New York: Atherton Press, 1964.

Pelz, D.C.   "Influence: A key to effective leadership in the first-line supervisor." *Personnel*, 1952, 29, 209–217.

Pettigrew, A.M.   "Information control as a power resource." *Sociology*, 1972, 6, 187–204.

Pfeffer, J.   "Power and resource allocation in organizations." In B. Staw and G. Salancik (Eds.), *New directions in organizational behavior*. Chicago: St. Clair Press, 1977.

Pfeffer, J.   "The ambiguity of leadership." In M.W. McCall, Jr., and M.M. Lombardo (Eds.), *Leadership: Where else can we go?* Durham, North Carolina: Duke University Press, 1978.

Pfeffer, J., and Salancik, G.R.   "Determinants of supervisory behavior: A role set analysis." *Human Relations*, 1975, 28, 139–153.

Pollard, W.E., and Mitchell, T.R.   "A decision theory analysis of social power." Technical Report 71–25, Department of Psychology, University of Washington, 1971.

Ponder, Q.D. "The effective manufacturing foreman." In E. Young (Ed.), Industrial Relations Research Association, *Proceedings of the Tenth Annual Meeting*, Madison, Wisconsin, 1957, 41–54.

Ponder, Q.D. "Supervisory practices of effective and ineffective foremen." Unpublished doctoral dissertation, Columbia University, 1958. *Dissertation Abstracts*, 1959, 20, 3983.

Porter, L.W., and Henry, M.M. "Job attitudes in management: V. Perceived perceptions of the importance of certain personality traits as a function of job level." *Journal of Applied Psychology*, 1964, 48, 31–36.

Powell, R., and Schlacter, J.L. "Participative management: A panacea?" *Academy of Management Journal*, 1971, 14, 165–173.

Preston, P., and Zimmerer, T.W. *Management for supervisors*. Englewood Cliffs, New Jersey: Prentice-Hall, 1978.

Prince, G.M. *The practice of creativity*. New York: Harper & Row, 1970.

Reddin, W.J. "The 3-D management style theory." *Training and Development Journal*, 1967, (April), 8–17.

Reitz, H.J. *Behavior in organizations*. Homewood, Illinois: Irwin, 1977.

Rice, R.W. "Construct validity of the least preferred co-worker score." *Psychological Bulletin*, 1978, 85, 1199–1237.

Ritchie, J.B., and Miles, R.E. "An analysis of quantity and quality of participation as mediating variables in the participative decision making process." *Personnel Psychology*, 1970, 23, 347–359.

Rosen, N.A. "How supervise?—1943–1960." *Personnel Psychology*, 1961, 14, 96–97.

Rosen, N.A. *Leadership change and work group dynamics: An experiment*. Ithaca, New York: Cornell University Press, 1969.

Runyon, K.E. "Some interactions between personality variables and management styles." *Journal of Applied Psychology*, 1973, 57, 288–294.

Rush, M.C., Thomas, J.C., and Lord, R.G. "Implicit leadership theory: A potential threat to the internal validity of leader behavior questionnaires." *Organizational Behavior and Human Performance*, 1977, 20, 93–110.

Salancik, G.R., Calder, B.J., Rowland, K.M., Leblebici, H., and Conway, M. "Leadership as an outcome of social structure and process: A multidimensional analysis." In J.C. Hunt and L.L. Larson (Eds.), *Leadership frontiers.* Kent, Ohio: Kent State University Press, 1975.

Sashkin, M. "The structure of charismatic leadership." In J.C. Hunt and L.L. Larson (Eds.), *Leadership: The cutting edge.* Carbondale: Southern Illinois University Press, 1977.

Sayles, L.R. *Leadership: What effective managers really do and how they do it.* New York: McGraw-Hill, 1979.

Schachter, S., Willerman, B., Festinger, L., and Hyman, R. "Emotional disruption and industrial productivity." *Journal of Applied Psychology,* 1961, 45, 201–213.

Schein, E. *Process consultation: Its role in management development.* Reading, Massachusetts: Addison-Wesley, 1969.

Schlesinger, L., Jackson, J.M., and Butman, J. "Leader–member interaction in management committees." *Journal of Abnormal and Social Psychology,* 1960, 61, 360–364.

Schneier, C.E. "Behavior modification in management: A review and critique." *Academy of Management Journal,* 1974, 17, 528–548.

Schoen, S.H., and Durand, D.E. *Supervision: The management of organizational resources.* Englewood Cliffs, New Jersey: Prentice-Hall, 1979.

Schriesheim, C.A. "Development, validation, and application of new leadership behavior and expectancy research instruments." Unpublished doctoral dissertation, Ohio State University, 1978.

Schriesheim, C.A., and Kerr, S. "Theories and measures of leadership: A critical appraisal." In J.G. Hunt and L.L. Larson (Eds.), *Leadership: The cutting edge.* Carbondale: Southern Illinois University Press, 1977.

Schriesheim, C.A., Kinicki, A.J., and Schriesheim, J.F. "The effect of leniency on leader behavior descriptions." *Organizational Behavior and Human Performance,* 1979, 23, 1–29.

Schriescheim, C.A., and Von Glinow, M.A. "The path-goal theory of leadership: A theoretical and empirical analysis." *Academy of Management Journal,* 1977, 20, 398–405.

Schwarz, F.C., Stilwell, W.P., and Scanlan, B.K. "Effects of management development on manager behavior and subordinate perception: I." *Training and Development Journal,* 1968, 22(4), 38–50.

Schwarz, F.C., Stilwell, W.P., and Scanlan, B.K. "Effects of management development on manager behavior and subordinate perception: II." *Training and Development Journal,* 1968, 22(5), 24–30.

Seeborg, I.S. "The influence of employee participation in job redesign." *Journal of Applied Behavioral Science,* 1978, 14, 87–98.

Seiler, J.A. "Diagnosing inter-departmental conflict." *Harvard Business Review,* 1963, 41 (September–October), 121–132.

Sheridan, J.E., and Vredenburgh, D.J. "Usefulness of leadership behavior and social power variables in predicting job tension, performance, and turnover of nursing employees." *Journal of Applied Psychology,* 1978, 63, 89–95.

Shetty, Y.K., and Perry, N.S. "Are top executives transferable across companies?" *Business Horizons,* 1976, 19(3), 23–28.

Shiflett, S.C. "The contingency model of leadership effectiveness: Some implications of its statistical and methodological properties." *Behavioral Science,* 1973, 18(6), 429–440.

Shull, F.A., Delbecq, A.L., and Cummings, L.L. *Organizational decision-making.* New York: McGraw-Hill, 1970.

Shutz, W.C. "What makes groups productive?" *Human Relations,* 1955, 8, 429–465.

Sims, H.P., Jr. "The leader as a manager of reinforcement contingencies: An empirical example and a model." In J.G. Hunt and L.L. Larson (Eds.), *Leadership: The cutting edge.* Carbondale: Southern Illinois University Press, 1977.

Sims, H.P., Jr. "Further thoughts on punishment in organizations." *Academy of Management Review,* 1980, 5, 133–138.

Sims, H.P., Jr. and Szilagyi, A.D. "Leader reward behavior and subordinate satisfaction and performance." *Organizational Behavior and Human Performance,* 1975, 14, 426–437.

Sims, H.P., and Szilagyi, A.D. "A causal analysis of leader behavior over three different time lags." Paper presented at the Eastern Academy of Management Meetings, New York City, 1978.

Skinner, E.W. "Relationships between leadership behavior patterns and organizational–situational variables." *Personnel Psychology,* 1969, 22, 489–494.

Slater, P.E. "Role differentiation in small groups." In A.P. Hare, E.F. Borgatta, and R.F. Bales (Eds.), *Small groups: Studies in social interactions.* New York: Knopf, 1955.

Slocum, J.W., Jr. "Supervisory influence and the professional employee." *Personnel Journal,* 1970, 49, 484–491.

Smith, C.G., and Tannenbaum, A.S. "Organizational control structure: A comparative analysis." *Human Relations,* 1963, 16, 299–316.

Smith, H.W. *Strategies of social research: The methodological imagination.* Englewood Cliffs, N. J.: Prentice-Hall, 1975.

Smith, P.E. "Management modeling training to improve morale and customer satisfaction." *Personnel Psychology,* 1976, 29, 351–359.

Solem, A.R. "An evaluation of two attitudinal approaches to delegation." *Journal of Applied Psychology,* 1958, 42, 36–39.

Stewart, R. *Managers and their jobs.* London: Macmillan, 1967.

Stewart, R. *Contrasts in management.* Maidenhead, Berkshire, England: McGraw-Hill (U.K.), 1976.

Stinson, J.E., and Johnson, T.W. "The path-goal theory of leadership: A partial test and suggested refinement." *Academy of Management Journal,* 1975, 18, 242–252.

Stogdill, R.M. "Personal factors associated with leadership: A survey of the literature." *Journal of Psychology,* 1948, 25, 35–71.

Stogdill, R.M. *Handbook of leadership: A survey of theory and research.* New York: Free Press, 1974.

Stogdill, R.M., Goode, O.S., and Day, D.R. "New leader behavior description subscales." *Journal of Psychology,* 1962, 54, 259–269.

Stogdill, R.M., Shartle, C.L., Scott, E.L., Coons, A.E., and Jaynes, W.E. *A predictive study of administrative work patterns.* Columbus: Bureau of Business Research, Ohio State University, 1956.

Stouffer, S.A., Suchman, E.E., Devinney, L.C., Starr, S.A., and Williams, R.M. *The American soldier: Adjustments during army life (Vol. 1).* Princeton New Jersey: Princeton University Press, 1949.

Strauss, G. "Some notes on power equalization." In H.J. Leavitt (Ed.), *The social science of organizations: Four perspectives.* Englewood Cliffs, New Jersey: Prentice-Hall, 1963.

Strauss, G. "Managerial practices." In J.R. Hackman and J.L. Suttle (Eds.), *Improving life at work.* Santa Monica, California: Goodyear, 1977.

Strauss, G., and Sayles, L.R. *Personnel: The human problems of management* (Third Edition). Englewood Cliffs, New Jersey: Prentice-Hall, 1972.

Stroud, P.V. "Evaluating a human relations training program." *Personnel,* 1959, 36 (November–December), 52–60.

Student, K.R. "Supervisory influence and work group performance." *Journal of Applied Psychology,* 1968, 52, 188–194.

Szilagyi, A.D. "Causal inferences between leader reward behavior and subordinate goal attainment, absenteeism, and work satisfaction." *Journal of Occupational Psychology,* 1980, 53 (in press).

Tannenbaum, A.S., and Allport, F.H. "Personality structure and group structure: An interpretive study of their relationship through an event structure hypothesis." *Journal of Abnormal and Social Psychology,* 1956, 53, 272–280.

Tannenbaum, R., and Schmidt, W.H. "How to choose a leadership pattern." *Harvard Business Review,* 1958, 36 (March–April), 95–101.

Tannenbaum, R., Weschler, I.R., and Massarik, F. *Leadership and organization.* New York: McGraw-Hill, 1961.

Taylor, J., and Bowers, D. *The survey of organizations: A machine scored standardized questionnaire instrument.* Ann Arbor, Michigan: Institute for Social Research, 1972.

Tenopyr, M.L. "The comparative validity of selected leadership scales related to success in production management." *Personnel Psychology,* 1969, 22, 77–85.

Terry, G.R. *Principles of management.* Homewood, Illinois: Irwin, 1972.

Thambain, H.J. and Gemmill, G.R. "Influence styles of project managers: Some project performance correlates." *Academy of Management Journal,* 1974, 17, 216–224.

Thibaut, J.W., and Kelley, H.H. *The social psychology of groups*. New York: Wiley, 1959.

Thomason, G.F. "Managerial work roles and relationships (Part 1)." *Journal of Management Studies*, 1966, 3, 270–284.

Thomason, G.F. "Managerial work roles and relationships (Part 2)." *Journal of Management Studies*, 1967, 4, 17–30.

Thurley, K.E., and Hamblin, A.C. *The supervisor and his job*. London: Her Majesty's Stationery Office, Department of Scientific and Industrial Research, 1963.

Tornow, W.W., and Pinto, P.R. "The development of a managerial job taxonomy: A system for describing, classifying, and evaluating executive positions." *Journal of Applied Psychology*, 1976, 61, 410–418.

Torrance, E.P. "The behavior of small groups under stress conditions of survival." *American Sociological Review*, 1954, 19, 751–755.

Trewatha, R.L., and Newport, M.G. *Management*. Dallas: Business Publications, 1978.

Underwood, W.J. "Evaluation of laboratory method training." *Training Director's Journal*, 1965, 19(5), 34–40.

Valiquet, M.I. "Individual change in a management development program." *Journal of Applied Behavioral Science*, 1968, 4, 313–326.

Van de Ven, A., and Delbecq, A.L. "Nominal versus interacting group processes for committee decision making effectiveness." *Academy of Management Journal*, 1971, 14, 203–212.

Van Fleet, D.D. "Toward identifying critical elements in a behavioral description of leadership." *Public Personnel Management*, 1974, (January–February), 70–82.

Van Fleet, D.D., Chamberlain, H., and Gass, W.K. "Some critical elements of leader behavior in a military cadet organization." *Organization and Administrative Sciences*, 1974, 5, 73–94.

Veen, P. "Effects of participative decision-making in field hockey training: A field experiment." *Organizational Behavior and Human Performance*, 1972, 7, 288–307.

Vinokur, A. "Review and theoretical analysis of the effects of group processes upon individual and group decisions involving risk." *Psychological Bulletin*, 1971, 76, 231–250.

Vroom, V.H. "Some personality determinants of the effects of participation." *Journal of Abnormal and Social Psychology*, 1959, 59, 322–327.

Vroom, V.H. *Work and motivation*. New York: Wiley, 1964.

Vroom, V.H. "Can leaders learn to lead?" *Organizational Dynamics*, 1976, 4(Winter), 17–28.

Vroom, V.H., and Jago, A.G. "On the validity of the Vroom–Yetton model." *Journal of Applied Psychology*, 1978, 63, 151–162.

Vroom, V.H., and Yetton, P.W. *Leadership and decision-making*. Pittsburgh: University of Pittsburgh Press, 1973.

Wager, L.W. "Leadership style, influence, and supervisory role obligations." *Administrative Science Quarterly*, 1965, 9, 391–420.

Wainer, H.A., and Rubin, I.M. "Motivation of research and development entrepreneurs: Determinants of company success." *Journal of Applied Psychology*, 1969, 53, 178–184.

Walker, C.R., Guest, R.H., and Turner, A.N. *The foreman on the assembly line*. Cambridge, Massachusetts: Harvard University Press, 1956.

Warren, D.I. "Power, visibility, and conformity in formal organizations." *American Sociological Review*, 1968, 6, 951–970.

Webber, R.A. *Time and management*. New York: Van Nostrand–Reinhold, 1972.

Webber, R.A. *Management: Basic elements of managing organizations*. Homewood, Illinois: Irwin, 1975.

Wexley, K.N., and Nemeroff, W.F. "Effects of positive reinforcement and goal setting as methods of management development." *Journal of Applied Psychology*, 1975, 60, 446–450.

Wexley, K.N., and Yukl, G.A. *Organizational behavior and personnel psychology*. Homewood, Illinois: Irwin, 1977.

White, J.H.R. *Successful supervision*. London: McGraw-Hill, 1975.

White, T.H. *The making of the president, 1960*. New York: Atheneum, 1965.

Whyte, W.F. *Organizational behavior: theory and applications*. Homewood, Illinois: Irwin, 1969.

Williams, R.E. "A description of some executive abilities by means of the critical incident technique." Unpublished doctoral dissertation, Columbia University, 1956.

Winter, D.G. *The power motive*. New York: Free Press, 1973.

Woodward, J. *Industrial organization*. London: Oxford University Press, 1962.

Wyndham, C.H., and Cooke, H.M. "The influence of quality of supervision on the production of men engaged in moderately hard work." *Ergonomics*, 1964, 9(2), 139–149.

Yanouzas, J.N. "A comparative study of work organization and supervisory behavior." *Human Organization*, 1964, 23, 245–253.

Yukl, G.A. "Leader characteristics and situational variables as co-determinants of leader behavior." Unpublished doctoral dissertation, University of California at Berkeley, 1967.

Yukl, G.A. "A situation description questionnaire for leaders." *Educational and Psychological Measurement*, 1969, 29, 515–518.

Yukl, G.A. "Leader LPC scores: Attitude dimensions and behavioral correlates." *Journal of Social Psychology*, 1970, 80, 207–212.

Yukl, G.A. "Toward a behavioral theory of leadership." *Organizational Behavior and Human Performance*, 1971, 6, 414–440.

Yukl, G.A., and Kanuk, L. "Leadership behavior and effectiveness of beauty salon managers." *Personnel Psychology*, 1979, 32, 663–675.

Yukl, G.A., and Nemeroff, W. "Identification and measurement of specific categories of leadership behavior: A progress report." In J.G. Hunt and L.L. Larson (Eds.), *Crosscurrents in leadership*. Carbondale: Southern Illinois University Press, 1979.

Zaleznik, A. "Power and politics in organizational life." *Harvard Business Review*, 1970 (May–June), 47–60.

Zand, D.E. "Trust and managerial problem solving." *Administrative Science Quarterly*, 1972, 17, 229–240.

INDICES

Name Index

Subject Index

DATE DUE

NO 4 '82	OCT 25 '82		

DEMCO 38-297